Democracy and Constitutionalism in India

Law in India is a series aimed at scholars, students, and law professionals, whose engagement with the law, especially in South Asia, reaches beyond standard black letter law towards an understanding of how law and legal institutions have an impact upon, and in turn are affected by, society as a whole.

Series advisors:
UPENDRA BAXI, RAJEEV DHAVAN, MARC GALANTER
Founding advisor:
Late S.P. SATHE

OTHER BOOKS IN THE SERIES

RONOJOY SEN
Articles of Faith
Religion, Secularism, and the Indian Supreme Court

RINA VERMA WILLIAMS
Postcolonial Politics and Personal Laws
Colonial Legal Legacies and the Indian State

FLAVIA AGNES
Law and Gender Inequality
The Politics of Women's Rights in India
(Oxford India Paperbacks)

ROBERT LINGAT
The Classical Law of India
(translated and edited by J.D.M. Derrett)
(Oxford India Paperbacks)

ARVIND SHARMA
Hinduism and Human Rights
A Conceptual Approach

B. SIVRAMAYYA
Matrimonial Property Rights
(Oxford India Paperbacks)

LAW
—IN—
INDIA
SERIES

Democracy and Constitutionalism in India
A Study of the Basic Structure Doctrine

SUDHIR KRISHNASWAMY

OXFORD
UNIVERSITY PRESS

OXFORD
UNIVERSITY PRESS

Oxford University Press is a department of the University of Oxford.
It furthers the University's objective of excellence in research, scholarship,
and education by publishing worldwide. Oxford is a registered trademark of
Oxford University Press in the UK and in certain other countries.

Published in India by
Oxford University Press
22 Workspace, 2nd Floor, 1/22 Asaf Ali Road, New Delhi 110002, India

First Edition published in 2009
Oxford India Paperbacks 2010
25th impression 2023

ISBN-13 (print edition): 978-0-19-807161-7
ISBN-10 (print edition): 0-19-807161-2

ISBN-13 (eBook): 978-0-19-908844-7
ISBN-10 (eBook): 0-19-908844-6

Typeset in Minion Pro 10.5/12.7
by Excellent Laser Typesetters, Pitampura, Delhi 110 034
Printed in India by Manipal Technologies Limited, Manipal

For
Ameya
and
Jayna

Contents

Contents

Acknowledgements

This book grew out of my Doctor of Philosophy in Law dissertation at Oxford University. Professor Paul Craig consistently supported this work over the years and gave it direction and purpose at times when it seemed to be too overwhelming. As my doctoral thesis supervisor he inspired by setting the highest personal example but was nevertheless tolerant of my failure to keep to most deadlines! At various points my examiners at Oxford gave critical inputs that shaped and re-shaped this work. So a special thanks to Professors Timothy Endicott, Nick Barber, Nicholas Bamforth, and Upendra Baxi.

The anonymous reviewers of this manuscript were encouraging and made useful suggestions and pointed out gaps in the coverage. The editors at OUP streamlined the text and put up with frequent delays in revising the work. I thank them for seeing value in this work and for seeing it through. Genuine thanks to my students, Ananth Padmanabhan, Don Mihsill, Madhav Khosla, and Sonam Kathuria, for providing valuable comments and editorial assistance at various points.

I thank my parents for their single minded insistence that I should complete this demanding task no matter what the odds and other competing concerns. Jayna for sacrificing our time together and for shielding me from domestic chores long enough for this book to get to print. Further, for providing me the urgent assistance to meet deadlines a big thank you to Jayna, Dev, and Nikita.

The two academic institutions I've been a part of while writing this work have often adjusted my teaching obligations to make this work happen. Heartfelt thanks to John Eekelaar at Pembroke College, Oxford and A. Jayagovind at the National Law School of India University, Bangalore.

Preface

The basic structure doctrine was announced by the Supreme Court in *Kesavananda Bharati* v. *State of Kerala* in 1973. This doctrine places substantive limits on the amending power and has subsequently been applied to other forms of state action. This work makes two arguments: first, that basic structure review is an independent and distinct type of constitutional judicial review which applies to all forms of state action to ensure that such action does not 'damage or destroy' 'basic features of the Constitution'. These basic features of the constitution are identified through a common law technique and are general constitutional rules which are supported by several provisions of the constitution.

Second, I argue that the basic structure doctrine like other types of constitutional judicial review possesses a sound constitutional basis and rests on a sound and justifiable interpretation of the constitution. The basic structure doctrine is founded on an interpretation of the provisions of the constitution granting amending, executive, and legislative power that relies on multi-provisional implications drawn from other important provisions of the constitution.

The legitimacy of basic structure review may be assessed under three categories: legal, moral, and sociological. The legal legitimacy of such review is established by defending a structuralist interpretation as a coherent and justifiable model of constitutional interpretation. The moral legitimacy of basic structure review rests on a rejection of majoritarian versions of democracy and the adoption of a dualist model of deliberative decision-making in a constitutional democracy. The sociological legitimacy of the doctrine is, to a large extent, contingent on the success of the moral and legal legitimacy arguments.

Introduction
The Basic Structure Doctrine in Indian Constitutional Adjudication

While we want this Constitution to be as solid and as permanent a structure as we can make it, nevertheless there is no permanence in Constitutions.

Jawaharlal Nehru, Constituent Assembly Debates, 1948[1]

The tension inherent in the desire to achieve radical social and political change while preserving the Constitution was recognized by Nehru at the founding of the Indian republic, and has remained at the fore of Indian constitutional development through the twentieth century. This paradoxical urge to ensure fixity in our constitutional arrangements while allowing for the possibility of constitutional change has returned to the forefront of national debates at the start of the twenty-first century. While this tension animates contemporary constitutional debates in varied ways, two significant developments in Indian constitutional law in the last decade merit special attention, namely, the prospect of radical constitutional change and the controversy surrounding judicial activism.

RADICAL CONSTITUTIONAL CHANGE

The growing electoral success of political parties ideologically committed to the complete overhaul of the Constitution of India has generated new proposals for radical constitutional change. In the year 2000, the Bharatiya Janata Party (BJP) led National Democratic Alliance (NDA) government constituted[2] the National Commission

[1] Constituent Assembly Debates, New Delhi: Lok Sabha Secretariat, Rep. 1999, vol. 7, p. 322.

[2] Cabinet Resolution No. A-45012(2)/98-Admn. III (LA), New Delhi, 22 February 2000.

to Review the Working of the Constitution to fulfil a promise made in its election manifesto. The party[3] has long argued that the post-independence Constitution adopted by India on 26 January 1950 is ill-suited to Indian society and should be comprehensively revised to reflect indigenous political institutions and values.[4] However, political pressure from its allies in government forced it to moderate these demands and frame more limited terms of reference for the Commission. The Commission was asked to:[5]

... examine, in the light of the experience of the past 50 years, as to how best the Constitution can respond to the changing needs of efficient, smooth, and effective system of governance and socio-economic development of modern India *within the framework of parliamentary democracy* and to recommend changes, if any, that are required in the provisions of the Constitution *without interfering with its basic structure or features* (emphasis added).

This effort by the BJP led government to set up a Constitution Review Commission at the turn of the century may be understood in one of two ways. Firstly, as an attempt to write a new constitution through an extra constitutional executive commission which was subsequentely abandoned due to a lack of political support. It was proposed that the Commission would set the broad principles and institutional outlines for a new constitution which would then be translated into a new constitutional document by a yet unspecified process. Secondly, it may be seen as a benign expert group studying proposals for constitutional reform. These proposals would set an agenda around which political mobilization and debate would take place, eventually leading to a substantial agenda for constitutional amendments through the formal amendment process outlined in

[3] R. Bhargava, 'Words Save Lives: India, the BJP and the Constitution', available at http://www.opendemocracy.net/themes/article-3-504.jsp (accessed on 10 April 2007).

[4] See J. Sharma, *Terrifying Vision: Golwalkar, the RSS and India*, New Delhi: Penguin Books, 2007, for the political vision of the Hindu Right. See also Christophe Jaffrelot, 'From Indian Territory to Hindu Bhoomi : The Ethnicization of Nation-State Mapping in India', in J. Zavos, A. Wyatt and V. Hewitt (eds) *The Politics of Cultural Mobilization in India*, New Delhi: Oxford University Press, 2004.

[5] Cabinet Resolution No. A-45012(2)/98-Admn.III(LA), New Delhi, 22 February 2000, at para 2.

the 1950 Constitution. In any case, the proposal for the Constitution Review Commission[6] was a proposal for radical constitutional change which severely underestimated the hurdles placed before it by the basic structure doctrine.

The Constitution Review Commission submitted its recommendations on 31 March 2002 and the report[7] has received little political or academic attention. This attempt at reviewing or rewriting the constitution is the most recent effort in what has been attempted on various occasions over the last fifty-eight years of the Republic. Significant previous efforts include the First Constitution Amendment Act, 1950, enacted by the Nehru government and the Indira Gandhi government's comprehensive 24th, 25th, and 29th Constitution Amendment Acts. Further, the Swaran Singh Committee established by the Congress party to comprehensively amend the constitution and overcome the basic structure doctrine in the late 1970s advanced the most radical agenda for constitutional change and has become the prototype[8] which inspires aggrieved governments that set out to rewrite the constitution.[9] The Committee's proposals for constitutional amendment were enacted through the 42nd Constitution Amendment Act, 1976. However some amendments were quickly undone through the 44th Constitution Amendment Act, 1979, while others were declared unconstitutional by decisions of the Supreme Court of India on the basic structure doctrine.[10]

[6] Commonwealth Human Rights Institute, 'Genesis of the Review Commission', available at http://www.humanrightsinitiative.org/publications/const/review_of_the_indian_constitution.pdf (accessed on 8 April 2007) pp. 17–19, for the political controversies surrounding the commission on the amending process.

[7] National Commission to Review the Working of the Constitution (Ministry of Law, Justice and Company Affairs, New Delhi, 2002) available at http://lawmin.nic.in/ncrwc/finalreport.htm (accessed on 8 April 2007).

[8] See Granville Austin, *Working a Democratic Constitution: A History of the Indian Experience*, New Delhi: Oxford University Press, 2002, pp. 348–70, for a vivid account of the political manoeuvring behind the Committee and the 42nd Constitution Amendment Act, 1976.

[9] Upendra Baxi 'Constitutional Changes: An Analysis of the Swaran Singh Committee Report' (1976) 2 SCC (Journal) 17, for a favourable review of the Committee's proposals.

[10] *Minerva Mills* v. *Union of India*, AIR 1980 SC 1789 and *Waman Rao* v. *Union of India*, AIR 1981 SC 271.

These attempts at radical constitutional amendment have often found some academic support. Upendra Baxi prefaced his analysis of the Swaran Singh Committee's efforts by observing:[11]

The Swaran Singh Committee on constitutional changes has performed its tasks with remarkable expedition and wisdom…The Committee's recommendations show high statesmanship; they accommodate the need for change within the framework of constitutional stability. Its major recommendations deserve close and sustained analysis by all citizens committed to fundamental social change through peaceful, democratic, and constitutional means.

More recently, the National Commission to Review the Working of the Constitution was anticipated by several academic proposals for constitutional change. Subhash Kashyap has consistently argued for radical[12] constitutional change. He suggests that the 'fundamental conflict between the needs of nation-building and the polity established by the constitution'[13] and the 'basic dichotomy between the constitutional values and the superstructure of the political system'[14] requires that the 'system has to be modified or replaced to match the character and meet the needs of the people.'[15] Such arguments have been criticized by some for being elite flirtations with an authoritarian government[16] and by Upendra Baxi as an effort to create the 'political space for manoeuvre'[17] to 'reconstruct the basic structure doctrine.'[18] One may make sense of Baxi's enthusiasm for the Swaran

[11] Supra n. 9.

[12] S.C. Kashyap, D.D. Khanna, and G.W. Kueck (eds) *Need to Review the Working of the Constitution*, New Delhi: Shipra Publishers, 2004, pp. 7–10 and S.C. Kashyap (ed.) *Reforming the Constitution*, New Delhi: UBS Publishers, 1992.

[13] S.C. Kashyap et al., *Need to Review the Working of the Constitution*, supra n. 12, p. 6.

[14] Ibid.

[15] Ibid., p. 7.

[16] M. Mohanty, 'Does India Need a New Constitution?', in S.N. Mishra, Subas Chandra Hazary, and A. Mishra (eds) *Constitution and Constitutionalism in India*, New Delhi: APH Publishing Corporation, 1999, p. 1.

[17] Upendra Baxi, 'Kar Seva of the Indian Constitution? Reflection on Proposals for Review of the Constitution', (2000) *Economic and Political Weekly*, vol. 35, p. 891.

[18] Ibid.

Singh Committee's proposals and disapproval of the setting up of the National Commission to Review the Working of the Constitution only by distinguishing between the political and ideological content of the constitutional revolutions promoted in each case.

In this work I am not concerned with arguments about the ideal type constitution to which all Indians should aspire and strive towards. Hence, I will not engage rigorously with the intellectual and political proposals for radical constitutional amendment considered above. Instead I will focus on the surprising failure of these proposals to understand the legal force and constitutional legitimacy of the basic structure doctrine and the limits this doctrine places on radical constitutional amendment. The basic structure doctrine, which was first propounded by the Supreme Court in *Kesavananda* v. *State of Kerala*[19] in 1973, places substantive and procedural limits on the amending process provided in the constitution.[20] Any constitutionally and politically nuanced project of radical constitutional change must integrate the pronouncements of the Supreme Court on the basic structure doctrine and this thesis responds to the failure to do so.

JUDICIAL ACTIVISM

A second controversial debate in Indian constitutional law over the last decade has been the widespread criticism of the expansion of the scope of the Supreme Court's power of judicial review. The broad interpretation of fundamental rights together with the relaxation of the rules of standing in constitutional writ litigation has allowed the court to expand its jurisdiction considerably and adjudicate on a wider range of issues than previously thought appropriate. Further, by arming itself with a wide array of remedies the court has sought to continually supervise the implementation of its orders and constitute committees for regulating diverse fields of activity. The scope of its constitutional judicial review power has extended far beyond the domain of rights to include the scrutiny of constitutional amendments, executive proclamations of national and state emergencies, executive

[19] (1973) 4 SCC 225.

[20] Venkatesh Nayak, 'The Basic Structure of the Indian Constitution' (Commonwealth Human Rights Initiative) available at http://www.humanrightsinitiative.org/publications/const/the_basic_structure_of_the_indian_constitution.pdf (accessed on 10 April 2007).

policy framing processes, and legislative inaction affecting core interests of citizens.[21]

Academic and political criticism of judicial activism by the Supreme Court has been wide ranging. The court is accused of widening the scope of judicial review beyond constitutional boundaries,[22] usurping the powers of the executive and legislature,[23] and employing techniques of adjudication and prescribing remedies considered inappropriate for courts.[24] While there is a substantial body of literature which investigates the range and significance of this expansion[25] and whether it is legitimate or optimal[26] there is little attention paid to the normative ideal of the judicial role in Indian constitutional democracy against which such instances of activism are to be measured.[27]

The contours of the debate on judicial activism are so blurred that even accomplished academics like Sathe, while introducing the framework of analysis in his latest work observes:[28]

Judicial activism is inherent in judicial review. Whether it is positive or negative activism depends upon one's own vision of social change. Judicial activism is not an aberration but is a normal phenomenon and judicial review is bound to mature into judicial activism.

The absence of clarity about the scope and character of the key terms—'judicial review' and 'judicial activism'—keeps us from making any progress in the task of understanding 'judicial activism'. This analytical confusion often leads to the use of the phrase 'judicial

[21] For a recent popular collection of articles on judicial activism see 'Judicial Challenge', *Frontline*, 9 February 2007.

[22] R. Dhavan, *Supreme Court and Parliamentary Sovereignty*, New Delhi: Sterling Publishers, 1976.

[23] A. Shourie, *Courts and their Judgments: Promises, Prerequisites, Consequences*, New Delhi: Rupa & Co., 2001, pp. 399–421.

[24] S.P. Sathe, *Judicial Activism in India*, New Delhi: Oxford University Press, 2002.

[25] A. Sangeeta, *People Power and Justice: A Casebook of Public Interest Litigation*, New Delhi: Orient Longman, 1997.

[26] S.P. Sathe, supra n. 24.

[27] See Margit Cohn, 'Judicial Activism in the House of Lords: A Composite Constitutionalist Approach', 2007 PL 95–115 for an analysis of judicial activism against different normative assumptions of the judicial role in a democracy.

[28] S.P. Sathe, supra n. 24, p. 6.

activism' as a rhetorical label to be attached to judicial decisions one finds politically unacceptable.

Arun Shourie, in a recent broadside against the higher courts in India, complains that judicial activism of Indian courts was motivated by the judges' 'exhibitionist and opportunist socialism' and a naive political 'progressivism' which paid inadequate attention to the circumstances in which the country was placed.[29] Moreover, he shows how several activist judgments did not clearly anticipate how they were to be implemented and often grabbed newspaper headlines without making much or any difference on the ground.[30] Shourie's polemical argument rests on a consequential analysis of the impact of judicial decisions but does not articulate the the means for assessing such impact. Further, he does not provide an account of the scope and extent of judicial review in the constitution or legal and normative reasons as to why certain forms of activism are good or bad. In the absence of these essential arguments on which a criticism of judicial activism may rest, one is left to make up one's mind about judicial activism in India by choosing whether one agrees or disagrees with his politics.

Sathe's and Shourie's interventions discussed above are illustrative of the character and form of the debates on judicial activism in India in the early part of the twenty-first century. Many more writings must be examined before a comprehensive analysis of these debates is possible. But this is not the main purpose of this part of the chapter or this work as a whole. In this chapter, I am concerned with the current debates on judicial activism only to show why the questions asked and the answers offered in the rest of this work are a significant contribution to the Indian debate.

I noted earlier in this chapter that the Indian debates on judicial activism lacked a nuanced understanding of the nature of constitutional adjudication and did not offer any analytical conception of the scope and extent of the judicial role under the Indian constitution. A sound understanding of the nature and practice of constitutional adjudication and its appropriate limits, however contested such an

---

[29] A. Shourie, supra n. 23, pp. 402–3.

[30] A careful examination of the proceedings in *Bandhua Mukti Morcha* v. *Union of India*, AIR 1984 SC 802 substantiates this argument; A. Shourie, supra n. 23, pp. 16–61.

understanding may be, is the only reliable basis on which the court's performance may be assessed. The first step towards criticizing the judicial role is to develop an accurate and complete analytical map of the types and models of constitutional judicial review currently employed by the courts. In the absence of clarity about the doctrinal framework in which the judicial role is nested, it is impossible for us to meaningfully assess claims of transgression or conservatism.

A significant part of the academic and popular criticism of judicial activism of the Supreme Court is directed to the courts' use of the basic structure doctrine to review constitutional amendments, executive proclamations of national and regional emergency, and ordinary executive and legislative action. I will argue that much of this criticism emerges from a failure to adequately map the contours of constitutional judicial review as practised in the courts today. As soon as basic structure review is recognized as a novel, independent, and distinct form of constitutional judicial review grounded in a sound constitutional basis and which operates independently of the other forms of constitutional judicial review, our understanding of the judicial role in Indian constitutional law will be reconfigured.

To support this argument, I will show how basic structure review is independent and distinct from rights based judicial review under Articles 13, 32, and 226, federal-state competence and constitutional compliance review under Articles 245 and 247, and common law administrative law review which has been partially assimilated into Articles 14 and 21 rights to equality, and life and liberty respectively. Next, I examine whether basic structure review may be understood as an appropriate exercise of judicial power or if it should be construed as an abuse of power and therefore abandoned or overruled. By reformulating the framework of constitutional judicial review in the Indian constitution which accomodates basic structure review and provides an adequate justification for this exercise of judicial power, I advance a new conception of the judicial role. This new understanding of the judicial role will serve as an essential benchmark against which judicial performance may be assessed thereby eliminating some of the confusions which currently plague the Indian debate on judicial activism. I turn to the task of rigorously analysing the courts' judicial output on basic structure review in the next chapter. In the next part of this chapter, I will review the existing secondary literature on this doctrine.

Basic Structure Review: The Debates so Far

The political project of radical constitutional amendment and the academic and popular criticism of excessive judicial activism are united in their lack of recognition of, and rigorous doctrinal and theoretical investigation into, the emergence and development of a new kind of constitutional judicial review: basic structure review. The failure to recognize and accommodate basic structure review as a form of constitutional judicial review has resulted in a partial and incomplete understanding of our constitutional inheritance. This failure cannot be attributed to inadequate attention paid to basic structure review by academic commentators or constitutional lawyers as this topic has arguably drawn more extensive commentary than any other aspect of Indian constitutional law. To investigate why basic structure review has escaped easy comprehension, I will survey the approach to the basic structure doctrine in the academic literature and identify the central questions to which the rest of this work must respond.

The basic structure doctrine initially developed in cases where the constitutionality of constitutional amendments was challenged, but is currently used in a wide range of constitutional law cases which are yet to be carefully mapped out and analysed. Given this path of historical evolution it is not surprising that the early criticisms of the basic structure doctrine concentrated on the cases where constitutional amendments were challenged. Some critics argued that plurality opinions in *Kesavananda* yielded no clear ratio decidendi[31] and for that reason was uncertain authority. Others pointed out that the case misunderstood the relationship between parliamentary sovereignty and judicial review in the constitution and should be set aside for that reason.[32] The lack of unanimity about the nature and character of

---

[31] P.K. Tripathi, 'Kesavananda Bharati v. State of Kerala: Who Wins?', (1974) 1 SCC (Journal) 3. For a contrary view see J. Minnatur, 'The Ratio in the Kesavananda Bharati Case', (1974) 1 SCC (Journal) 74. Rajeev Dhavan's precise account of the issues on which the court divided has come to be accepted as the most authoritative account of the problems related to the ratio of Kesavananda case: R. Dhavan, supra n. 22.

[32] R. Dhavan, supra n. 22.

the basic features of the constitution, and how they may be identified, led some critics to suggest that broad constitutional principles identified as basic features were not amenable to judicial application.[33] All these criticisms raise relevant concerns and I will develop a detailed response to these matters in the later chapters of this work.

The court's persistence with the doctrine in *Indira Gandhi* v. *Raj Narain*[34] and *Minerva Mills* v. *Union of India*[35] in dramatically different political circumstances[36] convinced many sceptics that this doctrine was worthy of respect. Baxi acerbically cast Chandrachud's transition, from his dissenting opinion in *Kesavananda* to his majority opinion affirming the doctrine in *Minerva Mills* and *Waman Rao* v. *Union of India*,[37] as the 'pilgrim's progress'.[38] This characterization was particularly harsh as several leading constitutional commentators including Seervai,[39] Sathe,[40] and to a lesser extent Baxi[41] himself, travelled through a similar change of convictions. In this sense, the basic structure doctrine has dented several reputations among judges and academic commentators alike.

[33] R.D. Garg, 'Phantom of Basic Structure of the Constitution: A Critical Appraisal of *Kesavananda* Case', (1974) 16 *Journal of the Indian Law Institute*, (1974) 16, p. 243. See Tripathi, supra n. 31.

[34] AIR 1975 SC 2299.

[35] AIR 1980 SC 1789.

[36] For a fuller account of the political circumstances in which these decisions were delivered see G. Austin, supra n. 8, pp. 370–90.

[37] AIR 1981 SC 271.

[38] U. Baxi, *Courage, Craft and Contention*, Bombay: N.M. Tripathi Ltd, 1985, pp. 64, 97.

[39] Contrast his sharp criticism of judicial review of constitutional amendments in the *Golaknath* opinion in H.M. Seervai, *Constitutional Law of India*, (1st edn) Bombay: N.M. Tripathi Ltd, 1967, p. 1117 and his convoluted endorsement of the basic structure doctrine, ibid. (4th edn) pp. 3109–70.

[40] Contrast his strident criticism in S.P. Sathe, 'Amendability of Fundamental Rights: *Golaknath* and the Proposed Constitutional Amendment', (1969) *Supreme Court Journal*, pp. 33–42 with his affirmation of basic structure review in S.P. Sathe, supra n. 24, pp. 63–98.

[41] Contrast the guarded endorsement of the reconciliation of parliamentary amending power and judicial review proposed by the Swaran Singh Committee recommendations in U. Baxi, ,Constitutional Changes: An Analysis of the Swaran Singh Committee Report', (1976) 2 SCC (Journal) 17 with the celebration of the *Kesavananda* opinion in U. Baxi, supra n. 38, pp. 64–110.

In the last three decades, the court has widened the scope of the doctrine to include a wide range of state action: executive proclamation of national and regional emergency, and ordinary legislation and executive action by those in the higher elected and the lower unelected executive authority. This expansion in the scope and application of the doctrine has either been ignored[42] or characterized as a mistaken application of the doctrine.[43] Sathe refers to cases where basic structure review is applied and where constitutional amendments are not being challenged and notes:[44]

> These utterances are made by individual judges in the judgements and cannot be called even *obiter dicta*. They are not decisions of the Court. A decision strictly speaking comes only when a constitutional amendment enacted by Parliament is challenged in court on the ground of its alleged violation of the basic structure of the Constitution.

By confining the application of basic structure review to constitutional amendments, Sathe labels all other applications of the doctrine as a mistake. The failure to recognize the evolution of basic structure review as an independent and distinct type of judicial review that applies to state action generally has deprived the existing literature of a critical and useful vantage point from which to assess the court's application of the doctrine in the later cases.

The few commentators who have examined the application of the doctrine to state action other than constitutional amendments assume that the doctrine applies to these different forms of state action in the same way as it applies to constitutional amendments.[45]

---

[42] P.B. Mehta, 'The Inner Conflict of Constitutionalism: Judicial Review and the Basic Structure', in Zoya Hasan et al. (eds) *India's Living Constitution*, New Delhi: Permanent Black, 2002, p. 181.

[43] A. Lakshminath, *Basic Structure* and *Constitutional Amendments*, New Delhi: Deep and Deep Publications, 2002.

[44] S.P. Sathe, supra n. 24, p. 97. Surprisingly, Sathe concludes that basic structure review will come to be increasingly used in cases not involving constitutional amendments.

[45] R. Ramachandran, 'The Supreme Court and the Basic Structure Doctrine', in *Supreme But Not Infallible*, New Delhi: Oxford University Press, 2000, pp. 122–6. A. Desai 'Constitutional Amendments and the Basic Structure Doctrine', in V. Iyer (ed.) *Democracy, Human Rights and the Rule of Law*, New Delhi: Butterworths, 2000, pp. 88–91.

In other words these writers suggest that basic structure review is of a singular character which is employed in the same manner irrespective of the state action being reviewed. This assumption leads them to the conclusion that it is inappropriate to apply basic structure review to cases which do not involve constitutional amendments. Careful analysis of the court's use of the basic structure review reveals that the court has developed several methods of applying such review depending on the kind of state action being challenged. Hence, in order to assess the character of the basic structure doctrine it is essential to map the various applications of the doctrine and then analyse its proper scope and utility.

In the last decade, diverse strands of constitutional commentary on the legitimacy of the basic structure doctrine have emerged. I examine three key strands of this literature: the historical approach, constitutional and political theory approaches, and lastly, journalistic criticism. I will address each of these in turn.

Granville Austin's political history of the Indian constitution has exerted considerable influence on the Indian judiciary. In his first work titled *The Indian Constitution: Cornerstone of a Nation*,[46] Austin identified three features: the spirit of democracy, pursuit of a social revolution, and the preservation of the unity and integrity of the country coming together to form a seamless web which animates the Indian constitution. For Austin this seamless web of normative goals embedded in the constitution exerts a mystical force which tethers India to an equilibrium point where these three normative impulses are in balance. The choice of this narrative device, which structures the enquiry in the book, may in some part be due to his claim to political history rather than legal theory.[47] He observes that, 'This is a history, and not a law book... It is about politics and economics and conditions and culture.'[48] By escaping the methodological and disciplinary boundaries of ordinary legal academic discourse, Austin deploys a master narrative which fuses historical data, anecdotal recollections of past events, and judgments to tell a compelling story

[46] G. Austin, *The Indian Constitution: Cornerstone of a Nation*, Oxford: Clarendon Press, 1966.

[47] See Upendra Baxi, '"The Little Done, The Vast Undone"—Some Reflections on Reading Granville Austin's *The Indian Constitution*', (1967) *Journal of the Indian Law Institute*, vol. 9, pp. 323, 325.

[48] G. Austin, supra n. 8, p. 1.

about India's constitutional inheritance. However, this account fails to give us any significant analytical insight into the development of Indian constitutional 'law'.

In any event, Austin persists with this model in his recent 669-page homage to the working of the Indian Constitution where he finds that the past 50 years of independent India's constitutional history is best captured by his metaphorical matrix of the 'seamless web'. To the three features identified in the first book he adds a fourth feature of 'culture' to the seamless web. He understands culture to include a range of elements from the citizen's cosmological view of life to her attitude to the government. The method and intent of Austin's analysis is exemplified by this sentence announcing this significant discovery: 'The seamless web had a fourth strand, omnipresent, visible and invisible: culture.'[49]

Having developed this historical, partly metaphysical, framework to assess India's constitutional history, Austin evaluates judicial performance by its ability to restore this mythical equilibrium point in the seamless web. He does not bother with the debates on judicial activism and the proper role of the different organs of government. While evaluating the basic structure doctrine he observes: 'With the basic structure doctrine, a balance, if an uneasy one, has been reached between the responsibilities of Parliament and the Supreme Court for protecting the integrity of the seamless web.'[50] The special character of the doctrine does not prompt Austin to undertake a careful doctrinal analysis or philosophical analysis of the content and scope of the doctrine. Having identified a positive role for the doctrine in maintaining the seamless web, he is content with an elaborate historical account of the emergence of the doctrine. The impact of Austin's writings on the bar and the bench is immense, as he is arguably the author most cited by the Supreme Court till date. Despite this influence, Upendra Baxi feels compelled to observe that 'St Granville is no longer a safe navigator to the politics of dominant and insurrectionary desires that shape the future practices of Indian constitutionalism'.[51] To this we may add that Austin's labours do not significantly contribute to the pursuit of an analytical and normative

[49] Ibid., p. 637.

[50] G. Austin, supra n. 8, p. 652.

[51] U. Baxi, 'St Granville's Gospel: Reflections', (2001) *Economic and Political Weekly*, vol. 36, p. 921.

analysis of the basic structure doctrine in Indian constitutional law with which this work is concerned.

The constitutional law and political theory literature promises to be of greater assistance to the questions posed in this work. Sathe in *Judicial Activism in India* presents a complex but confusing account of judicial activism in India. In his discussion of the evolution of the basic structure doctrine he observes that '*Golaknath* marks a watershed in the history of the Supreme Court of India's evolution from a positivist court to an activist court.'[52] More recently he charts the history of the Supreme Court of India as a shift from a 'legal positivist' model of constitutional interpretation to a 'structuralist' approach.[53]

Sathe's characterization of the legal positivist model of adjudication seems to be misplaced. He takes the separation of law and morals, which is a fundamental element of a positivist theory of identifying law, to be a necessary ingredient of a positivist model of constitutional adjudication. In other words, Sathe assumes that a legal positivist theory of law entails a formalist mode of adjudication in which judges rely on some version of constitutional literalism eschewing any reliance on non-legal sources.[54] He may well be right to suggest that the Supreme Court in its early years tended to be formalist or literalist in its approach to constitutional interpretation, but labelling the court as adopting a 'legal positivist' model of interpretation confuses the matter.

The label 'structuralism' as a model of constitutional interpretation in Sathe's work is a placeholder for many distinct approaches to the task of interpretation in which the constitution is 'interpreted liberally, as a totality, in the light of the spirit pervading it and the philosophy underlying it.'[55] Moreover he suggests that structuralist interpretation may be called 'teleological'[56] as it 'understands the constitution

---

[52] S.P. Sathe, supra n. 24, p. 67.

[53] S.P. Sathe, 'India: From Positivism to Structuralism', in J. Goldsworthy (ed.), *Interpreting Constitutions: A Comparative Study*, Oxford: Oxford University Press, 2006, p. 226.

[54] H.L.A. Hart strove hard to eliminate this error in H.L.A. Hart, *The Concept of Law*, Oxford: Clarendon Press, 1961, ch. 5.

[55] S.P. Sathe, supra n. 53, p. 226.

[56] Ibid., p. 226. See also R. Dhavan, supra n. 22, for his concluding argument that the Supreme Court must recognize the teleological character of its interpretation and offer adequate justification for such an exercise.

to be intended to achieve certain purposes.'[57] Structuralism as an interpretive approach may offer some assistance to understand and help justify the Indian courts' judicial output on the basic structure doctrine. However, I first need to clarify what structuralism means as an interpretive method and assess its justificatory potential. I return to this argument about methods of constitutional interpreatation in greater detail in Chapter 6 of this work.

The legal and political legitimacy of the basic structure has drawn sharply conflicting views. Raju Ramachandran, in an important essay to celebrate the 50th Anniversary of the Supreme Court, argues that 'the basic structure doctrine is anti-democratic and counter-majoritarian in character, and that unelected judges have assumed vast political power not given to them by the constitution.'[58] Moreover, he concludes that 'the doctrine can now stand in the way of political and economic changes which may be felt necessary'.[59] He concludes by noting that:

The basic structure doctrine has served a certain purpose: it has warned a fledgling democracy of the perils of brute majoritarianism. Those days are however gone ... The doctrine must now be buried. The nation must be given an opportunity to put half a century's experience of politics and economics into the Constitution.[60]

A similar combination of principled and pragmatic reasons for curtailing the basic structure doctrine is advanced with lesser[61] and greater[62] clarity in other book-length works.

[57] S.P. Sathe, supra n. 53, p. 226.

[58] R. Ramachandran, supra n. 45, p. 108.

[59] Ibid.

[60] Ibid., p. 130.

[61] Lakshminath does not emphatically state whether he considers the basic structure doctrine to be legitimate and justifiable. At times he criticizes the doctrine for being symptomatic of the 'megalomaniacal assumption of power by the judiciary' and at other times suggests that the doctrine is essential for 'the preservation of the constitutional roots of our democratic process': A. Lakshiminath, supra n. 43, p. 301.

[62] S. Raman argues that the constitution is in desperate need of revision as the 'political, social, economic and legal systems are under great strain ...' and that judicial review is a politically inappropriate instrument to impose limitations on the amending power. S. Raman, *Amending Power under the Constitution of India: A Politico-Legal Study*, Calcutta: Eastern Law House, 1990, p. 314. Bhandari, *Basic Structure of the Indian Constitution: A Critical Reconsideration*, New Delhi: Deep & Deep Publications, 1993.

The debate on the anti-democratic character of judicial review has generated an extensive literature in the common law world. Basic structure review has attracted criticisms similar to those articulated in other jurisdictions: namely, that unelected judges review, and sometimes reject, decisions made by elected representatives.[63] Arguably the scope and application of basic structure review to constitutional amendments and executive proclamations of emergency invites more formidable legitimacy challenges than the judicial review of legislation, but these have not been clearly made out in the existing literature. The response to the legitimacy challenge to basic structure review has developed along two lines. First, it has been suggested that such a criticism is founded on 'an impoverished conception of democracy'[64] and that the basic structure doctrine reflects a 'democratic conception of constitutionalism'.[65] This argument has considerable promise to be an effective counter to the anti-democratic challenge but needs to be elaborated with greater clarity. The continued invocation of the doctrine of parliamentary sovereignty in constitutional argument and decision making even in the absence of textual support for such a doctrine has cast a long shadow on the interpretation of key constitutional provisions. In Chapter 6 I return to address the arguments relating to the democratic legitimacy of the basic structure doctrine and show that a doctrine with the nature and character of basic structure review may be justified to be legitimate.

The second response to the legitimacy challenges to basic structure review is rooted in the post-war German constitutional tradition. The exceptionally brilliant lectures and writings of Dietrich Conrad had an enduring influence on the bar and the bench and no doubt[66]

---

[63] For a recent argument against strong judicial review of legislation see J. Waldron, 'The Core of the Case Against Judicial Review', 115 *Yale LJ* 1346 (2006).

[64] P.B. Mehta, 'The Inner Conflict of Constitutionalism', in Zoya Hasan (ed.), *India's Living Constitution*, New Delhi: Permanent Black, 2004, p. 181.

[65] Ibid.

[66] A.G. Noorani, 'Behind the 'Basic Structure' Doctrine: On India's debt to a German Jurist, Professor Dietrich Conrad', *Frontline*, 18(9), 28 April–11 May 2001, available at http://www.hinduonnet.com/fline/fl1809/18090950.htm (accessed on 15 March 2006); M.P. Singh, 'Bridging Legal Traditions: Dietrich

contributed to the conception of the basic structure doctrine. Conrad's richly illustrated analogies between the abuse of amending power under the Weimar Constitution by Hitler and the amending power under the Indian constitution played a significant role in persuading the court to reach its conclusion on the limits to amending power in *Kesavananda*.[67] The influence of European philosophical approaches to constitutionalism[68] on Indian constitutional jurisprudence has been modest. These perspectives have not found their way explicitly into constitutional argument in the court or the judicial reasoning of the Supreme Court. While I will examine Conrad's arguments on the nature of constituent power in greater detail in Chapter 6, any further exploration into the influence of European Constitutional philosophy on Indian Constitutional law would require a different analytical framework from that adopted in this work and a broader account of the history of constitutional philosophy in the European tradition and the transmission of these ideas across legal jurisdictions and cultures. Hence, I will not engage in a more wide ranging enquiry into the undoubted value that European approaches to constitutional philosophy can contribute to an understanding of basic structure review. This limitation on the scope of enquiry allows me to keep the enquiry within manageable proportions.

I conclude this part of the chapter by briefly taking note of another strand of commentary on the basic structure doctrine that may be best described as being of a 'journalistic' character. Of the many such accounts[69] I will elaborate on a recent effort by Pran

---

Conrad 1932–2001', *Frontline*, 18(18), 1–14 September 2001, available at http://www.hinduonnet.com/fline/fl1818/18181240.htm (accessed on 15 March 2006).

[67] Dietrich Conrad, 'Limitation of Amendment Procedures and the Constituent Power', in Dieter Conrad (ed.) *Zwitschen den Traditionen: Problememe des Verfassungsrechts und der Rechtskultur in Indien und Pakistan*, Stuttgart: Franz Steiner Verlag, 1999, pp. 52–72.

[68] R. Sudarshan, 'Stateness and Democracy in India's Constitution', in Zoya Hasan (ed.) *India's Living Constitution*, New Delhi: Permanent Black, 2004, pp. 159–78.

[69] For a recent positive journalistic account of the basic structure doctrine see A. Shourie, 'Protector of our Freedoms', *Indian Express*, 20 January 2005, available at http://www.indianexpress.com/res/web/pIe/full_story.php?content_id=63028 (accessed on 10 April 2007).

Chopra, a prominent political analyst and newspaper editor, who organized a conference on the basic structure doctrine and published the proceedings. His lead essay provocatively titled 'The Supreme Court Versus the Constitution' suggests that the basic structure is 'not provided in the text of the Constitution'[70] and 'cannot be derived from an interpretation of the text with the normal scope of interpretation.'[71] Such a claim must rest on a fuller account of the nature of constitutional interpretation which pays attention to the complex nature of the interpretive task, but Chopra gives this crucial subject a very superficial treatment.[72] His second major argument against the basic structure doctrine is that it impedes the principle and practice of federalism which he takes to be foundational to the amending power in the Indian Constitution. This is a curious argument as it misunderstands the nature of the amending power. The proviso to Article 368(2) requires the ratification of at least half the states before certain parts of the constitution are amended. However, this procedural limit on amending power is not limited to parts of the Constitution which are related to federalism. Basic structure review does not disturb this procedural limit on the exercise of amending power in the Constitution and supplements it with substantive limits. Moreover, it is arguable that by identifying 'federalism' as a basic feature of the constitution this aspect of our constitutional arrangement has been strengthened under basic structure review.

Despite these glaring inadequacies, legal journalism, like the example explored above, has had a significant impact on the constitutional discourse in India. This impact has magnified the absence of a vibrant law journal tradition which addresses these issues with academic rigour. Despite this impact this writing does not respond to the core legal and philosophical questions regarding basic

---

[70] P. Chopra, *The Supreme Court Versus the Constitution*, New Delhi: Sage Publications, 2006, p. 29.

[71] Ibid.

[72] By relying on H.M. Seervai's constitutional commentaries as the last word on constitutional interpretation, the chapter falls very short of a competent account of the very complex and contested terrain of constitutional interpretation; P. Chopra, supra n. 70, pp. 40–5.

structure review addressed in this work. Hence, I do not engage with this writing sparingly hereafter.

So far in this section, I have surveyed and analysed an extensive body of academic and journalistic literature which has developed around the basic structure doctrine. I have distinguished between writings which will be addressed in greater detail from others on which no further comment will be made. Further, this survey of the literature has assisted me to identify some of the critical questions to be addressed in the rest of this work. In the concluding section of this Chapter, I will set out the key arguments of this work and the manner in which they will be addressed in the chapters to follow.

The Argument

This work makes two central arguments. First, that basic structure review is an independent and distinct type of constitutional judicial review which applies to all forms of state action to ensure that such action does not 'damage or destroy' 'basic features of the constitution'. Second, it will show that the basic structure doctrine like any other constitutional law doctrine possesses a sound constitutional basis—by which we mean that the doctrine rests on a sound and justifiable interpretation of the constitution and is legally, morally, and sociologically legitimate. These two arguments are sketched out in greater detail below.

The tendency in the existing literature on the basic structure doctrine, surveyed in the section above, to criticize or applaud the 'basic structure doctrine' in an omnibus fashion robs any critical enquiry into basic structure review of analytical clarity and focus. An enquiry into any form of judicial review may usefully be divided into arguments about the scope and extent of review, the nature and standards of review, and the grounds of review. Where the legitimacy of constitutional foundations of this form of judicial review is in doubt one must critically examine its constitutional or legal basis and show that it has legitimate foundations. By breaking down a form of judicial review into its constituent parts our attention is focused on the particular challenges to such review and thereby avoids sweeping generalizations. Further, it helps us to reason comparatively across the types of judicial review which our courts presently engage in, thereby allowing us to rightly identify the normal from the exceptional character of different types of judicial review.

The division of judicial review into its component parts proposed above does not assume that these component parts are necessarily discrete and unrelated aspects of judicial review: strong constitutional justifications for rights based judicial review allows for a more substantive type, and rigorous standards, of rights compliance review, while administrative law review may rest on weaker theoretical justifications and therefore be a procedural and less intrusive form of review which primarily ensures that executive action is within jurisdiction and follows proper process. Moreover arguments about identifying the grounds of review and the constitutional and legal basis of review may both require careful attention to the legitimacy of particular models of constitutional interpretation. As the existing literature on the basic structure doctrine is analytically unstructured and theoretically diffused, an essential first step is to isolate and organize the Supreme Court's doctrinal output in the analytical categories of a model of judicial review described above.

The next four chapters of the work explore basic structure review cases to uncover and clarify, and then criticize, the Supreme Court's output on the basic structure doctrine. In Chapters 2 and 3, I outline the scope and extent of basic structure review and examine what forms of state action it applies to. Basic structure review could potentially apply to constitutional amendments, executive proclamations of emergency, ordinary legislation, and executive action. By examining its application to each of these types of state action in isolation, I assess whether basic structure review of these state actions possesses a sound constitutional basis. In Chapter 4, I explore the nature and standard of basic structure review as applied to these varied forms of state action. Does basic structure review apply in a similar fashion to all these forms of state action and can it be from the other types of constitutional judicial review? If, basic structure review is an independent type of judicial review then it must possess distinct grounds of review. In Chapter 5, I examine the issues surrounding the grounds of basic structure review. Are these grounds of review a closed or open set and how are these grounds of review identified?

In Chapters 2 to 5, I will show how basic structure review, which emerged from the landmark decision in *Kesavananda Bharati* v. *State of Kerala*[73], has in the last 34 years evolved into a full-fledged doctrine of constitutional judicial review which operates independently from other forms of constitutional judicial review authorized under Articles 13, 32, 246, and 247. I argue that the basic structure doctrine has in this period evolved into a mature doctrine of constitutional judicial review in which each of its component elements has been developed in a sophisticated manner. Unlike other forms of constitutional judicial review which rests on express constitutional provisions, basic structure review has developed as a doctrine of constitutional common law. Despite this unique origin, like other forms of judicial review, a critical review of the case law of the Supreme Court reveals that the doctrine has a sound constitutional basis, nuanced and justified standards of review, and a stable method for identifying the grounds of review. In the chapters below I will turn to each of these ingredients of a mature doctrine of constitutional judicial review and show that the court has developed a justifiable approach to these questions. Where there is a multiplicity of approaches, I will argue that some of these approaches are superior and more justifiable than others and should therefore be adopted in the further development of the doctrine.

The constitutional legitimacy of the basic structure doctrine has provoked the most extensive critical debates in Indian constitutional history. However, much of this debate has been carried out without paying adequate attention to the analytical elements of basic structure review. Having clarified the doctrinal contours of basic structure review in Chapters 2 to 5 and broken it down to its compnent parts, we are able to set aside some preliminary objections as being overstatements of the impact, or simply misunderstandings, of the doctrine. Some critical legitimacy arguments remain and in Chapter 6 I respond to these criticisms and address the question of constitutional legitimacy of the basic structure doctrine. The debate around constitutional legitimacy of the doctrine is diverse and I may organize them into discrete enquiries of legal, sociological, and moral legitimacy. As constitutional legitimacy is a scalar category, any assessment of the constitutional legitimacy of judicial doctrines is unlikely to yield categorical and unanimously accepted answers.

[73] (1973) 4 SCC 225.

Hence I will try to show that the court's development of basic structure review is minimally legitimate, even if not incontrovertibly or ideally so.

Having set out the central argument and the manner in which it is organized in the rest of this thesis, we conclude this section with an important caveat. A title like 'Basic Structure Doctrine in Indian Constitutional Adjudication' raises the expectation that this work would contain an expansive analysis of constitutional law cases decided by the Supreme Court of India and a justification of this doctrine as it is practised by the court. This expectation will be adequately satisfied. Some readers may also expect a general justification of a doctrine of judicial review of constitutional amendments and emergency power which may apply irrespective of the constitutional jurisdiction in which it is practised.[74] Such readers are likely to be disappointed. By tailoring this work to the constitutional text and case law in India, I seek to justify propositions which are justifiable in Indian constitutional law. Though some of the arguments made and theoretical perspectives considered would be relevant in other jurisdictions, it would be a mistake to assume that all these propositions would be equally valid in other constitutional jurisdictions.

A particular constitutional theory may be understood as interpretation of the constitutional text and constitutional practice of one particular jurisdiction. It pays attention to the political history of the jurisdiction and the salience of particular modes of thinking about, or discourses around, constitutional legitimacy in that jurisdiction. Such analysis does consider general themes in constitutional theory that may be relevant to the study of any constitution: the scope and existence of parliamentary sovereignty, the role of constitutional judicial review, among others. However, the conclusions reached are partial to the constitutional text and practice of a particular jurisdiction.

---

[74] Charles A. Kelbley, 'Are There Limits To Constitutional Change? Rawls On Comprehensive Doctrines, Unconstitutional Amendments, and the Basis of Equality', *Fordham L. Rev.*, 72(5), p. 1487 (2003–4). Ronald Dworkin, 'Rawls and the Law', *Fordham L. Rev.*, 72 (special issue), (2003–4), p. 1387. Frank I Michelman 'Justice as Fairness, Legitimacy, and the Question Of Judicial Review: A Comment', *Fordham L. Rev.*, 72(5), (2003–4), p. 1487.

Varied issues are salient or prominent in different countries as different political, social, and historical backgrounds influence the way constitutional discourse operates in a country. This insight, coupled with the more commonplace observation regarding the particular phrasing of constitutional documents may lead some to conclude that a particular constitutional theory is the only theoretically coherent, or at any rate useful, mode of doing constitutional theory. It is not the argument of this work that constitutional theory may only be done by situating it in particular jurisdictions[75] or that a 'particular' or a 'general' approach to constitutional theory is to be preferred. I justify basic structure review as a legitimate doctrine in Indian constitutional law. As the legal doctrine on the constitutional judicial review of amendments is best developed in Indian constitutional law the conclusions of this work may have significance for a general constitutional theory.[76]

The formulation and practice of the basic structure doctrine mediates between two important political values: namely, democracy and constitutionalism. While there have been many important and useful theoretical efforts at reconciling these values, there is no constitutional jurisdiction where this reconciliation has been carried out as richly and with as much sophistication as in India. In the next chapter I begin the task of carefully analysing and reconstructing the basic structure doctrine to identify and establish its scope and constitutional basis.

[75] See A. Kavanagh, 'Fidelity and Change in Constitutional Adjudication' (D Phil. Thesis, Oxford University, 2000) pp. 10–16, for an argument for a general constitutional theory.

[76] G.J. Jacobsohn, 'An Unconstitutional Constitution? A Comparative Persepective' (2006) 4 *International J. Constitutional L.* pp. 460–87 at 462.

1

Amending Power
The Constitutional Basis for Basic Structure Review

The basic structure doctrine evolved in the context of challenges to the constitutionality of land reform legislation. In the early 1950s the constitutional validity of land reform legislation was challenged before the courts and some of this legislation was declared unconstitutional. Hence, the constitution was amended to undo the constitutional basis for these challenges to the validity of this legislation. The court was petitioned to judicially review these constitutional amendments and declare them to be unconstitutional. Land reform related constitutional amendments were challenged before the Supreme Court in a series of cases beginning with *Sankari Prasad* v. *Union of India*[1] in 1951 and culminating in *Kesavananda Bharati* v. *State of Kerala*[2] in 1973. Between 1951 and 1973 the Supreme Court accepted two separate arguments for judicial review of constitutional amendments: first, constitutional amendments are subject to judicial review under Article 13 (express limits) and second, that constitutional amendments are subject to basic structure review (implied limits).

This chapter critically evaluates these two arguments in support of judicial review of constitutional amendments. The first argument rests on the claim that the express limits on all forms of 'state action'

[1] *Sankari Prasad* v. *Union of India*, AIR 1951 SC 458.
[2] *Kesavananda Bharati* v. *State of Kerala*, (1973) 4 SCC 225 .

in Article 13, to comply with fundamental rights[3] in the constitution, should be extended to include constitutional amendments. This argument is considered at length in the part on 'express limits' on amending power and is rejected as constitutional judicial review constitutional amendments under Article 13 would require the court to contort the meaning of constitutional text and apply constitutional principles inconsistently.

The second argument offers an alternative constitutional basis for judicial review of constitutional amendments other than the express limits under Article 13. It is argued that constitutional amendments may be subject to implied limits whereby the courts may review a particular constitutional amendment to assess whether it destroys or abrogates the basic features of the constitution.[4] This chapter assesses the relative merits of these two forms of review paying particular attention to the constitutional basis for such a review. I conclude that basic structure review, at least the version of the doctrine defended in this chapter, is by the second argument accounted for a coherent reading of the constitutional text and the application of sound constitutional principles.

Rights review under Article 13 and basic structure review do not exhaust the scope of judicial review of constitutional amendments. The court may also review whether constitutional amendments have been made in compliance with the procedure outlined in Article 368. Judicial review to ensure compliance with the procedural limits to constitutional amendments has been carried out in several cases considered below. As I am concerned primarily with substantive limits on amending power in this work I do not pay any more attention to challenges based on procedural limits to amending power.

In *Kesavananda* the Supreme Court used the basic structure doctrine for the first time to subject constitutional amendments to judicial review. Since that ruling, the doctrine has been used by the Supreme Court in several significant constitutional law cases not all of which relate to constitutional amendments. In Chapter 1,

[3] This was first proposed in *Sankari Prasad* and finally accepted in *Golaknath* v. *State of Punjab*, AIR 1967 SC 1643.

[4] The doctrine was announced in *Kesavananda* and has been continuously developed since.

I suggested that the constitutional basis of basic structure review is best addressed by focusing our enquiry on the particular forms of state action being reviewed. In this chapter the constitutional basis of basic structure review as it applies to constitutional amendments is examined. In Chapter 3, I go on to analyse basic structure review as it applies to other forms of state action.

In this Chapter, I will show why basic structure review, when understood as an implied limit on the power of amendment under Article 368 which arises from several provisions of the constitution taken together, provides a sounder constitutional basis for the judicial review of constitutional amendments for two reasons: first, it does not rely on the particular phrasing of a single provision of the constitution thereby avoiding the possibility that the Parliament may amend such provision of the constitution to oust judicial review. Second, implied limits review requires a type of review which distinguishes between constitutional limits on ordinary state action and constitutional amendments. Moreover, it avoids focusing on the detailed fundamental rights provisions in the constitution and proposes a set of general constitutional principles as the limit on the amendment power in the constitution. By distinguishing between fundamental rights review and basic structure review, the court gives the amendment process an opportunity to express democratic conceptions of basic constitutional values with out derogating from the fundamental constitutional principles protected by basic structure review. Before I get too far ahead of the story let us turn to the arguments around Article 13 in detail.

EXPRESS LIMITS ON AMENDING POWER: JUDICIAL REVIEW UNDER ARTICLE 13

The operative part of Article 13(2) provides that: 'The State shall not make any law which takes away or abridges the rights conferred by this Part and any law made in contravention of this clause shall, to the extent of the contravention, be void.'[5] For constitutional amendments to be subject to judicial review under Article 13, the courts need to find that constitutional amendments are 'law' under Article 13(2). The inclusive definition in Article 13(3)(a) makes no

---

[5] Constitution of India, 1950, Article 13(2).

mention of constitutional amendments. Hence in order to include constitutionhal amendments, petitioners advance arguments about the nature and purpose of judicial review for rights compliance in the constitution and about whether parliamentary amending power is a species of residuary legislative power. I will examine each of these in turn.

First, let me briefly examine the role that Article 13 judicial review plays in the constitution. Article 13 is often characterized as the guarantor of fundamental rights in the constitution. It provides that 'the state' shall not make any 'law' that abridges any of the fundamental rights guaranteed in Part III of the constitution.[6] Article 12 defines 'the state' widely to include 'Government and the Parliament of India' as well as other authorities 'all local and within the territory of India or under the control of the Government of India' to be subject to judicial review under Article 13. The fundamental rights protected in Part III include the rights to life and personal liberty[7] and rights guaranteeing equality of all persons before law.[8] Read with Articles 32 and 226, Article 13 authorizes the Supreme Court and the High Courts in the States to declare invalid any 'law' which abridges these rights. The arguments in the constitutional amendment cases focus on whether the scope of the term 'law' is wide enough to include constitutional amendments. 'Law' is defined in Article 13(3)(a) to include 'any Ordinance, order, by-law, rule, regulation, notification, custom or usage having in the territory of India the force of law.'[9]

A lean version of the argument that constitutional amendments are 'law' under Article 13 was first raised in *Sankari Prasad* v. *Union of India*.[10] Although Patanjali Sastri considered this to be a more 'plausible argument'[11] than the others advanced in the case, he eventually rejected it by 'harmonizing' the wide scope of the amending power in Article 368 with the scope of judicial review under Article 13. Mudholkar and Hidayatullah expressed doubts on the soundness

---

[6] Constitution of India, 1950, Article 13(2).

[7] Ibid., Article 21.

[8] Ibid., Article 14.

[9] Ibid., Article 13(3) (a).

[10] *Sankari Prasad*, supra n. 1, p. 458 (Patanjali Sastri, CJ).

[11] Ibid., p. 463.

[12] AIR 1965 SC 845.

of Sastri's ruling a few years later in their concurring opinions in *Sajjan Singh v. State of Rajasthan*.[12] A revised, stronger version of this argument was endorsed by the majority in *Golaknath v. State of Punjab*[13] and it is this version of the argument that I will focus on.

If the argument that constitutional amendments can be reviewed under Article 13 is to succeed either one of the following two independent claims need to be accepted. First, that constitutional amendments in the Indian Constitution are the product of the exercise of legislative power through an essentially legislative process and are therefore correctly described as 'law' under Article 13(3)(a). Second, it is proposed that all state action including constitutional amendments are subject to judicial review under Article 13 as a necessary condition of a written constitution protecting immutable fundamental rights guaranteed under the constitution. These arguments are assessed separately below.

The Legislative Character of Constitutional Amendments

The legislative character of constitutional amendments is supported by the interpretation of two distinct sets of constitutional provisions first, provisions on the source of amending power and second, provisions relating to the process of amendment of the constitution. These arguments bring varied resources and interpretive strategies to advance their claims. Some judges relied exclusively on a close reading of the constitutional text while others drew on broader constitutional principles gleaned from historical data, a comparative approach, and theoretical literature.

The argument about the source of amending power in the constitution rests on a close reading of the constitutional text. The marginal note to an unamended Article 368,[14] which provides for the general amending power of Parliament, read 'The Procedure for the amendment of the Constitution'. The word 'power' was conspicuously missing in the marginal title and the several clauses of Article 368. Hence, it is argued that the power to amend the

[13] *Golaknath*, supra n. 3, p. 1643.

[14] The marginal note to Article 368 was amended by section 3 of the Constitution (24th Amendment) Act, 1971 to read 'Power of Parliament to amend the Constitution and procedure thereof'.

constitution is not provided for in Article 368 and instead is to be found in the residuary legislative power of Parliament.[15] A corollary to this argument is that Article 368 merely provides for a special process to be followed when exercising the amending power. By declaring that amending power draws from the plenary legislative power of Parliament the *Golaknath* majority alludes to the doctrine of parliamentary sovereignty in the United Kingdom; a constitutional principle which is not easily accommodated by the text of the constitution. While it is true that Article 368, as it then stood, did not contain the word 'power' and its marginal title employed the word 'procedure', the conclusion that amendments were an exercise of legislative power leads to absurd consequences.

Article 245 which confers legislative power on the Union and the States begins with the phrase 'Subject to the provisions of this Constitution, Parliament may make laws …'.[16] The effect of this phrase is to establish a hierarchy between ordinary laws and constitutional law by disabling Parliament from using its ordinary legislative power to alter the constitution. Hence, no law enacted under Article 245 may amend any provisions of the constitution. In the absence of this hierarchy, the Indian Constitution would more closely resemble the British constitutional arrangement in which Parliament may enact ordinary legislation on any subject matter including constitutional matters. The doctrine of implied repeal resolves any problems arising out of conflicting laws. The doctrine of implied repeal is an adequate device to settle conflicts among laws provided all the laws are considered to be of equal status. The majority opinion in the *Golaknath* case does not appear to have grasped the essence of this limitation on Parliamentary legislative power.

Rao's response to this problem is that the 'limitations in Article 245 are in respect of the power to make a law and not of the content of the law made'.[17] He suggests that limit on the power of Parliament to make a law amending the Constitution under Article 245 depends on whether the constitutional provision

---

[15] Constitution of India, 1950. Articles 245 and 246 read with entry 97 of List I of the 7th Schedule confers on Parliament the power to legislate on any item not included in any other list of the 7th Schedule.

[16] Ibid., Article 245.

[17] *Golaknath*, supra n. 3, p. 1658 (Subba Rao, CJ).

to be amended expressly provides or impliedly suggests that it cannot be amended. In other words, he seems to suggest that in order to determine whether a provision in the constitution can be amended using Article 368 one must read the provision for verbal cues which suggest whether it is immutable or open to change. Therefore, he concludes that Article 245 does not prevent all laws that amend the constitution from being enacted. However, the distinction between the limits on amending power and the limits on the content of the amending law which Rao seeks to identify in Article 245[18] is not clear. Further it is difficult to imagine how such a distinction allows us to overcome the limitations on legislative power in Article 245. At any rate, Rao's proposal presents us with a tortured reading of the constitutional text with insufficient reasons to support it.

The majority opinions in *Golaknath* eliminate the hierarchy between ordinary and constitutional law in Article 245, drawing inspiration from a British constitutional model of parliamentary sovereignty.[19] However, they do not embrace the implications of this model of illimitable sovereignty and assert that both law making and constitutional amendment are equally subject to judicial review under Article 13. Their equivocating use of the text and comparative constitutional analogies to support their interpretive conclusions about different parts of the constitution leads to a constitutional collage that is incoherent and inconsistent. This becomes clearer with the analysis of the arguments related to the scope of judicial review later in this chapter.

The second argument advanced to support the conclusion that constitutional amendments are 'law' under Article 13 relies on the strong resemblance between the legislative process and the amending process set out in the constitution. The essentially 'legislative character' of the amending process is sought to be demonstrated by comparing: first, the rules followed to enact ordinary legislation as well as the process of amendment adopted under the special amending articles in the constitution and second, the rules adopted by the

---

[18] Hidayatullah's eloquent concurring judgment in the case does not even visit this controversy.

[19] *Golaknath*, supra n. 3, p. 1695 (Hidayatullah, J).

Lok Sabha to administer the amendment process under the general Article 368 power.

The Indian constitution may be amended in two ways: first, a general amending power under Article 368 which applies to all subject matter and second, a 'special' amending power that applies to specified subjects. The special amending powers allow Parliament to amend the constitution for the purposes identified under the Article by enacting an ordinary law using the ordinary legislative process. For example, Articles 2 and 3 of the Constitution[20] allow the Parliament to admit new states into the Union and alter the boundaries of existing states in the Union by making law. Though these laws alter some provisions of the constitution, they are deemed as not being amendments to the constitution under Article 368.[21]

As the constitution expressly allows for amendment in particular cases by the exercise of ordinary legislative power, it is argued that the constitution adopts a legislative model of constitutional amendment. This conclusion strains the constitutional text and is difficult to accept without further reasons. The constitution distinguishes between two types of amending power and sets out the different processes by which they may be exercised. A plain reading of the constitutional text suggests that Article 368 is the general power of amendment, while other articles which provide for an easier mode of amendment of specific subject matter are exceptions to this general power. As the constitutional text clearly sets out further process requirements—two-thirds majority in Parliament and the consent of half the states in some cases—for the exercise of the general amending power under Article 368 which are unnecessary for the exercise of special amending power, it is difficult to understand why the majority concludes that both types of constitutional amending powers are exercised in an identical fashion. Further, this comparison between general and special amending power does not itself provide us with any principled reasons to decide the scope of judicial review under Article 13.

The Rules of Procedure adopted by the Lok Sabha under Article 18 for the passage of a bill amending the Constitution bear a close

---

[20] Other articles which confer special amending powers include Article 169, Para 7 of the 5th Schedule and Para 21 of the 6th Schedule.

[21] Constitution of India, 1950, Article 4(2).

resemblance to those adopted for ordinary legislation.[22] Rao concludes from the above evidence that amendments in the Indian constitution are essentially 'legislative'[23] in character. He considers the requirements of an enhanced majority of two-thirds of the members present and voting[24] to pass any amendment and of ratification by half the states in certain circumstances[25] as safeguards against hasty action and the protection to the states respectively which did not alter the 'legislative character' of amendments. Hence, he concluded that these safeguards did not alter the 'legislative character' of constitutional amendment.

The majority opinions in the *Golaknath* case offer any further arguments to extend the analogy between legislative process and amending process to control the scope of judicial review under Article 13. The analogy may be extended if one considers that the Indian constitution does not submit constitutional amendments to a unique process—like referendums, or to a specially convened constitutional convention—as prescribed by other constitutions. This may be because Rao decries the use of the comparative method in constitutional interpretation as he considers that differences between constitutions can be traced to the 'spirit and genius of the nation in which a particular constitution has its birth'.[26] Keeping aside the merits of his constitutional particularism, it is nevertheless difficult to conclude from the evidence and arguments of the majority in *Golaknath* that the constitution makes no distinction between the process of legislation and constitutional amendment.

Moreover, even if the process of amendment is legislative in character it is not necessary for us to conclude that the outcome of the amending process is 'law' for the purpose of Article 13. To extend this analogy between the amending process and the legislative process to the nature and quality of the outcomes which result from these respective processes one needs more substantive reasons. These arguments could be about the definition of 'law' in Article 139(3)(a) or about the constitutional principles which guide the scope of

---

[22] Lok Sabha Rules of Procedure, 1951, Rules 155, 156, 157, and 158.

[23] *Golaknath*, supra n. 1, p. 1659 (Subba Rao, CJ).

[24] Constitution of India, 1950, Article 368(2).

[25] Ibid., Proviso to Article 368(2).

[26] *Golaknath*, supra n. 3, p. 1661 (Subba Rao, CJ).

judicial review under Article 13. However, none of these arguments are offered in *Golaknath*.

In this section I have considered the arguments, advanced in support of the conclusion that constitutional amendments are 'law' under Article 13: first, the source of the amending power and second, the analogy between the amending process and the legislative process. The arguments offered by the *Golaknath* majority about the source of amending power are motivated by the British constitutional model and ignores the text of the Indian constitution. Further, this constitutional model erases the relationship between ordinary laws and constitutional laws which is among the basic facets of any written constitution. As a result, amending power is located in a constitutional provision that does not lend support to the constitutional practices of amendment. The analogy proposed between the legislative and amending process does not, without further support from constitutional text and principle, provide us with any guidance on the nature of amending power in the constitution. In the next part of this chapter, I consider whether the arguments about the nature and scope of judicial review under Article 13 offers us compelling reasons as to why constitutional amendments are law.

The *Golaknath* judgment provoked a strong reaction from Parliament which amended the marginal title of Article 368 to read 'Power of Parliament to amend the Constitution and the procedure therefor'[27] and inserted a new clause (1) which expressly provides for Parliament's 'constituent power'[28] to amend any of the articles in the Constitution. When the 24th Constitution Amendment Act, which made these changes, was challenged in *Kesavananda*,[29] counsel for the appellant conceded the arguments about the source and nature of amending power in the constitution. Both majority and minority judgments agreed that this amendment was valid insofar as it clarified the source of amending power. Khanna, who wrote the controlling opinion in the case, emphatically concluded that once the procedure prescribed in Article 368 was followed the 'end-product is the amendment of the constitution.'[30] The issue has remained settled by

[27] Constitution (24th Amendment) Act, 1971, section 3.
[28] Ibid.
[29] *Kesavananda Bharati*, supra n. 2, p. 225.
[30] Ibid., p. 739 (Khanna, J).

these constitutional amendments and has not been raised thereafter in any case before the Supreme Court.

Scope of Judicial Review

Four major arguments were advanced in support of the conclusion that constitutional amendments are subject to judicial review under Article 13. First, it is argued that 'law' under Article 13 is wide enough to include constitutional amendments. Second, it is suggested that the nature of judicial review provided for in written constitutions requires the review of amendments. This is closely related to the third argument about the nature of fundamental rights guaranteed by the constitution. Finally, it is argued that a common law doctrine of implied limitation on the sovereignty of Parliament was applicable in India. I will consider each of these arguments in turn.

The scope of Article 13 is controlled by clause 2 which provides that no 'law' shall contravene the fundamental rights in the constitution. Article 13(3)(a) defines 'law', for the purpose of judicial review under Article 13 to include 'any ordinance, order, bye-law, rule, regulation, notification, custom, or usage having in the territory of India the force of law'.[31] This open-ended inclusive definition of 'law' used in the Article does not provide sufficient linguistic resources to decisively settle the question of whether constitutional amendments should be regarded as 'law'. This definition allows for the argument that constitutional amendments, although not expressly included, may be accommodated within the definition of law in this Article. It is argued that the ordinary meaning of the word 'law' would include constitutional law and hence constitutional amendments should be considered law for the purposes of Article 13. Further, it is argued that the term 'law' should be read consistently in Article 13(1) on pre-constitutional laws, and Article 13(2) on post-constitutional laws.

Article 13(1) allows for the continuity of all laws existing in the territory of India before the adoption of the 1950 constitution provided that such laws are not inconsistent with the fundamental rights. As the 1950 constitution is the first constitution of independent India it is difficult to imagine what 'constitutional laws' are saved under clause 1. It seems likely that petitioners had important

---

[31] Constitution of India, 1950, Article 13(3)(a).

colonial enactments like the Government of India Act, 1935 and the Indian Independence Act, 1947 as examples of laws of 'constitutional character' prior to 1950. However, these enactments are expressly repealed by Article 395 of the Constitution of India, 1950 leaving no laws of constitutional significance to be covered under Article 13(1).

The attempt by some judges to arrive at a definitive conclusion about the scope of the term law by semantic stipulation or an interpretation of Article 13 standing alone is unsatisfactory. Such an approach to interpretation is devoid of any consideration of constitutional principles that illuminate the role and function that Article 13 judicial review plays in the constitution. Moreover, it is far from convincing to arrive at a conclusion about the proper scope of the term 'law' in Article 13 without paying attention to other provisions of the constitution and its overall structure which allows us to develop a view about the purpose of judicial review in the constitution. I now consider two arguments about the scope of the term 'law' which go beyond the language of Article 13.

One argument defines the scope of the term 'law' by examining the relationship between Articles 13 and 368 with the aid of doctrines of statutory and constitutional interpretation. However, this attempt to resolve the conflict between the two widely phrased articles using standard techniques of statutory interpretation—'the technique of harmonious construction'—is deeply flawed. In *Sankari Prasad*, Sastri sought to harmoniously reconcile the amending power of Parliament and the judicial review power of the courts by reading down the scope and application of the judicial review power to not include constitutional amendments.[32] Rao utilized the same principle of construction to read down the amending power of Parliament under Article 368 to be subject to the judicial review power under Article 13 in *Golaknath*.[33] Both these judgments correctly apply the rule of harmonious construction as this interpretive strategy provides equal support to opposite outcomes. It is unlikely that judges may convincingly resolve complex questions about the judicial review of amending power by resorting to semantic stipulation or applying doctrines of statutory construction like the doctrine of harmonious

[32] *Sankari Prasad*, supra n. 1, p. 463 (Patanjali Sastri J, Kania CJ).
[33] *Golaknath*, supra n. 3, p. 1664 (Subba Rao, CJ).

construction without further substantive argument. Both these text-based strategies of interpretation need arguments of principle to support the conclusions they advance. The second argument about the nature of judicial review in written constitutions promises to offer more substantive reasons.

A second, more promising, argument about the nature of judicial review in written constitutions emerged from Kania's observation in *A.K. Gopalan* v. *Union of India*.[34] He took the view that funda-mental rights guaranteed in the constitution are paramount and inviolable even in the absence of Article 13. Hence, he concluded that the judiciary has the power to review the constitutional validity of any legislative enactment to the extent that it violated fundamental rights irrespective of the particular phrasing of Article 13. He was echoing Marshall in *Marbury* v. *Madison*[35] when he proposed that the Indian Constitution, by virtue of being a written constitution, conferred an inherent power on the Supreme Court to review state action. Patanjali Sastri, concurring in the case, added that the people of India, as sovereigns, delegated to government the right to govern but reserved to themselves certain fundamental rights.[36]

Gajendragadkar rejected these arguments in *Sajjan Singh* v. *State of Rajasthan*[37] on the grounds that both opinions pre-supposed a 'theoretical concept' of sovereignty which was not necessary to interpret the provisions of the Constitution. Arguably, any concept of judicial review pre-supposes some principled justification in political theory assigning to different institutions their respective powers and functions. By refusing to engage in a full-fledged discussion about the proper role of judicial review, Gajendragadkar foreclosed the opportunity of providing a substantive justification for an interpretation of Article 13 to include constitutional amendments. This eschewal of justifications from political theory resulted in a premature abandonment of this line of argument. The unwillingness of the court to revisit it in later constitutional amendment cases including *Golaknath* has deprived the court of a significant argument in support of Article 13 judicial review to constitutional amendments.

[34] AIR 1950 SC 27 at p. 34 (Kania, CJ).
[35] 5 US 137 (1803).
[36] *A.K. Gopalan*, supra n. 34, p. 72 (Kania, CJ).
[37] *Sajjan Singh*, supra n. 12, p. 858 (Gajendragadkar, CJ).

Inspite of the court's reluctance, I will explore whether the view taken by the court in *Gopalan* provides an adequate justification for judicial review of constitutional amendment as this advances the argument in this thesis.

Three distinct lines of argument emerge out of the dicta in *A.K. Gopalan*. First, the court proposes that judicial review is inherent in a written constitution. This conclusion about the nature of judicial review was important in *Marbury* as the United States Constitution does not expressly provide for judicial review, its relevance of the argument to the Indian constitution which expressly provides for such review is unclear. Perhaps, one could argue that the inherent character of judicial review in a written constitution allows for judicial review of a wider scope than that suggested by the text of Article 13. However, to extend the scope of *Marbury* principle beyond ordinary legislation to cover constitutional amendments, principled arguments must be offered to justify such an extension. Further, it is not necessary that the constitutional judicial review justified by the *Marbury* principle needs to be rights based review under Article 13. It is plausible to suggest that judicial review of constitutional amendments may be an extension of legislative competence review which the courts conventionally exercise under Article 245. Moreover, besides developing a justification for such a review, we will also need to find textual support from the constitution to accommodate this expanded model of judicial review.

Secondly, Sastri proposes a model of delegated sovereignty in which the people as popular sovereigns delegate limited powers under the constitution to the government. Though this model was rejected as an inaccurate description of the political arrangements in the Indian constitution, Hidayatullah's concurring judgment in *Golaknath* implicitly adopts it. He suggests that a Parliament which sought to amend fundamental rights in the Constitution should reconstitute a Constituent body of the people which would be authorized to make such changes.[38] I will consider both these arguments in greater detail in Chapter 6.

The third line of argument in *A.K. Gopalan* about the nature of judicial review rests on an understanding of the nature and status of

---

[38] *Golaknath*, supra n. 3, p. 1705 (Hidayatullah, J).

fundamental rights in the constitution. The immutable character of fundamental rights guaranteed in Part III of the constitution was a critical ingredient of the argument for judicial review of constitutional amendments under Article 13 in the majority opinions in *Golaknath*. Rao took the view that 'fundamental rights are given a transcendental position under our constitution and are kept beyond the reach of Parliament.'[39] He surveyed various provisions of the constitution, a wide range of historical sources from declarations adopted by the Congress party during the freedom movement, and speeches made by leaders in the Constituent Assembly to arrive at the conclusion that fundamental rights are only a modern name for 'natural rights'.[40] Hidayatullah, in his concurring opinion in *Golaknath*, agreed for different reasons that fundamental rights were immutable in character though he did not go so far as to endorse the view that they were natural rights. He reiterated the position which he first adopted in *Sajjan Singh* where he observed that 'The Constitution gives so many assurances in Part III that it would be difficult to think that they were the playthings of a special majority'.[41] Moreover he took a different view from Rao about the immutable character of these rights where he was willing to admit that fundamental rights may be tinkered with in minor ways but that they could not be abridged or removed. Notably, Wanchoo's dissenting opinion in *Golaknath* does not respond to any of the arguments about the immutable character of fundamental rights in the constitution.

So far, we have identified three of the arguments in support of the majority opinions in *Golakanath* that fundamental rights should not be modified by constitutional amendments: first, that because fundamental rights are natural rights and such rights are by definition beyond the reach of the state; second, that the elevated status of fundamental rights in the constitution may be discerned from the historical process by which these rights came to be included in the constitution; and third, that the constitutional provisions together as a whole, organic document the conclusion that constitutional amendments are subject to judicial review under Article 13. I will critically analyse each of these arguments below.

[39] *Golaknath*, supra n. 3, p. 1656 (Subba Rao, CJ).
[40] Ibid.
[41] Ibid., p. 1693 (Hidayatullah, J).

The Indian Constitution does not spell out the rationale for the 'fundamentalness' of the rights guaranteed by Part III of the constitution. Unlike the United States Constitution, which confers rights using broad and general phrases, the Indian Constitution contains a detailed catalogue of rights providing for exceptions and allowing for restrictions under specific circumstances. Moreover, the constitution allows for rights to be abridged or suspended in times of national emergencies.[42] Nothing in the text of the constitution supports the conclusion that these rights are 'natural rights'. To the contrary, these modestly stated rights, weighed down by several exceptions, grate against the overarching monolithic vision of immutable natural rights which Rao proposes. While it is clear that the constitution guarantees a wide range of fundamental rights there is no reason a priori to assume that such rights have to be 'natural rights'.[43] The constitution may just as well have adopted an interest-based theory or will-based justification of fundamental rights.[44]

The crucial question posed in *Golaknath* is about the level of entrenchment that these rights enjoy—it is clear that they limit ordinary state legislative and executive action. The courts have to determine whether rights are immune to constitutional amendments as well. By positing that the rights in the Constitution are natural rights, without making any argument about how the constitutional text supports such a conclusion, Rao seeks to settle the question in an unconvincing way. To accept the conclusion that constitutional amendments are subject to judicial review under Article 13, we need further argument about the nature of rights or the manner of their entrenchment in the constitution.

The second argument supports the conclusion that rights are entrenched against amendment by relying on historical evidence. There are two kinds of histories that this argument relies on: first, a historical evolutionary perspective on how rights came to be included in the Indian constitution and secondly, the drafting

---

[42] Constitution of India, 1950, Articles 352 and 356.

[43] G.J. Jacobsohn, 'An Unconstitutional Constitution: A comparative perspective', 4 *International J Constitutional L* 474 (2006), where he analyses why 'the era of natural rights in India was short-lived'.

[44] J. Waldron (ed.), *Theories of Rights*, Oxford: Oxford University Press, 1984, pp. 1–20 for an excellent introduction to theories of rights.

history of the relevant articles of the Constitution being interpreted. The reliance on historical evidence raises complex theoretical problems about the appropriate methods to be adopted in constitutional interpretation. Even assuming that both these kinds of histories aid constitutional interpretation, we must enquire into the scope and kinds of historical evidence which are relevant and the nature of inferences that one may draw from such evidence. Below, I consider the use of these techniques in the cases under judicial review of constitutional amendment cases and assess whether they support the conclusions reached.

The Supreme Court has developed a rule of construction which allows any court to examine the Constituent Assembly debates when there is ambiguity in the constitutional text. The court may use these debates to establish the broader historical background to any provision but prohibits the use of such materials to interpret the text of the constitution.[45] It is not altogether clear whether courts are able to apply this distinction in the way that these materials are to be used in practice. In any event the evidence on the applicability of Article 13 judicial review to constitutional amendment is scanty and unhelpful. Both sides of the argument are able to mobilize evidence to support their conclusions.

The Constitutent Assembly considered draft article 304-A,[46] corresponding to Article 368, which cast express limits on the power of constitutional amendment. There is no clarity from the historical record as to why the Constituent Assembly rejected this proposal. Draft article 8,[47] corresponding to Article 13, proposed to include a specific clause which prevented Parliament from amending any fundamental rights. This draft Article was subsequently dropped without specific reasons. While petitioners concluded that these draft articles were abandoned because the framers envisaged that the existing provisions of the constitution already provided for these contingencies, the respondents suggested that these draft articles were dropped in order to give Parliament a wider amending power.

[45] *Golaknath*, supra n. 3, p. 1682 (Wanchoo, J).

[46] Constituent Assembly Debates, 17 September 1949.

[47] Constituent Assembly Debates, October 1948. See also Shiva Rao, *The Framing of India's Constitution* (Vol. IV) p. 26.

Both sides to the argument led further evidence of the importance that the eminent leaders speaking in the Constituent Assembly attached to fundamental rights or to the supremacy of Parliament in support of their respective claims. In the absence of further clinching historical evidence or agreement on a judicial technique of drawing suitable inferences from historical materials one must safely conclude that this approach to constitutional interpretation cannot settle the question before us decisively.

The second argument from history seeks to establish the immutable character of rights in the constitution by developing a broad historical evolutionary perspective on the exalted status of rights in the freedom movement which resulted in their 'fundamental' status in the 1950 Constitution. However, the evidence presented falls far short of establishing the proposition asserted—that fundamental rights are immune from amendment. Rao selectively excerpts from speeches made, and declarations adopted, by the freedom movement between 1850 and 1947. He relies heavily on a speech delivered by Motilal Nehru in 1928 in which it is asserted that fundamental rights guaranteed in the constitution should not be withdrawn '… under any circumstances.'[48] The attempt to control the interpretation of concretely expressed articles of the constitution using scanty historical record of this sort is fraught with danger. This is particularly so when there is an attempt to reduce a wide array of often contradictory historical events and expressions to support or sustain narrow propositions in constitutional law. This does not rule out the use of historical evidence by courts to arrive at broader propositions about the central ideas animating a constitution such as whether the constitution should be understood to be of a transformative character as opposed to status-quoist character. For the moment it is sufficient to note that both arguments from history are inadequate to support the conclusion that fundamental rights are immutable and beyond the reach of the amending power in Article 368.

The third interpretive strategy advanced in support of immutable fundamental rights is an interpretation of the relationship between amending power and fundamental rights which situates it in the

---

[48] *Golaknath*, supra n. 3, p. 1656 (Subba Rao, CJ).

context of wider provisions of the constitution. Rao was of the opinion that the proper place of fundamental rights in the constitution could not be appreciated unless we first undertake a survey of the objectives of the constitution and the particular provisions employed to achieve these objectives.[49] He first looked to the preamble and identified the other provisions of the Constitution which establish the principle of the rule of law and the supremacy of the constitution as central themes in the constitution. He concluded from his broad survey that the Constitution sought to achieve the overarching goal of social justice while ensuring that the country did not slide down an authoritarian path.

This is not the first time that the court has considered the role of the preamble in constitutional interpretation. In a previous case, the Supreme Court had ruled that the preamble could not be a source of substantive power[50] and Wanchoo's dissenting opinion in *Golaknath* inferred from this ruling that the preamble could not be a source of prohibition or limitation on power either.[51] Rao's use of the preamble does not offend this rule of construction. He does not take the view that the preamble directly imposes limitations on the amending power in Article 368 and uses it as an aid to interpret the relationship between Articles 13 and 368. The preamble in the constitution is a compact statement of the ideals and aspirations of the constitution and should not be read as a mere platitude. If the language of Article 13 and 368 allow for conclusions which take into account the preamble's aspirations then such an interpretation is certainly more attractive than the strategy of harmonizing conflicting articles in an opaque and inarticulate manner adopted by the courts in some decisions we considered earlier in this section.

However, it is not clear which values in the preamble can provide us assistance in interpreting the relationship between Articles 13 and 368. The chief values that Rao employs to interpret the relationship is the supremacy of the constitution and the rule of law. Neither of these values is expressly stated in the preamble. Moreover, both the rule of law and supremacy of the constitution as general constitutional

---

[49] Ibid., p. 1655 (Subba Rao, CJ).
[50] In *Re Berubari Union*, AIR 1960 SC 845.
[51] *Golaknath*, supra n. 3, p. 1683 (Wanchoo, J).

principles do not compel us to the conclusion that constitutional amendments should be subject to judicial review under Article 13. We can think of other constitutions, like that of the United States, which profess both these ideas but do not recognize the judicial review of constitutional amendments.

A structural interpretation of the Constitution which uses the preamble to assist in the interpretation of other constitutional provisions may well be a legitimate and useful interpretive approach. Rao needs to engage in further argument to establish why either supremacy of the constitution or the rule of law should require the conclusion that constitutional amendments are subject to judicial review. This may have something to do with the kinds of conclusions that such a structural interpretation of the constitution can support. Such interpretations support the identification of constitutional themes and institutional arrangements at a level of abstraction that supplements plausible readings of the constitutional text. In other words, these constitutional principles assist us in choosing between two possible interpretations of the text but do not support the use of constitutional principles to override the express provisions in the constitution. In Chapter 5, I will examine whether structural interpretation is a defensible model of interpretation and the kinds of conclusions that such an interpretation can support.

The fourth, and final, argument advanced to support the conclusion that amending power is subject to judicial review under Article 13 is the doctrine of implied limits. I must clarify that judicial opinions and commentaries have used the phrase 'implied limitations' differently. Some judges and commentators use the implied–express distinction to signal whether the limitations they seek to impose on parliamentary amending power are expressed in particular provisions of the constitution or are inferred from the constitution as a whole, respectively. In this sense, Article 13 is an express limit whereas any limitation which is inferred from the constitution as a whole is considered an implied limit. The express–implied limit distinction is used in a second sense to distinguish between limits that may be traced to the structure and origin of the constitution at its founding moment—historically implied limits—and express limits which may be traced to the constitutional text. It is the second sense of the distinction that we are concerned about here.

There are two strands of arguments advanced in the majority opinions in *Golaknath* about the doctrine of implied limits. First, regarding the status and power enjoyed by colonial legislatures as distinguished from Westminster Parliament[52] and second, arising from the distinction between states and governments in European jurisprudence. In *Golaknath*, both strands of argument were raised in a rather confused and underdeveloped fashion.

Rao relied on two important judgments of the Privy Council[53] which deal with arguments about limits on the power of amendment enjoyed by colonial legislatures as authority to conclude that the Indian Constitution may be amended legislatively. These cases address the important question in British constitutional law of how the sovereignty of colonial assemblies may be limited by statute in ways that Westminster Parliament is not. Rao does not enquire into whether the Indian Parliament is similarly situated. Instead he relies on these cases as authority for the proposition that constitutions may be amended legislatively, an issue settled by these cases in a legal system which was crucially different from the provisions of the Indian constitution. The argument for special limits on the power of colonial legislatures is one that autochthonous constitutional traditions such as India's reject. An improved version of the doctrine of implied limits is raised more appropriately in a more fleshed-out fashion in the *Kesavananda* case which developed the doctrine of basic structure. I will carefully analyse the applicability of this modified version of the doctrine in India in the next part of this chapter where I consider the *Kesavananda* case.

The second strand of the argument for implied limits draws on the distinction in European constitutional jurisprudence between the state and the government. Hidayatullah suggests that this distinction may be mapped onto the Indian constitution to distinguish between the status of the constituent body which drew up the constitution and that of Parliament exercising its powers of amendment. He concludes that 'kompetenz–kompetenz' or the unlimited ability to

[52] Geoffrey Marshall, *Constitutional Conventions*, Oxford: Clarendon Press, 1984, pp. 206–9.

[53] *McCawley* v. *The King*, AIR 1920 PC 691; *Pederick Ranasinghe* v. *Bribery Commissioner*, [1964] 2 WLR 1301.

alter the constitution 'does not flow from the amendatory process'[54] in the constitution. Once rights have been declared to be fundamental by 'the people', Parliament may not abridge them in any way through the amending process. It must 'convoke another Constituent Assembly'[55] which may be empowered to look at the constitution afresh. Hidayatullah conducts a sketchy survey of constitutions where similar limits have been placed on the amending body to buttress this conclusion.

The entrenchment of fundamental rights against constitutional amendment is an outcome that may be justified differently by varied philosophical traditions. The German Basic Law sets out that certain portions of law are immune from amendment in order to overcome the defects of the Weimar Constitution exploited during the Hitler years.[56] Some common law constitutional jurisdictions view limits on amending power as being anti-democratic in character, which would require us to provide a revised account of the relationship between constitutions and democracy.[57] We will engage with these philosophical arguments in greater depth in Chapter 6.

Irrespective of the merits of these arguments we must recognize that the task of constitutional interpretation is not merely to conceive of the best theoretical reconciliation between popular sovereignty of the people and the amending power of Parliament, but to direct one's attention to the interpretation of the text of the constitution. Hidayatullah's opinion in *Golaknath* fails to address the limits which the constitutional text imposes on the kinds of insights from political philosophy which may legitimately be used to interpret the constitution. For the moment, it is sufficient for us to conclude that though a doctrine of implied limits which relies on the distinction in power between a constituent and constituted body may be a plausible philosophical argument, more reasons to conclude that

---

[54] *Golaknath*, supra n. 3, p. 1697 (Hidayatullah, J).

[55] *Golaknath*, supra n. 3, p. 1705 (Hidayatullah, J).

[56] R. Sudarshan, 'Stateness in the Indian Constitution' in Zoya Hasan et al. (eds) *India's Living Constitution*, Delhi: Permanent Black, 2002, p. 159. Sudarshan enquires into the European philosophical influences on the Indian Supreme Court.

[57] P.B. Mehta, 'The Inner Conflict of Constitutionalism: Judicial Review and the Basic Structure', ibid., p. 181.

this distinction extends the scope of judicial review to constitutional amendments under Article 13.

CONCLUSION

In this part of the chapter, I have considered whether parliamentary amending power is subject to judicial review under Article 13. I have argued that the claim that the source and nature of amending power is legislative in character is unsustainable for two reasons: first, Article 245 cannot be a source for amending power as the powers under the article are to be exercised subject to the other provisions of the constitution, and second, the analogy between legislative and amending process is a weak one which cannot support the conclusion that the substantive output of both processes is legislation and therefore should be subject to judicial review. I then considered three types of arguments on why the term 'law' should be considered to include amendments. I have argued that the definition of 'law' should not be stipulated semantically or merely by reference to the structure of Article 13 as these arguments are inconclusive and avoid principled arguments about whether 'law' should be construed to include amendments or not.

The argument that all written constitutions allow for judicial review—irrespective of the phrasing of Article 13—thereby making constitutional amendments subject to judicial review, is that it moves from a principle which relates to the source of judicial review to unsupported conclusions about the nature and scope of such review. In order to apply the *Marbury* principle in these cases further arguments are necessary to justify its application to constitutional amendments and to clarify whether it requires rights based review as opposed to competence review.

I conclude this part of the chapter by considering the four arguments about why fundamental rights in the constitution are immutable in character. The claim that fundamental rights are natural rights is devoid of any support from the text of the constitution and one may argue that the constitution is motivated by other justifications for making some rights 'fundamental' but open to amendment. Both types of arguments from history are indecisive. Reliance on the Constituent Assembly debates is unreliable as there is evidence that supports alternative conclusions. The attempt to develop a historical evolutionary perspective on the status of fundamental rights in the constitution is sketchy and utilizes inadequate historical data. Even if a comprehensive historical perspective is developed such a technique cannot support an interpretation of the constitution which is inconsistent with the constitutional text.

Structural interpretations of the constitution which use the preamble and other constitutional provisions to establish constitutional values and principles such as supremacy of the constitution or rule of law can be useful aids to judicial interpretations. However, none of these principles or values can be used to support the narrow legal proposition that amendments are subject to judicial review under Article 13. Moreover, such principles and values derived through a structural interpretation of the constitution cannot override the constitutional text and cannot be used in a general context or independent fashion to settle interpretive questions about whether constitutional amendments are 'law' under Article 13.

There are two versions of the doctrine of implied limitations advanced in support of the immutable character of rights. The argument which rests on the limited sovereignty of colonial legislatures misapplies precedent and is unable to withstand the claim of autochthonous constitutions, like the Indian Constitution, to enjoy full sovereignty. The second version which relies on the distinction in the powers of constituent and constituted bodies is a useful distinction which needs to be developed in two senses: to assess if it fits with the Indian Constitution and whether it offers a reasoned understanding of the interaction between the ideas of democracy and constitutionalism. The version put forward in the *Golaknath* case does neither. Hence, for the reasons addressed above, the Supreme Court was mistaken in ruling that constitutional amendments are subject to judicial review under Article 13.

IMPLIED LIMITS ON AMENDING POWER: BASIC STRUCTURE REVIEW

In this part of this chapter, I argue that the Supreme Court was right in concluding that the Constitution imposes implied limits on the power of constitutional amendment under Article 368. I must make clear at the outset that this is a modest argument about limits on this mode of constitutional change—constitutional amendment—which may or may not apply with equal rigour to other modes of constitutional change beyond constitutional amendment. In the first part of this chapter I had suggested that the argument for express limits on the power of amendment under Article 13 was unsustainable on a reasonable interpretation of the constitutional text as it led to a complete breakdown of the relations between the legislative and amending powers of Parliament envisaged in the constitution. It may then seem odd that while I deny that the constitution imposes express limits I argue that it nevertheless imposes implied limits.

I will try to show by the end of this chapter that what, at first glance, seems to be a rather surprising conclusion turns out to be a reasonable and well supported one. Significantly, not much turns on the distinction between 'express' and 'implied' limits. The distinction between the two types of limits is prompted by the arguments advanced in court in these cases and in the academic literature commenting on these cases.[58] The doctrine of implied limits which has previously been applied in diverse constitutional cases in several other jurisdictions came to be strenuously argued as the basis on which amending power was restricted. This use of the doctrine is both confusing and unhelpful. What is at stake here is whether an interpretation of the Constitution which limits Parliamentary amending power is valid and legitimate? The phrasing of these limits as implied or express is not indicative of the nature or source of the limit and is at best a placeholder for arguments about whether these limits were previously recognized or not. It is only to signal the temporal novelty of these new limits in the Indian constitutional context that I use the term 'implied limit' to characterize basic structure review.

In this work, I mark out arguments which extend previously recognized constitutional models of judicial review to cover constitutional amendments—express limits—from arguments that devise a novel form of judicial review that applies especially to constitutional amendments—implied limits. This distinction is useful to the extent as it identifies the different models of judicial review developed by the court. This work argues that the distinction between types of

---

[58] See N. Palkhivala, *Our Constitution Defaced and Defiled*, Delhi: Macmillan Co. of India, 1974.

constitutional judicial review has not been amplified or well understood in the academic literature on the subject. However, it is a misleading distinction insofar as it suggests that while express limits are somehow based on the text of the constitution, implied limits are divined free from the constitutional text by some imaginary value-laden ether. Such a use of the distinction is a reminder that the constitutional basis for both models of judicial review is arguments about the interpretation of the constitutional text. What distinguishes the constitutional basis of implied and express limits on amending power is the reliance on different provisions in the constitution and different methods of constitutional interpretation.[59]

The *Kesavananda* Ratio

In *Kesavananda* v. *State of Kerala*,[60] the majority among a 13-judge bench of the Supreme Court ruled that the 24th, 25th, and 29th Constitution (Amendment) Acts passed by Parliament exercising its powers under Article 368 were unconstitutional to the extent that they damage the 'basic structure of the constitution'. In doing so the court overruled the majority opinion in *Golaknath* v. *State of Punjab*,[61] that Article 13 provided a constitutional basis for the judicial review of constitutional amendments. The *Kesavananda* opinion is among the longest judicial opinions delivered by any superior court in any jurisdiction and it is almost impossible to deal with every argument raised in the case exhaustively. In this part of the chapter, I will consider in great detail the important arguments considered by the Supreme Court in *Kesavananda* on the constitutional basis for basic structure review. I will argue that though the court was right in concluding that the constitution included implied limits on the power of amendment it did not ground this conclusion on a satisfactory interpretation of the constitution.

In *Kesavananda* a special bench of 13 judges was constituted to hear a bunch of six writ petitions that raised several common

---

[59] For a fuller account of the approach to constitutional interpretation in this thesis see Chapter 6.

[60] *Kesavananda Bharati*, supra n. 2, p. 225.

[61] *Golaknath*, supra n. 1.

questions of constitutional law. The judges took seriously Mathew's suggestion that it 'was desirable for the future development of the law that there should be a plurality of opinion even if the conclusion reached is the same'.[62] Eleven opinions were delivered making the task of identifying the majority holding on any question of law an arduous exercise. Nani Palkhivala, writing soon after the judgment was delivered, took the view that Khanna's view 'became the law of the land' as it agreed with the majority six led by Sikri on the question of limitations on the amending power and with the minority six led by Ray on the validity of Article 31C.[63] Very many interesting things may be, and have been, said about the judgment of the court in this case and whether one may ascertain a clear majority holding in the case.[64] Rajeev Dhavan's painstaking analysis accurately identifies the plurality opinion to comprise six majority, four minority, and three cross-bench opinions. He notes that even the nine judges who subscribed to some version of the doctrine of implied limits did not do so for the same reasons.[65] With the passage of time, the legal debate over the existence of a majority holding or ratio has ebbed away. I will not go any further into this question in this work. The analysis in this part of the chapter will focus on the two main questions before it: the scope of amending power under Article 368 and the power of the court to subject constitutional amendments to judicial review.

The eleven opinions in the case concentrated almost exclusively on the scope of amending power of the constitution. The arguments

[62] *Kesavananda Bharati* (Mathew J), supra n. 2, p. 825.

[63] N.A. Palkhivala, 'Fundamental Rights Case: Comment', (1973) 4 SCC (Journal) 57.

[64] Editor's Note, (1973) 4 SCC 225, 226. Compare Granville Austin, *Working a Democratic Constitution: A History of the Indian Experience*, New Delhi: Oxford University Press, 1999, pp. 258–69; P.K. Tripathi, '*Kesavananda Bharati* v. *State of Kerala*: Who wins?' (1974) 1 SCC (Journal) 3; 'In view of such radical divergence of approach and reasoning, it is submitted that any attempt to cull out a common ratio between the six judges led by the Chief Justice and Khanna, J., would be highly artificial and insupportable', at 28. For a contrary opinion see J. Minnatur, 'The Ratio in the *Kesavananda Bharati* Case' (1974) 1 SCC (Journal) 73.

[65] R. Dhavan, *Parliamentary Sovereignty and the Supreme Court*, New Delhi: Sterling Publishers, 1978, p. 141.

advanced crystallized along two nodes: the scope of the term 'amendment' in Article 368 and the doctrine of implied limitations. None of the opinions developed any extensive argument about the role of the court in judicially reviewing these amendments. The opinions seem to assume that once it is clear that some implied limits on amending power are identified, it follows that the court is empowered to police these limits. This assumption about the role of the courts is central to the issues before the Court and in Chapter 5, I analyse the constitutional arguments that support, and counter-arguments which object, to the court's power to judicially review amendments. In the rest of this chapter, I will consider the arguments relating to amending power in Article 368.

In *Kesavananda*, the court considered whether the power of constitutional amendment under Article 368 was subject to implied limits. All the opinions delivered by the court were agreed that where the language used by the constitution was capable of more than one plausible meaning, then the court was right to call into aid various rules of construction. The argument for implied limits took many forms: it was argued that the source of limits lie in the word 'amend' in Article 368 which allowed Parliament to modestly alter the constitution but not radically change it. I will argue that this 'textualist' interpretation adopts a semantic approach to the constitutional text, and standing alone, fails to offer any convincing reasons to conclude one way or the other.

Other opinions concluded that implied limits on amending power emerge when one reads Article 368 together with the other provisions of the constitution. It was argued that the amending power in Article 368 could not extend to alter the values espoused in the preamble to the constitution and all the rights guaranteed by the constitution. This was not an argument about the scope of Article 368 amending power considered in isolation but one that determines the scope of amending power by reading Article 368 in the context of the other relevant provisions of the constitution and the institutional structure envisaged by the constitution. This 'structural interpretation' of the constitutional document as a whole offers more compelling reasons for the court to uphold a particular interpretation of the scope of the amending power. This chapter will analyse the court's use of structural interpretation and argue that the conclusions arrived at by the court using this model of interpretation upholds the integrity of the constitutional document and can be the basis for imposing limits on the amending power.

A third type of argument that played a significant role in the court's reasoning was one that investigated the historical origins and purpose of the constitutional document. This argument took many forms: there were 'originalist' arguments about the intent of the constitutional framers. The constitutional assembly debates on which these originalist arguments rely do not offer significant support to the conclusions arrived at by the court on the point at issue and hence do not settle the issue of whether there are limits on the amending power. In addition, the court considered the historical context and motivations of the nationalist freedom movement to identify the purposes and aspirations that they ascribed to the constitution. This 'grand historical narrative' provided the court with a teleological argument that a constitution which advanced such noble aims would necessarily impose limits on parliamentary amending power. It is often suggested that such grand narratives are unsophisticated in their historical technique and provide malleable frameworks that are amenable to the courts' whims and fancies. In this chapter I will argue that such historical arguments provide the court with valuable information and orientation while interpreting historically self-conscious constitutions which are adopted in a particular historical context to achieve clearly identified transformative ends.

By adopting an approach to interpreting the constitution which was analogous to the tasks of statutory interpretation, the court avoided any engagement with the theoretical arguments that the issue of constitutional judicial review of constitutional amendments raises. I will take the lead of the court and avoid such enquiries for the moment. In Chapter 5, I return to these debates and consider some issues in constitutional interpretation which arise in the context of basic structure review. Before I engage with these normative problems that the court's decision raises, we would do well to analyse carefully the precise grounds on which the court reached its conclusions.

Textualism

In *Kesavananda*, the court's attention was riveted on the language used in Article 368. Khanna's opinion laid down two key propositions from his analysis of Article 368. First, that the article laid down no limitations on the power of amendment particularly with respect to fundamental rights and second, that this power did not include the power to 'abrogate the constitution and replace it with an entirely new constitution.'[66] He found support for both these propositions in the language of Article 368. In support of the first proposition, he observed that 'no words are to be found in Article 368 as may indicate that a limitation was intended on the power of making amendment'.[67] Similarly, he found that the 'words "amendment of this Constitution" and "the Constitution shall stand amended" in Article 368 show that what is amended is the existing constitution and what emerges as a result of amendment is not a new and different constitution...'.[68]

By strongly denying the utility of relying on dictionary meanings,[69] historical resources,[70] and the support of the doctrine of implied limitations,[71] Khanna rested his conclusions on the scope of the amending power in Article 368 on very narrow ground. Though generally short on constitutional theory arguments, he hints at his normative understanding of the basic structure by quoting Dietrich Conrad on structural limits on an amending body and Carl J. Friedrich on the constitution as a 'living, organic system'.[72] I will explore the use of these theoretical resources in greater detail in the next section of this chapter. But first I will turn to the arguments against such a view.

The lead dissenting judgment in *Kesavananda* was by Ray. He agreed with Khanna that the 'crux of the matter is the meaning of the word "amendment"'.[73] He was of the view that the Constitution used 'the word "amendment"... in an unambiguous and clear manner' to 'mean any kind of change'.[74] On considering the various provisions of the Constitution which uses the word, and paying attention

[66] *Kesavananda Bharati*, supra n. 2, p. 767 (Khanna, J).
[67] Ibid., p. 739 (Khanna, J).
[68] Ibid., p. 768 (Khanna, J).
[69] Ibid., p. 770 (Khanna, J).
[70] Ibid., p. 743 (Khanna, J).
[71] Ibid., p. 776 (Khanna, J).
[72] Ibid., pp. 768 and 769 (Khanna, J).
[73] *Kesavananda Bharati*, supra n. 2, p. 537 (Ray, J).
[74] Ibid., p. 539 (Ray, J).

to the constitutional practice of amendment up to that point, Ray concluded that the amending power was 'unlimited so long as the result is an...organic instrument which provides for the making, interpretation, and implementation of law.'[75] So he concludes that Article 368 conferred an amending power of the widest amplitude but even his dissent remarkably concedes that the scope of amending power does not extend to the abrogation of the Constitution itself.

Mathew's approach to the question exposed the textualist assumptions that plagued a bulk of the opinions in the case. He eloquently observes that 'although the word "amendment" has a variety of meanings, we have to ascribe to it in the article a meaning which is appropriate to the function to be played by it in an instrument apparently intended to endure for ages to come and to meet the various crises to which the body politic will be subject'.[76] By confronting linguistic indeterminacy squarely, Mathew correctly points out that the scope of the term 'amendment' in Article 368 cannot be settled by resorting to linguistic resources alone. In other words, to identify the better interpretation of Article 368 on a linguistic basis, one must provide other means of resolving this interpretive dispute. Mathew adopts a functional approach by enquiring into the role played by the article in the constitutional document. This interpretive approach is promising regardless of the conclusions reached.

Structural Interpretation

In difficult cases, judges draw on a wide variety of interpretive aids to assist them in reaching a justifiable interpretation of the constitution. Sikri took the lead in setting out the motivations for this task: 'I must interpret Article 368 in the setting of our constitution, in the background of our history and in the light of our aspirations and hopes...I am not interpreting an ordinary statute, but a Constitution which apart from setting up a machinery of government, has a noble and grand vision.'[77] This purposive orientation to the interpretive activity meant that Sikri would 'look to the whole scheme of the constitution'[78] to construe the expression 'amendment of this

---

[75] Ibid., p. 557 (Ray, J).
[76] Ibid., p. 830 (Mathew, J).
[77] *Kesavananda Bharati*, supra n. 2, p. 306 (Sikri, CJ).
[78] Ibid., p. 316 (Sikri, CJ).

Constitution.' He found support for such an interpretive approach in the precedents of the Federal Court[79] and the House of Lords[80] on statutory construction.

He then went on to consider the various parts of the Constitution in a haphazard fashion. He lays great stress on the preamble and part III which deals with fundamental rights and considers the relevance of part XVII which deals with Official languages with a cursory line.[81] This long drawn, and often erratic, examination[82] began with the provisions themselves but often included their respective drafting histories. Sikri ties together this varied and disparate analysis with the pithy conclusion that all these provisions of the Constitution lead to some necessary implications: that the expression 'amendment of this constitution' allows Parliament to amend or change any part of the Constitution as long as it does not 'abrogate or take away fundamental rights or to completely change its fundamental features of the Constitution so as to destroy its identity.'[83] The conclusion rests on an interpretive approach which may be put forth as a single proposition: 'In a written constitution it is rarely that everything is said expressly. Powers and limitations are implied from necessity or the scheme of the Constitution.'[84]

I have examined Sikri's opinion very carefully not because it is the strand of reasoning for the majority views in *Kesavananda* which has come to be accepted in subsequent decisions as the constitutional basis for the basic structure doctrine. As Khanna expressly subjects fundamental rights[85] to the amending power of Parliament, that part of Sikri's conclusions relating to the unamendability of fundamental rights is a minority opinion. A structural interpretation of the constitution, as proposed by Sikri, overcomes some of the defects of a textualist reasoning adopted by Khanna in support of his version of the basic structure doctrine. By bringing various elements of

[79] The Central Provinces and Berar Act, 1939, FCR 18, 42 (Gwyer, CJ).

[80] *Bidie* v. *General Accident, Fire and Life Assurance Corporation* (1948) 2 AllER 995, 998 (Lord Greene).

[81] *Kesavananda Bharati*, supra n. 2, p. 335 (Sikri, CJ).

[82] Ibid., pp. 321–46 .

[83] *Kesavananda Bharati*, supra n. 2, p. 405 (Sikri, CJ).

[84] Ibid., p. 346.

[85] Ibid., p. 824 (Khanna, J).

constitutional design and aspiration to bear on the interpretation of constitutional phrases like 'amendment of the Constitution' this approach offers a more persuasive bouquet of reasons for the conclusion reached in this case.

The Use of History

The opinions in *Kesavananda* considered different types of history and engaged in a debate on the relevance of these sources and the legitimate inferences that may be drawn for the interpretation of the constitution. Earlier in this chapter, the extensive use of history to determine the express limits on the scope of amendment was briefly discussed. This approach to constitutional interpretation continued in *Kesavananda* where the court considered a wide range of historical evidence on several issues before it. Both sides of the argument drew strong support from these sources, which forced the court to acknowledge the indecisiveness of such authority. When coupled with other restraints on the use of such sources in constitutional interpretation, no opinion rested any key proposition or reasoning supported by these historical sources. For the sake of analytical clarity I will divide up these histories by the sources on which they rely, namely, constituent assembly proceedings; social and political history of India; and world history. Though the court does not adopt a clear distinction with respect to historical sources, arguably the distinction above has significant insights to offer as to the nature of historical evidence and the arguments it can support. I will analyse the use of each type of history in turn.

The proceedings in the Constituent Assembly included a wide range of activity: some central and others peripheral, to the crafting of the constitutional text. Seervai breaks these proceedings into four classes: the presentation of the draft constitutions; the consideration of amendments proposed to draft Articles or sub-Articles; the reports of the various committees appointed by the Assembly; and the speeches made in the Assembly. He points out that the court addressed itself to the wrong question with respect to the use of such evidence. 'The right question to ask was not whether speeches in the Constituent Assembly are admissible as extrinsic aids to construction, but whether, any, and if so what, part or parts of the proceedings in the Constituent Assembly are admissible as extrinsic aids to construction.'[86] By lumping together these diverse sources the court erred in indiscriminately relying on these sources without paying attention to their probative value. Even if we consider the court's approach to speeches made in the Constituent Assembly one becomes immediately aware of the complex questions that arise from the use of these materials.

Sikri speaking for the majority articulated a Janus-faced approach to the use of speeches made by members in the Constituent Assembly. While he found it, on the strength of precedent and other reasons, 'a sound rule of construction that speeches made by members of a legislature in the course of debates relating to the enactment of a statute cannot be used as aids for interpreting any provision of the statute'[87] he nevertheless saw 'no harm in finding confirmation of one's interpretation in debates...'[88]. Khanna was less equivocal in his reliance on speeches in the Constituent Assembly and took the view that they may 'be referred to for finding the history of the Constitutional provision and the background against which the said provision was drafted...' but cannot 'form the basis for construing the provisions of the Constitution.'[89]

Mathew, dissenting in the case, sought to approach the question from first principles: 'Logically, there is no reason why we should exclude altogether the speeches made in the Constituent Assembly by individual members if they throw any light which resolve latent ambiguity in a provision of the Constitution.'[90] Relying on the speeches made by Ambedkar on draft Article 304 (now Article 368), draft Article 25 (now Article 32) and on the nature of fundamental rights, he found 'it difficult to understand why the constitution-makers did not specifically provide for an exception to Article 368 if they wanted that fundamental rights should not be amended in such a way as to take away or abridge them.'[91]

[86] H.M. Seervai, *Constitutional Law of India*, Bombay: N.M. Tripathi Pvt Ltd, (1st Ed.), p. 1202.

[87] *Kesavananda Bharati*, supra n. 2, p. 339 (Sikri, CJ).

[88] Ibid., p. 340.

[89] Ibid., p. 743 (Khanna, J).

[90] Ibid., p. 841 (Mathew, J).

[91] *Kesavananda Bharati*, supra n. 2, p. 843 (Mathew, J).

There is no dispute about the veracity of the speeches cited by Mathew, but other opinions in the case cite these very same speeches to infer the opposite conclusions. These inferences are only buttressed by conflicting speeches made by Ambedkar on various provisions of the Constitution which are not easily reconciled. Seervai, after a detailed analysis of the use of Constituent Assembly proceedings,[92] comes to the conclusion that courts may rely usefully on the first three classes of Constituent Assembly proceedings but not on speeches in the Constituent Assembly.[93] The analysis of the complexities which arise out of the use of speeches made in the Constituent Assembly in *Kesavananda* confirm that caution needs to be exercised in using these materials in constitutional interpretation. Further, argument on the probative value of these speeches and other proceedings in the Constituent Assembly more generally, as well as the manner of drawing inference from historical evidence is necessary before such materials may be employed in constitutional interpretation. Under these circumstances it is best not to rest the constitutional basis of judicial review of constitutional amendments on these historical resources. As none of the majority opinions in *Kesavananda* or subsequent decisions have relied exclusively on the speeches made in the Constituent Assembly, I need not engage in any further analysis of these arguments.

I will now briefly consider the use of social and political history of colonial India and snapshots of world history that were salient in the arguments raised in *Kesavananda*. The various opinions in *Kesavananda* summoned up very different sets of events under these categories, and used them with varying degrees of sophistication. Hegde and Mukherjea expressed their reliance on the former sources succinctly: 'What was the purpose intended to be achieved by the Constitution? To answer this question it is necessary to make a brief survey of our Nationalist movement... since 1885 and the objectives sought to be achieved by that movement.'[94] The survey that followed allowed them to identify the two primary objectives of the Constitution to be: '(1) to constitute India into a Sovereign

---

[92] H.M. Seervai, supra n. 86, pp. 203–5.

[93] Ibid., pp. 200–2.

[94] *Kesavananda Bharati*, supra n. 2, p. 477 (Hegde and Mukherjea, JJ).

Democratic Republic and (2) to secure to its citizens the rights mentioned therein'.[95] Taking these objectives into account they were unwilling to 'accept the contention that our Constitution-makers after making immense sacrifices for achieving certain ideals made provision in the Constitution itself for the destruction of these ideals.[96] This grand historical narrative covering almost 100 years of pre-Independence history allows the judges to impute a teleological orientation to constitutional interpretation, thereby avoiding the need for other normative arguments about the validity of the propositions advanced in the case.

Khanna's treatment of the 'argument of fear' offers us a more careful methodological approach to the use of history as well as a cautionary retort to the attempt by the majority to weave an elaborate historical justification for their conclusions. It was argued that that 'unless there are restrictions on the power of amendment...the danger is that the Indian Constitution may also meet the same fate as did the Weimar Republic at the hands of Hitler.'[97] Khanna refuted this argument strongly and observed that it 'is wholly misconceived and is not based upon correct appreciation of historical facts'. First he pointed out that Hitler made use of Article 48 of the Weimar Constitution which dealt with emergency powers and not amending power. He pointed out that the Weimar example illustrated that while 'Hitler made a show of following the Constitution...the acts of his party in and out of the government in practice violated the basic law.'[98] The lesson he learnt from this historical reference was that 'the best guarantee against the abuse of the power of amendment is good sense of the majority of members of Parliament and not the unamendability of Part III of the constitution...'.[99]

Khanna's approach highlights some critical issues on the use of history. First, he insists on a close correlation between the factual history examined and the proposition sought to be supported. The factual inaccuracies in the historical analogy proposed between the Weimar Germany and 1970s India, he casts doubt on the inference

---

[95] Ibid., p. 479.

[96] Ibid., p. 480 .

[97] Ibid., p. 765 (Khanna, J).

[98] *Kesavananda Bharati*, supra n. 2, p. 766 (Khanna, J)

[99] Ibid.

to be drawn in the case. Second, even assuming that the analogy is factually correct, one must still work out the inferences which may be drawn by reference to history. Khanna relies on the analogy to the Weimar Republic to conclude that the judiciary should not intervene in this political context.

To these cautions on the use of history I may add one other. Pierre de Vos analyses the South African Constitutional Court's efforts to interpret the 1996 Constitution using a 'contextual approach'.[100] He argues that the court, while mobilizing a grand narrative history in support of its conclusions, adopts an idea of history which pays inadequate attention to theoretical developments in historiography. In particular he is concerned with the lack of reflexivity of the judges' use of history which, while denying the agency of the historian, seeks to portray history as somehow objectively true. Even if one were to insist, as Hobsbawm does, that 'relativism will not do in history any more than in law courts',[101] there must rest a critical responsibility on the user of historical argument to pay careful attention to the plural historical accounts available and the normative lessons that may be inferred from these accounts.

From the discussion above I conclude that the use of historical arguments in *Kesavananda* did not evidence a sophisticated understanding of the historical method. Further, the opinions fail to develop normative reasons for the use of historical sources to support the legal propositions on limited amending power.

The Use of Social, Political, and Philosophical Theory

The use of social, political, and philosophical theories in constitutional interpretation was a topic on which there was a rare consensus across the majority and minority opinions in the case. Different opinions handled these materials with varied ability. Mathew displayed a strong felicity with this type of argument, Chandrachud signalled the approach of the court to these opinions: 'We were taken through the writings of scores of scholars, some of whom express their beliefs

[100] Pierre de Vos, 'A Bridge too Far? History as Context in the Interpretation of the South African Constitution', (2001) 17 *South African J of Human Rights*, 1, 7.

[101] E. Hobsbawm, *On History*, London: Weidenfeld and Nicolson, 1997, p. viii.

with a dogmatism not open to a Judge. There was a faint controversy regarding the credentials of some of them … but brushing aside such considerations, the conflicting views of these writers, distinguished though they may be, cannot conclude the controversy before us, which must be decided on the terms of our Constitution and the genius of our nation.'[102]

Though theoretical argument was not taken to be conclusive of the questions before the court, the extended investigation and attention paid to such materials beg explanation. The doctrine of implied limits was one proposition for which much theoretical support was invoked in the opinions, albeit in a most confused and disparate fashion. Nani Palkhivala, lead counsel for the petitioners, argued before the court, and in other secondary writing, that the doctrine of inherent and implied limits was in principle supported by a correct theoretical understanding of the relationship between amending power and the basic elements or fundamental principles of the written constitution in a democracy.[103] At other points 'implied limits' was put forward as a principle of the common law pertaining to the interpretation of statutes in general and written constitutions in particular. Decisions of the Australian Federal Court on implied rights in the Australian Constitution, those of the Privy Council interpreting post-colonial constitutions, and the US Supreme Courts' review of constitutional amendments were canvassed in support of such a doctrine. Often courts are confronted by arguments for a legal proposition which simultaneously rely on political theory, legal theory, and comparative law. However, it is rare that such an intricately threaded and tightly woven argument is likely to get a satisfactory response from the judges as they first need to untangle the varied strands of such arguments and then assess them.

Mathew, who approached such arguments with great sophistication, framed the argument in normative constitutional theory precisely when he observed that inherent and implied limitations 'flow from the fact that the ultimate legal sovereignty resides in the people; that Parliament is a creature of the Constitution and not a constituent body and that the power to alter or to destroy the essential features

[102] *Kesavananda Bharati*, supra n. 2, p. 961 (Chandrachud, J).
[103] N. Palkhivala, *Our Constitution: Defaced and Defiled*, Delhi: Macmillan Co. of India, 1974.

of the Constitution belongs only to the people, the ultimate legal sovereign.'[104] He then went on to examine the argument in its abstract theoretical form, removed from the constitutional text, in great detail but reached the conclusion that this was an 'impossible position'.[105]

Dhavan, after conducting an extensive analytical examination of *Kesavananda* insightfully observes, 'We might ask the question: was the theory of implied limitations securely established? The answer must be that despite the attempt to give the theory credibility by reference to history, cosmopolitan jurisprudence, and word play, it was really advanced on a common sense basis. Never did a Court take so long a route to reach so simple a proposition, and never were so many fundamental propositions left unanswered.'[106] This may well be an accurate assessment of the reasoning advanced in plurality opinion in *Kesavananda*. However, the question of judicial review of constitutional amendments requires a fuller account of the relevant normative constitutional theory and more crucially, the extent of reliance that a court should place on such argument while interpreting the Constitution. I return to these concerns in Chapter 5.

In *Kesavananda* the court was presented with novel arguments for the constitutional judicial review of constitutional amendments. The court heeded Seervai's counsel, advanced in the first edition of his treatise, *Constitutional Law of India*, that the majority judgment in *Golaknath* was 'clearly wrong, is productive of the greatest public mischief, and should be overruled at the earliest opportunity'.[107] The court replaced explicit limits on amending power with implied limits whereby the plenary amending power of Parliament could be exercised so long as it did not 'damage or destroy the basic features of the Constitution'. The detailed analysis above considers the various arguments advanced in support of this proposition and is not exhaustive of all the arguments considered in the opinion: the use of comparative law judgments and the discussion surrounding the relationship between the directive principles and fundamental rights are notable omissions.

---

[104] *Kesavananda Bharati*, supra n. 2, pp. 844–5 (Mathew, J).
[105] Ibid., p. 852. The entire discussion extends from pages 844–52.
[106] R. Dhavan, supra n. 65, p. 191.
[107] H.M. Seervai, supra n. 86, p. 1117.

Though both petitioners and respondents canvassed their opinions using comparative law materials, no opinion relies exclusively on these precedents in support of their conclusion. More significantly, no opinion develops a sophisticated approach to the relevance and utility of these materials in aid of a conclusion with the issues at hand.[108] As comparative law sources are not critical to any arguments about the constitutional basis of the basic structure doctrine I say no more about such materials in the rest of the work. The relationship between the directive principles and fundamental rights has been the subject of extensive discussion in some secondary literature on *Kesavananda*. Dhavan suggests that the 'Supreme Court missed a great opportunity of evaluating the relative priority of right based notions, and goal oriented principles entrenched in the Directive Principles.'[109] Whatever the merits of this view, this is not an argument in support of the proposition that the basic structure doctrine has a sound constitutional basis. The relative priority of fundamental rights and directive principles is important to assess the constitutional validity of land reform legislation under rights compliance review as well as the validity of constitutional amendments under basic structure review. The enquiry into whether constitutional amendments which protected land reform legislation satisfies judicial scrutiny under the basic structure standard is about the nature and standards of basic structure review—a topic fully considered in Chapter 4.

CONSTITUTIONAL BASIS FOR BASIC STRUCTURE REVIEW OF AMENDING POWER

In the preceding sections I have considered the judicial reasoning in support of a constitutional basis for implied limits to the amending power in *Kesavananda*. I have argued that a structural interpretation of the Constitution may offer good reasons to interpret amendment under Article 368 to be subject to implied limits.

This chapter endorses Sikri's interpretive approach in support of the basic structure doctrine, as the best constitutional interpretation

---

[108] For a detailed exploration of the use of comparative law in *Kesavananda* see A. Thiruvengadam, 'Comparative Law' (SJD Thesis, New York University, unpublished) on file with author.

[109] R. Dhavan, supra n. 65, p. 228.

advanced by the *Kesavnanda* bench despite it not securing a majority support. He sought to imply necessary limitations on amending power by drawing on a broad survey of various constitutional provisions. This approach needs closer examination of the text and more careful reasoning to persuade one to a conclusion regarding the necessity of such implication. I will need to show the conditions under which the provisions of the constitution may be said to yield text-emergent, but otherwise unwritten, principles which constrain the exercise of powers and functions under the Constitution.

Unfortunately, subsequent decisions of the court in *Indira Gandhi* v. *Raj Narain*[110] or *Minerva Mills* v. *Union of India*[111] do not undertake these essential tasks. These cases affirm the holding in *Kesavananda* on the strength of the bench rather than the persuasiveness of its reasons. However, Seervai claims that:[112]

A critical discussion of *Kesavananda's* case, taken by itself, would be inaccurate and misleading without a discussion of the deeper analysis of the amending power in the *Election* case ... It appears to me that the most satisfactory method of exposition would be to defer a critical examination of *Kesavananda's* case till the full implications of the *Election* case have been brought out by a critical examination.

This astonishing claim about the constitutional basis of the basic structure doctrine merits a clarification. Seervai suggests the constitutional basis of the doctrine is more clearly set out in *Indira Gandhi* and not in *Kesavananda*. In *Indira Gandhi*, all the judges accepted the constitutional basis of the doctrine as set out in *Kesavananda* as binding precedent and ignored this issue in their opinions. Hence, Seervai's comment is best understood as a convoluted attempt to locate the constitutional basis of the doctrine in *Indira Gandhi* as he had already denounced the *Kesavananda* holding as a bad law. It is certainly true that various other aspects of the basic structure doctrine—nature and standards of review and the identification of basic features of the constitution—was developed

---

[110] AIR 1975 SC 2299 at 2242 (Ray, CJ).

[111] AIR 1975 SC 1789 at 1818 (Bhagwati, J) relying on the *Indira Gandhi* opinion as binding on him.

[112] H.M. Seervai, *Constitutional Law of India*: Bombay: N.M. Tripathi Ltd., (4th Edn) Vol. 3, 1996, pp. 3109–10.

significantly in *Indira Gandhi* and this is a matter we will turn to in Chapters 4 and 5 respectively. Most recently, in *I.R. Coelho* v. *State of Tamil Nadu*,[113] a nine-judge bench had the opportunity to articulate a stronger constitutional basis for the basic structure doctrine but did not apply itself to this task.

Despite such refusal by the courts to engage with the foundational questions relating to basic structure review of constitutional amendments, in this chapter I have made significant progress in uncovering a constitutional basis for the basic structure doctrine by eliminating a range of plausible but nevertheless inappropriate arguments. I have not proposed a basic structure doctrine which rests on any version of natural rights or metaphysically derived fundamental values, or suggested that a semantic stipulation on the scope of the term 'amend' in Article 368 would provide a sufficient constitutional basis. I propose that implied limitations which may be inferred from other relevant provisions of the constitution can offer us a sound constitutional basis for the basic structure doctrine. Before I can assert that such a model of basic structure review has a sound constitutional basis, I will need to consider normative arguments on the appropriate model of constitutional interpretation and provide a coherent normative constitutional theory which supports basic structure review. These arguments are addressed in Chapter 5.

The evolution and constitutional practice of basic structure review in the 30 years since it was established in Kesavananda has gone beyond judicial review of amendments. In Chapter 3, I examine the judicial debates on the constitutional basis of basic structure review as it applies to legislation and executive action. Chapters 4 and 5 address aspects of basic structure review which apply equally to all forms of state action and in Chapter 6, I examine the theories of interpretation necessary to support the claim of the legitimate constitutional basis of basic structure review. In the next chapter I go on to investigate the constitutional basis of the basic structure doctrine to review two other species of state action: the exercise of executive emergency power and ordinary legislative and executive action.

---

[113] (2007) 1 Sup Ct Almanac 45.

2

The Broadening Scope of Basic Structure Review
Emergency, Legislative, and Executive Powers

The basic structure doctrine was developed as a rare residuary power to be used by the Court to control the excesses of a transitory majority... But there is a problem. The formulation of the doctrine has not been precise and it is tempting for a judge with the best of intentions to invoke it and try to mould the Constitution in his own image.[1]

Much of the debate over the basic structure doctrine, both within the Supreme Court and outside, has often been at cross-purposes for a number of reasons. The court has itself compounded the confusion by refusing to be clear about the scope of the doctrine.[2]

The doctrine of basic structure review was developed in the context of challenges to the validity of constitutional amendments. In the previous chapter we argued that the constitutional basis for basic structure review may be understood to be the result of implied limitations on the amending power under Article 368. The extension of basic structure review to emergency powers, as well as legislative and executive action, requires the court to either articulate a novel constitutional basis for such a power or offer good reasons for extending to these forms of state action the implied limitations

[1] Ashok Desai, 'Constitutional Amendments and the "Basic Structure" Doctrine', in V. Iyer (ed.) *Democracy, Human Rights and the Rule of Law*, New Delhi: Butterworths India, 2000, p. 90.

[2] Pratap B. Mehta, 'The Inner Conflict of Constitutionalism', in Zoya Hasan (ed.), *India's Living Constitution*, New Delhi: Permanent Black, 2002, p. 180.

which form the constitutional basis for basic structure review of constitutional amendments. The analysis of the relevant cases in this chapter reveals that the court fails to articulate the constitutional basis for basic structure review in either of these ways. I conclude by arguing that the constitutional basis of basic structure review of emergency power, legislation, and executive power is best understood as having the same constitutional basis as constitutional amendments: namely, implied limitations which circumscribe the grant of executive and legislative powers in the constitution.

The exercise of federal emergency power, either at the national level under Article 352 or at the regional level under Article 356, is through an executive action carried out in the name of the President of India. The court is yet to use basic structure review to strike down a proclamation of emergency as unconstitutional.[3] Where it has applied basic structure review to evaluate the validity of such a proclamation, it has found them to be valid on the particular facts and circumstances of the case. In these cases the court has not held that basic structure review emerged from any particular phrase in the provisions authorizing the President to proclaim an emergency. This chapter will argue that even in such cases the constitutional basis of basic structure review emerges from the implied limitations which place substantive restraints on the scope of the emergency power conferred by the constitution.

Ordinary legislative power and executive power is subject to judicial review by the High Courts and the Supreme Court for competence and compliance with fundamental rights. The question of whether basic structure review would apply to these species of state action was considered and dismissed in *Indira Gandhi* v. *Raj Narain*.[4] Subsequently, the court has moved away from this position and utilized basic structure review in conjunction with other available forms of review.[5] In a recent case,[6] the court has reverted to the view that basic

---

[3] The court considered national emergency proclamations in *Waman Rao* v. *Union of India*, AIR 1981 SC 271, *Minerva Mills* v. *Union of India*, AIR 1980 SC 1789; and regional emergency provisions in *S.R. Bommai* v. *Union of India*, AIR 1994 SC 1918; and *Rameshwar Prasad* v. *Union of India*, (2006) 2 SCC 1.

[4] AIR 1975 SC 2299.

[5] *Union of India* v. *Association of Democratic Reforms*, AIR 2002 SC 2113.

[6] *Kuldip Nayar* v. *Union of India*, (2006) 7 SCC 1.

structure review does not apply to legislation by relying on the *Indira Gandhi* case and ignoring subsequent precedent. As these divergent holdings have been delivered by coordinate constitutional benches of equal strength, the law on the point is unsettled. Moreover, as is the case with emergency proclamations, the court has not articulated a constitutional basis for basic structure review by interpreting the provisions granting executive or legislative power. I will show that the extension of implied limitations to regulate ordinary legislative and executive powers offers us the best constitutional basis for basic structure review in these cases.

EMERGENCY POWER

Indeed, the temptation to invoke the basic structure doctrine even in areas which do not involve constitutional amendments is so strong that the Court has sometimes referred to the doctrine even when considering challenges to executive orders … An instructive example of the imprecise radiations of the doctrine arose in *Bommai*.[7]

This section investigates former Attorney General, Ashok Desai's concerns with the 'imprecise radiations' of the basic structure doctrine leading to the judicial review over executive proclamations of emergency of a national and regional character. These exercises of emergency power had previously been challenged in the courts on administrative law grounds. It was initially in *Waman Rao* and later in *Bommai* that the court considered the application of the basic structure doctrine to such action. As with the critical commentary on the use of basic structure review with respect to amendments, the quotation above indicates unease with the use of the doctrine to review proclamations of emergency. Some of this unease arises from the inability of the court to articulate a precise constitutional basis for this form of judicial review. This section of the chapter investigates the cases on this point of law and shows that there are good reasons for this unease. The court has not applied itself to the constitutional basis for basic structure review of constitutional amendments. The concluding part of this section explores options available to the court and advances the most justifiable constitutional basis for basic structure review of executive proclamations of Emergency.

[7] Ashok Desai, supra n. 1.

The court's first expansion of the doctrine beyond amendment cases was to test the executive proclamation of Emergency. The Indian Constitution allows the executive to proclaim two kinds of Emergency—national and regional. In *Waman Rao*,[8] the court had the opportunity to apply the basic structure doctrine to the proclamation of a national emergency in 1975. As the emergency had been revoked before the court reached its decision, the court did not find it necessary to apply the doctrine. However, the court did not rule out the application of the doctrine to such cases. In *Bommai*,[9] the proclamation of regional emergency in several states was challenged and the court ruled that secularism, which was among the basic features of the constitution, provided a basis to distinguish between legitimate and illegitimate proclamations of emergency. I will now investigate the court's justification for the use of the basic structure doctrine as a limit on the executive's power to proclaim emergency and whether the reasoning and justification for such an exercise is consistent with that adopted in the amendment cases.

National Emergency

The complex political factors which gave rise to the petition in *Waman Rao*[10] forced the court to consider a unique constitutional challenge. The 40th Constitution Amendment Act, 1976 placed several land reform statutes in the 9th Schedule, thereby immunising them from judicial review for violation of fundamental rights. This amendment was enacted during an extended term of the Lok Sabha beyond its usual term of 5 years. This extension was carried out by statutes[11] enacted during the period of national emergency under Article 352. The petitioners challenged the vires of the constitutional amendment, the statutes which extended the term of Parliament, and the proclamation of emergency. Though these challenges were intricately connected in the facts and circumstances of the case,

[8] *Waman Rao*, supra n. 3 on proclamations of national emergency under Article 352.

[9] *Bommai*, ibid., on proclamations of state emergencies under Article 356.

[10] *Waman Rao*, supra n. 3.

[11] House of the People (Extension of Duration) Act, 1976 and the House of the People (Extension of Duration) Amendment Act, 1976 respectively.

for the purposes of this chapter I will consider the challenge to the emergency proclamation in isolation.

Counsels for the petitioner raised two issues: was the power to proclaim an emergency under Article 352 properly exercised and if there were any circumstances justifying the continuance of the emergency? The petitioners relied extensively on factual averments designed to show that the government acted injudiciously to advance partisan political considerations.[12] These arguments used administrative law judicial review understandings of substantive unreasonableness to challenge the executive proclamation. Given that there is scope for abuse of power by a government which extends such a proclamation indefinitely, petitioners urged the court that the provisions of Article 352 should 'be interpreted in a liberal and progressive manner so that the democratic ideal of the Constitution will be furthered and not frustrated'.[13]

A constitutional challenge to the proclamation of emergency before the courts invites two objections: first, lack of jurisdiction and second, the absence of a judicial standard which provides a basis for such review. Chandrachud amplified these concerns and observed that courts 'have severe constraints which deter them from undertaking a task which cannot judicially be performed'.[14] Further, as the emergency proclamation was no longer in force and the 42nd Constitution Amendment Act, 1976 had inserted safeguards against such possible abuse in clauses (2) to (8) in Article 352, the court declined to engage with the issue in the hope that similar issues will not arise in the future.

Besides this pious hope, Chandrachud carefully considered the reasons for his decision to decline jurisdiction. As the challenge to the proclamation of emergency under Article 352 in this case was tangential to the core challenge to the constitutionality of Article 31-A, 31-B, and 31-C, he took the view that it was best adjudicated in a case where it was the central issue. The more substantive reasons were the inability of the court to marshal evidence from diverse sources, or apply the preponderance of probabilities standard that the extension

[12] *Waman Rao*, supra n. 3, pp. 292–3 (Chandrachud, CJ).

[13] Ibid., p. 293 (Chandrachud,CJ).

[14] *Waman Rao*, supra n. 3, p. 294.

of the emergency was motivated by mala fides. Distinguishing between the standards applied by lay persons, newspapers and public men, and those applied by the court, Chandrachud took the view that the court could not reach a binding conclusion in such a case based on public commentary and newspaper editorials and reports.

The petitioners and the judgments in the case failed to develop two key arguments in this case: first, the applicability of the basic structure doctrine to the proclamation of emergency under Article 352 and second, the task of fashioning a mode of review suitable for administrative action by high constitutional functionaries. I will examine each in turn.

Chandrachud applied the basic structure doctrine in a nuanced and complex fashion in *Waman Rao* to uphold Article 31-A as it furthered the basic values and aspirations of the Constitution. By applying the basic structure doctrine to constitutional amendments in *Kesavananda*, the court had overcome arguments about the justiciability of constitutional amendments under Article 368 which are similar to the respondents' arguments against the judicial review of executive proclamations of national emergency under Article 352 in *Waman Rao*. The petitioners and the judges failed to notice that the *Kesavananda* court had already disposed arguments about the absence of judicial standards in basic structure review and these conclusions could be applied with minor modifications to the review of executive proclamations of emergency. If the court had identified basic structure review as a model of judicial review independent from administrative law review then the court could have applied a set of judicially manageable standards developed in the constitutional amendment cases, thereby bypassing the constraints of administrative law judicial review which was hitherto inapplicable to these forms of higher executive action.

The second element that needed careful attention was the nature of the action that was being challenged in this case. The proclamation of a national emergency under Article 352 is an executive decision of the Cabinet carried out in the name of the President of India. The petitioners in *Waman Rao* set out to establish that this action was motivated by mala fides. In judicial review of ordinary executive action this standard is the most exacting for any petitioner to satisfy in order to succeed in the action. Even if the petitioner was able to provide extensive evidence to the court it is unlikely that the court would find that this ground was satisfied. Hence, administrative law review is unsuited for application to the executive action by higher constitutional authorities. Moreover, even if the court was to apply basic structure review to executive action it would have to mould it to apply effectively to such a case.

In cases where the court reviews constitutional amendments, the court conducts a substantive review to enquire if the constitutional amendments 'destroy or damage' the basic structure of the constitution. Before the court applies basic structure review to executive action, it must clarify whether it is merely extending this substantive review model or adopting a modified administrative law review model which evaluates whether the executive action accords with basic features of the constitution. By testing the proclamation of emergency under Article 352 only on the grounds of mala fides and not subjecting such proclamations to other grounds available in administrative law review the court adopts a very low level of scrutiny of such executive action. Further, the court failed to tackle the complex issues which arose in the judicial review of executive orders by high constitutional functionaries, missing a significant opportunity to develop constitutional judicial review jurisprudence in a coherent and rational manner.

Thus far, I have argued that the court in *Waman Rao* failed to accommodate basic structure review while reviewing the national emergency proclamations challenged in that case. Even if the court were to develop the doctrine along the strategies advanced above, a significant issue remains unaddressed. I will have to consider carefully whether the constitutional basis for the basic structure doctrine is inextricably tied to the courts' interpretation of Article 368 in *Kesavananda* or if it may equally be applied to an executive action under Article 352. The court at this stage has two options: first, it may develop an interpretation of the Article 352 which entails basic structure review or second, recognize that the constitutional basis of the basic structure is non-textual and is derivative of the 'spirit of the Constitution' in some sense. In the next section, we will examine if the court addressed any of these concerns while reaching its conclusion in *Bommai* before returning to these fundamental questions about the constitutional basis for basic structure review.

Regional Emergency

In the section above I outlined the various obstacles that the basic structure doctrine which evolved in the context of constitutional amending power must overcome to be properly used in the review of national emergency powers. A 9-judge bench in *S.R. Bommai v. Union of India*[15] addressed these concerns when the presidential proclamation of a regional emergency under Article 356, whereby six state governments were dismissed and their legislative assemblies dissolved, was challenged as being unconstitutional. The court was invited to consider the scope, type, and extent of judicial review that the courts could exercise over presidential discretion in exercise of this power. In this section, I am particularly concerned with the constitutional basis for basic structure review of emergency proclamations.

Earlier in *State of Rajasthan* v. *Union of India*[16] Bhagwati had established the extent and scope of judicial review of a presidential proclamation under Article 356. He began with a broad statement of principle: 'So long as a question arises whether an authority under the Constitution has acted within the limits of its power or exceeded it, [this] can certainly be decided by the Court. Indeed it would be its Constitutional obligation to do so ...'.[17] However, he translated this broad principle of constitutional accountability into a very narrow holding on the scope of the court's enquiry into the 'satisfaction' of the President that the conditions set out in Article 356 are satisfied. He surprisingly concluded that 'the satisfaction of the President is a subjective one and cannot be tested by reference to any objective tests ... '[18] and hence such a decision cannot be based on 'judicially discoverable and manageable standards'.[19] It was only in the 'narrow minimal area' where the satisfaction of the President required for the exercise of power under Article 356 was 'mala fide or is based on wholly extraneous and irrelevant grounds' that the court would have jurisdiction to review it. Bhagwati did not advance any reasons for narrowing down a constitutional basis for judicial review of executive

---

[15] *Bommai*, supra n. 3.
[16] AIR 1977 SC 1361.
[17] *State of Rajasthan* v. *Union of India*, supra n. 16, p . 1413 (Bhagwati, J).
[18] Ibid.
[19] Ibid.

action by the higher executive to a select few grounds of common law administrative law review.

It was Sawant who developed this line of reasoning in *Bommai*. He surmised that on previous authority[20] it was safe to conclude that presidential powers under Article 356 'is subject to judicial review at least to the extent of examining whether the conditions precedent to the issuance of the proclamation have been satisfied or not.'[21] Hence the court could ensure that there indeed 'existed material for the satisfaction of the President'.[22] Though the court could not enquire into 'the sufficiency or otherwise of the material'[23] the 'legitimacy of inference drawn from such material is certainly open to judicial review'.[24] Hence he concluded that 'the material in question has to be such as would induce a reasonable man to come to the conclusion in question'.[25] This incremental approach to expanding the scope of review outlined in *State of Rajasthan* was modest in two respects: first, it did not respond to the broader constitutional role of the court as guardian of the constitution proposed by Bhagwati as the abiding rationale for judicial review. Second, it remained trapped in the language of administrative law review and merely supplements the malafides ground of review with a general reasonableness ground of review.

While the major part of his opinion related to the principles of administrative law review applicable to Article 356 proclamation, Sawant changed track late in his opinion. He recognized that as provisions such as Article 356 'have a potentiality to unsettle and subvert the entire constitutional scheme' the exercise of powers 'needs ... to be circumscribed to maintain the fundamental constitutional balance lest the Constitution is defaced and destroyed.'[26] He recognized that

---

[20] Besides *State of Rajasthan* v. *Union of India* he relied on *Kehar Singh* v. *Union of India*, AIR 1989 SC 653, which deal with the presidential power of pardon under Article 72. The cases discussed in this section would be discussed under the category of prerogative power in British public law.

[21] *Bommai*, supra n. 3, p. 1994 (Sawant, J).

[22] Ibid.

[23] Ibid., p. 1995.

[24] Ibid.

[25] Ibid.

[26] *Bommai*, supra n. 3, p. 1976 (Sawant, J).

basic structure review could be 'achieved ... without bending, much less breaking, the normal rules of interpretation, if the interpretation is alive to the other provisions of the Constitution and its bearing on them.'[27] Identifying the principles of democracy and federalism to be at stake in such cases, he was of the view that 'any interpretation' of Article 356 must preserve and not subvert these values. These principles would authorize the court to 'scrutinize the material on the basis of which the advice is given and the President forms his satisfaction more closely and circumspectly'.[28]

The Supreme Court recently applied[29] the ruling in the *Bommai* case to hold a proclamation of regional emergency under Article 356 to be illegal and unconstitutional. However, this case did not develop on the application of basic structure review to such executive proclamations. Hence, the analysis of basic structure review of executive proclamations of emergency in this chapter will stay focused on the *Bommai* ruling. The application of basic structure review to Article 356 proclamations in *Bommai* lacked two crucial ingredients: first, Sawant proposed an interpretive strategy in support of his conclusions but failed to apply this strategy to the provisions of Article 356. He seems to identify a potential abuse of the provision and conclude that it is for the courts to check for such abuse. Second, this inability to identify basic structure review as a free standing constitutional doctrine for judicial review is confirmed when Sawant concludes that this enhanced review to protect essential features 'can be done by the courts while confining themselves to the acknowledged parameters of the judicial review as discussed above, viz., illegality, irrationality, and mala fides'.[30] In the next chapter I consider the limitations of such a view and the potential for the courts to develop a distinct doctrine of basic structure review with respect to executive action more generally. In the rest of this section I will propose a sounder constitutional basis for basic structure review of emergency proclamations by exploring the manner in which the interpretive strategy proposed by Sawant—namely a structural interpretation—will modify the scope of judicial review of emergency powers.

[27] Ibid.
[28] Ibid.
[29] *Rameshwar Prasad* v. *Union of India*, (2006) 2 SCC 1.
[30] *Bommai*, supra n. 3, p. 1976.

Articles 352 and 356 require that the President be 'satisfied' that certain 'pre-conditions' are fulfilled before a proclamation of emergency may be issued. In *Bommai*, Sawant sought to interpret these two facets—the Presidential satisfaction common to both articles and the different preconditions set out by them—in the light of other provisions of the Constitution. Such an interpretation needs to identify what implied limitations may apply to these two aspects of the proclamation. I will examine each in turn.

The President is the only officer under the Constitution who takes oath under Article 60 to 'preserve, protect and defend the Constitution...'.[31] Article 74 which requires the president to carry out his 'functions' in accordance with the advice tendered by the prime minister as the head of the Council of Ministers has cast a long shadow on the potential for independent action by the president. This provision enshrines the working principles of the British parliamentary model of government with respect to the ordinary executive functions of the president. However, doubt is cast on the scope of this principle with respect to the exercise of 'prerogative powers' including the power to proclaim an emergency. The unique role of the president as defender of the constitution, and by implication its basic structure, arguably requires him to exercise an independent role in the exercise of such powers. As the president, together with the prime minister, who is the leader of the Parliamentary majority party, should promote the observance of constitutional values, the court would be justified in utilizing basic structure review to scrutinize the advice offered by the prime minister and the presidential decision under these circumstances.

The pre-conditions required to be satisfied before a valid proclamation of emergency may be issued are distinct under each article. Article 352 establishes a narrow necessity standard for the proclamation of emergency—a grave emergency arising out of armed rebellion or external aggression which threatens the security of the nation[32]—and does not expressly invoke or otherwise integrate the wider constitutional principles that basic structure review is concerned with. Article 356 by contrast allows the President to

[31] Constitution of India, 1950, Article 60.
[32] Constitution of India, 1950, Article 352(1).

proclaim an emergency where the 'government of the State cannot be carried on in accordance with the provisions of the Constitution'[33] and thereby presciently accommodates the preservation of basic features of the constitution. Although the article does not specify the particular constitutional provisions which need to be complied with, surely the provisions relating to federalism, democracy, and republicanism are among those protected. The Sarkaria Commission on Centre-State Relations interprets this phrase[34] to deal primarily with political problems within the State or between the Centre and State(s). The report's recommendations have been cited with approval in *Bommai*[35] and have tended to dominate public discussions on this topic. Sawant supplements this narrow formulation of the range of concerns of Article 356 and interprets the scope of the phrase 'breakdown of constitutional machinery' to include an assessment of normative constitutional principles identified under the basic structure doctrine.

The analysis above suggests that there are adequate reasons to integrate the implied limitations on the exercise of state power inherent in basic structure review into our interpretation of both aspects of executive proclamations considered above—the presidential role and the pre-conditions to be satisfied. If such an interpretation were to rest on the nature and content of the presidential role as defender of the constitution, the court would apply similar standards to both state and national emergencies. However, if the court pays attention only to the pre-conditions to the exercise of the power, as its present analysis of these provisions suggests, then basic structure review would require a greater level of scrutiny of state emergency while conceding a wider zone of autonomy to the political process in the case of national emergency.

This differential approach to the two provisions may arise from the different character of the power in each case. National emergency power is a conventional prerogative power to deal with security— external and internal—a subject frequently considered to be beyond judicial standards. Regional emergency power on the other hand

---

[33] Ibid., Article 356 (1).
[34] Sarkaria Commission Report on Centre–State Relations, para 6.4.01
[35] *Bommai*, supra n. 3, pp. 1972–3 (Sawant, J).

responds to conditions of political instability and disregard for basic features of the constitution which are capable of judicial scrutiny. It is more likely though that this distinction between the scope of judicial review of these two types of emergency power arises from an inability of the court to isolate the character of basic structure review and consider how it might integrate such review with the administrative law review model previously applied to executive proclamations. But this is a topic that I return to in the next chapter.

ORDINARY EXECUTIVE AND LEGISLATIVE POWER

The Indian Constitution confers, and distributes, legislative and executive powers between the Union and the states in an identical fashion.[36] Besides these general powers, some special powers are conferred on each unit through special provisions.[37] These special powers are subject to particular conditions that need to be satisfied before they are exercised. In this section, I will investigate the courts' approach to basic structure review of ordinary legislative and executive power and will argue that there are good reasons to construe the constitutional provisions regulating executive and legislative powers to accommodate basic structure judicial review.

As the court has not distinguished pointedly between the application of the basic structure review to legislative and executive power, I will not emphasize this distinction either. I treat these two types of state action to be of the same status and requiring the same constitutional basis. The distinction between these two types of state action assumes greater significance when I examine the nature and standard of basic structure review in the next chapter. As legislative and executive powers are conferred by similarly phrased constitutional provisions, an argument for the application of basic structure review which turns on the interpretation of either constitutional provision should apply equally to the other type of state action. Although legislative and executive power are distinct types of power, they are

[36] Articles 245 and 246 confer legislative power while Articles 73 and 162 confer executive power on the same subject matter.

[37] Articles 247 to 254 confer significant special legislative powers while Articles 256 to 263 confer significant special executive powers. Several other provisions of the constitution confer minor executive and legislative powers.

both constitutional powers conferred on the organs created by the constitution and in this sense pose similar problems for the extension of basic structure review. Before I go further, I will briefly survey the provisions of the constitution which confer ordinary executive and legislative powers.

Executive powers are vested in, and distributed between, the Union and State governments in separate articles of the Constitution. Articles 53 and 154 invest executive power of the Union and State governments on the President and Governor respectively. Clause 1 in both articles vests the powers and provides that they may be exercised either directly or through subordinate officers. The nature of executive power and manner of its exercise has provoked significant judicial attention and critical commentary, but these controversies are unrelated to basic structure review with which I am concerned in this section. The extent of executive power of the Union and the State is determined by Articles 73 and 162 respectively. The extent of the general executive power of the Union and State is co-extensive with the distribution of legislative powers discussed below. As with legislative powers, the extent of executive power is circumscribed by the phrase: 'Subject to the provisions of this Constitution ...'. These articles set out the scope and extent of general executive power while others like Articles 75 and 164 provide for the power of the president and governor to appoint the prime minister at the Union, and the chief minister of a State, respectively. In this section I address the constitutional basis for basic structure review of general executive power and the implications for special executive powers by paying attention to the governor's power to appoint chief ministers.

Unlike what I observed with executive power, the constitution does not expressly confer legislative power on the Parliament and State Legislatures. For that matter, the judicial power is not expressly vested in the judiciary either. In practice, the absence of an exclusive vesting clause for legislative and judicial power has not assumed any significance in the interpretation of the constitution. Notably, legislative power is distributed between the Union and State by Articles 245 and 246 of the constitution. Article 245 makes the Parliament's and the State legislatures' power to make laws *subject to the provisions of the Constitution ...*' While Article 245 sets out the territorial jurisdictional limits of the respective legislatures, Article

246 read with the three lists in Schedule VII distributes subject matter between the legislatures. A precise account of the distribution of powers is crucial for any account of the federal arrangements in the Indian Constitution but this is not the focus of this section of the chapter.

Besides this general power of legislation, other provisions of the Constitution confer special legislative powers on the Union government to enact laws relating to citizenship[38] or on state subject matters 'in the national interest'.[39] In some exceptional circumstances legislative powers are conferred on the executive branch of government to make temporary laws.[40] The exercise of special legislative powers may potentially threaten the basic structure doctrine, but this is yet to happen. Moreover the analysis in the rest of this chapter, confined though it is to the general legislative power, offers us sufficient guidance as to how one may approach the basic structure review of special legislative powers.

The brief survey conducted above of the constitutional provisions related to the scope and extent of executive and legislative power highlight the centrality of the phrase 'subject to the provisions of the Constitution' which circumscribes both these powers. The courts have deployed this phrase in support of their conclusion that two significant limits emerge from it: first, that no state action shall take away or abridge fundamental rights conferred in Part III of the constitution[41] and second, that jurisdictional boundaries of the Union and State[42] set out in the Constitution are to be maintained. Judicial review for the protection of fundamental rights and for competence has developed extensively taking into account the relevant constitutional provisions and the courts' interpretations of these provisions. One may then anticipate that the legal arguments about the application of basic structure review to these powers would concentrate on an interpretation of this phrase. Surprisingly, this is yet to happen!

[38] Constitution of India, 1950, Article 11.
[39] Ibid., Article 249.
[40] Ibid., Articles 123 and 213.
[41] Constitution of India, 1950, Article 13.
[42] Ibid., Article 246.

The *Election* Case

The concept of a basic structure as a brooding omnipresence in the sky apart from the specific provisions of the Constitution ... is too vague and indefinite to provide a yardstick to determine the validity of an ordinary law.[43]

The Representation of the People (Amendment) Act, 1974 and the Election Law (Amendment) Act, 1975 were enacted to validate the disputed election of the then Prime Minister, Indira Gandhi. These statutes together with the constitutional amendments sought to fortify her legal position in the election dispute. These were challenged in *Indira Gandhi* v. *Raj Narain*[44] where the doctrine of basic structure was invoked as binding precedent for the first time. Three of the judges who dissented in *Kesavananda* were part of the 5–judge constitutional bench which decided this case. The Respondents counsel argued an alluringly simple proposition: 'that ordinary legislative measures are subject like Constitution amendments to the restrictions of not damaging or destroying the basic structure or basic features'.[45] Three judges rejected the proposition outright, while two others[46] found it unnecessary to consider the argument as they decided the case on other grounds. Mathew's observations, quoted above, signal the difficulties faced by a court dealing with a new doctrine, particularly one which they had to reluctantly apply by the force of precedent.

Ray, in his lead opinion, characterized arguments which subject ordinary legislation to the basic structure doctrine to mistakenly 'equate legislative measures with Constitution amendment'.[47] He took the purpose of the doctrine to render the change of constitutional norms 'more difficult by regulating the manner and form of ... amendments'.[48] As seven judges in *Kesavananda* had rejected the theory of implied limits in the constitution, he took any attempt at using the basic structure doctrine to review legislation to be an exercise in 'rewriting the Constitution and robbing the legislature of acting within the framework of the Constitution'.[49] He concluded

[43] *Indira Gandhi* v. *Raj Narain*, supra n. 4, pp. 2388–9 (Mathew, J).
[44] Ibid.
[45] *Indira Gandhi* v. *Raj Narain*, supra n. 4, p. 2331 (Ray, CJ).
[46] Ibid., p. 2365.
[47] Ibid.
[48] Ibid.
[49] Ibid.

by reiterating that the 'constitutional validity of a statute depends entirely on the existence of the legislative power and the express provision in Article 13'.[50] Chandrachud concurred that the existing two-tier model of judicial review exhausted the potential for useful judicial review of ordinary legislative action and pointed out that as the basic structure was 'not a part of the fundamental rights nor indeed a provision of the Constitution'[51] it could not form the basis of review of ordinary legislation.

Mathew addressed the constitutional basis of the basic structure doctrine more directly. First, he noted that there was no support for the review of ordinary legislation in the *Kesavananda* opinion[52] which he correctly understood to be a 'limitation on the power of amendment under Article 368'.[53] Then it fell to the respondents to show that such a limitation is found in Articles 245 and 246 which provide for the legislative power of Parliament and the State legislatures. By rejecting the idea that the concept of basic structure was an abstract model of review, removed from the Constitutional text, Mathew sharpens the enquiry into the constitutional basis for basic structure review of ordinary legislation. At this point in his opinion, he conflates the enquiry into the constitutional basis for basic structure review of ordinary legislation with an important, but analytically unrelated, enquiry into the process of identifying basic features of the Constitution.[54] As I discuss the identification of basic features in Chapter 5, I now turn to address the other important questions raised by Mathew.

Three aspects of the conclusion in *Indira Gandhi* require scrutiny. First, the judges in this case offer little explanation for the constitutional basis and rationale for the basic structure doctrine in *Kesavananda*. They assume the doctrine to be authoritative precedent for judicial review with respect to amendments but offer no justifying reasons for the doctrine. Unless, the court develops an understanding of the role and scope of basic structure review as an independent model of judicial review, it will be difficult to use it to

[50] Ibid., p. 2332.
[51] *Indira Gandhi* v. *Raj Narain*, supra n. 4, p. 2472 (Chandrachud, J).
[52] Ibid., p. 2388 (Mathew, J).
[53] Ibid., p. 2385.
[54] Ibid., pp. 2383–7.

review amendments or any other species of state action convincingly. Second, despite the interpretive approach adopted in *Kesavananda* to Article 368, the judges in *Indira Gandhi* revert to a limited view of the role of the court in interpreting the constitution by adopting a formalist approach to construing the scope of the legislative power of Parliament and the State legislatures set out in Articles 245 and 246. Moreover, none of the opinions in *Indira Gandhi* considers the impact of the *Kesavananda* opinion on the content of the phrase 'subject to the provisions of the Constitution'. Finally, the court is reluctant to subject Parliament's legislative power to limits which are uncertain and indeterminate. As this is the first case where the basic structure doctrine was applied, the court was unsure about the process by which basic features are to be identified and the nature and scope of basic structure review. These concerns, though strictly unconnected to whether the scope of basic structure review should apply to ordinary legislation and executive action, play a significant role in the court's conclusion.

Of the three aspects considered above, I address the first and the third in Chapters 4 and 5 respectively. In this part of the Chapter I will confine the discussion to the interpretation of Articles 245 and 246. In Chapter 2 I have proposed that the constitutional basis for basic structure review of constitutional amendments is the operation of implied limitations on the amending power in Article 368. In order to develop the argument for basic structure review of executive and legislative action, in the next section I consider a few relevant cases where the court has utilized the basic structure doctrine.

The *Inquiries* Case

I specifically said there that the doctrine of the basic structure of the Constitution could be used to test the validity of laws made by Parliament either in its constituent or ordinary law making capacities because 'ordinary law making cannot go beyond the range of constituent power'.... But, if, as a result of the doctrine, certain imperatives are inherent in or logically and necessarily flow from the Constitution's 'basic structure', just as though they are its express mandates, they can be and have to be used to test the, validity of ordinary laws just as other parts of the Constitution are so used.[55]

[55] *State of Karnataka* v. *Union of India*, AIR 1978 Supreme Court 68 (Beg, CJ)

In *State of Karnataka* v. *Union of India*[56], through an original civil suit under Article 131 of the Constitution, the State of Karnataka challenged a notification issued by the Union government in exercise of its powers under Section 3 of the Commissions of Inquiry Act, 1952, constituting a Commission of Inquiry into allegations of corruption on the part of the chief minister and other ministers of the state government. Despite the proceeding taking the form of a civil suit for a declaration, this executive order was challenged on administrative law grounds of mala fide motives and constitutional grounds of a lack of competence on 'the terms of the Constitution as well as the federal structure implicit and accepted as an inviolable basic feature of the Constitution'.[57] The court brushed off the administrative law challenges with relative ease and concentrated on the challenge to the plenary power of the Union to legislate on Commissions of Inquiry. Though it was the exercise of executive power in the form of a Union notification that was challenged in the case, the court focused on the legislative competence of the Union to enact the parent statute. The court seems to assume that if the legislation passed the competence enquiry, the executive action would be competent too. The court conflated the two types of state action and did not anticipate the possibility that though the executive action may satisfy judicial review on competence grounds, it may fail to satisfy administrative law review and basic structure review. Further, the court also failed to distinguish between competence review and basic structure review as the court did not apply itself to the problems related to the basic structure review of executive action.

Basic structure review of ordinary legislative and executive action did not emerge through a single logical step as suggested by Beg in his lead opinion in the *Inquiries* case. I had concluded the discussion of the *Election* case by pointing out that before a court could extend basic structure review to ordinary legislative and executive powers, it must apply itself to an understanding of the constitutional basis of the basic structure doctrine in *Kesavananda* as well as an approach to constitutional interpretation. Beg, in his lead opinion in the *Inquiries*

[56] AIR 1978 SC 68.

[57] Supra n. 56, para 1.

case, responded to these concerns. Hence, his opinion deserves close analysis.

Reading Kesavananda

Beg while reviewing the *Kesavananda* holding, where he took a dissenting view, observed that:

although a majority of learned Judges of this Court ... rejected the theory of 'implied limitations' upon express plenary legislative powers of constitutional amendment, yet, we accepted, I say so with the utmost respect, again by a majority, limitations which appeared to be not easily distinguishable from implied limitations upon plenary legislative powers even though they were classed as parts of 'the basic structure of the Constitution'.[58]

In Chapter 2 I had noted that several justifications were advanced in support of a doctrine of implied limitations—natural rights, historical commitments of the freedom movement, constitutional common law, limited sovereignty of a post-colonial state—which had been expressly rejected by the majority in the court. Beg revives the implied limitations argument despite its express rejection by the *Kesavananda* majority and seeks to justify it by turning to the provisions of the constitution.

He begins by clarifying that he did not consider *Kesavananda* 'to lay down some theory of a vague basic structure floating, like a cloud in the skies, above the surface of the Constitution and outside it or one that lies buried beneath the surface for which we have to dig in order to discover it' and then draws us back to the constitutional text. He then sets out a restatement of the *Kesavananda* holding with clarity that is yet to be found in any other opinion of the Supreme Court and deserves to be quoted in full:[59]

I prefer to think that the doctrine of 'a basic structure' was nothing more than a set of obvious inferences relating to the intents of the Constitution makers arrived at by applying the established canons of construction rather broadly, as they should be so far as an organic Constitutional document, meant to govern the fate of a nation, is concerned. But, in every case where reliance is placed upon it, in the course of an attack upon legislation, whether ordinary or constituent (in the sense that it is an amendment of the Constitution), what

---

[58] *State of Karnataka* v. *Union of India*, supra n. 56.
[59] *State of Karnataka* v. *Union of India*, supra n. 49, para 121.

is put forward as part of 'a basic structure' must be justified by references to the express provisions of the Constitution. That structure does not exist in vacuo. Inferences from it must be shown to be embedded in and to flow logically and naturally from the bases of that structure. In other words, it must be related to the provisions of the Constitution and to the manner in which they could indubitably be presumed to naturally and reasonably function ... So viewed, the doctrine is nothing more than a way of advancing a well recognised mode of construing the Constitution ... Thus, it is clear that whenever the doctrine of the basic structure has been expounded or applied it is only as a doctrine of interpretation of the Constitution as it actually exists and not of a Constitution which could exist only subjectively in the minds of different individuals as mere theories about what the Constitution is. The doctrine did not add to the contents of the Constitution. It did not, in theory, deduct anything from what was there. It only purported to bring out and explain the meaning of what was already there.

This rather long extract is clear but confused. Beg rightly identifies three aspects of the *Kesavananda* holding. First, that the court developed a particular approach to constitutional interpretation; second, that applying this method of interpretation the court concluded that the amending powers of Parliament did not extend to the basic structure of the Constitution. Finally, he isolates an interpretive technique for the identification of basic features which pays attention to the textual provisions of the Constitution and not to abstract political or moral theory. We will return to this third aspect of the judgment in Chapter 5 but for the moment it is crucial to disentangle these distinct enquiries to overcome their jumbled presentation in the above quotation.

By presenting these three distinct enquiries together, Beg comes to the conclusion that the 'basic structure' doctrine is nothing more than a principle of construction of the Constitution. In Chapter 2, I had argued that the basic structure doctrine was the result of a 'structural interpretation' of important constitutional provisions which give rise to limits on the amending power. The doctrine which results from such an interpretive approach has developed into a full-fledged doctrine of judicial review which includes well worked out standards of application and carefully identified grounds of review. The structural interpretation of the Constitution allows the court to articulate a constitutional basis for the basic structure doctrine, which in *Kesavananda* resides in an interpretation of the amending power in Article 368. In the *Inquiries* case, Beg rightly identifies the technique of interpretation but fails to apply this technique to interpret Articles 245 and 246 which confer legislative power on Parliament.

He reviews the refusal of the court in the *Election* case to extend basic structure review to ordinary legislation and observes that the reason for that decision was 'that there was no ambiguity to be resolved about the ordinary law making powers of Parliament. It was applied to interpret the ambit of the Constituent power as there was some uncertainty about its scope'.[60] Although he accepts the reasoning of the court in the *Election* case he does not apply this to the provisions of the Constitution which grants executive and legislative power.

We had noted earlier that the Constitution confers executive and legislative power by making them expressly 'subject to the provisions of the Constitution.' The application of the method of constitutional interpretation identified by Beg would require that the courts determine whether the scope of this phrase is limited to the provisions of the Constitution or include the implied limits developed by the court while interpreting these constitutional provisions. For example, as the court has interpreted Article 14 of the Constitution to include the Wednesbury unreasonableness principle,[61] executive power which is 'subject to the provisions of the Constitution' is therefore subject to the Wednesbury standard. Clearly, the court has accepted the proposition that the 'provisions' of the Constitution include its interpretation of these provisions. The key issue then is whether the basic structure doctrine announced in *Kesavananda* is a limit on the legislative and executive powers. Though the *Election* case did not address this question, Beg did so in the *Inquiries* case albeit in a roundabout fashion:

[I]f, as a result of the doctrine, certain imperatives are inherent in or logically and necessarily flow from the Constitution's 'basic structure', just as though they are its express mandates, they can be and have to be used to test the validity of ordinary laws just as other parts of the Constitution are so used.[62]

This observation, though unrelated to an interpretation of Article 245 or 246 in Beg's opinion, does articulate a constitutional basis for the basic structure review of legislative and executive power through

---

[60] *State of Karnataka* v. *Union of India*, supra n. 56 (Beg, CJ).

[61] *R.C. Cooper* v. *Union of India*, (1970) 1 SCC 248.

[62] *State of Karnataka* v. *Union of India*, supra n. 56, p. 679 (Beg, CJ).

an interpretation of the phrase 'subject to the provisions of the Constitution.' Such an argument pre-supposes that an interpretation of the constitutional provisions generates emergent basic features which operate as implied limitations on the power-conferring provisions of the Constitution. As these implied limitations are a result of an interpretation of the 'provisions' of the Constitution, all legislative and executive powers which must be exercised subject to the 'provisions' of the Constitution are therefore subject to basic structure review.

Reading the Election Case

Even if the above interpretation of the Constitution is persuasive, the 7-judge bench in the *Inquiries* case had to deal with the refusal to apply basic structure review to ordinary legislation by another 5-judge bench in the *Election* case. I had noted earlier that Beg interpreted the basic structure doctrine to be a principle of interpretation of the Constitution. Therefore, he read the majority opinion in the *Election* case to affirm that the basic structure was a valid principle of construction but that 'it was not available to test the validity of the impugned provisions of the Representation of People Act because the expressly laid down ordinary law making powers of Parliament are clear enough. In other words, it was held to be inapplicable here on the view that there was no ambiguity to be resolved about the ordinary law making powers of Parliament.'[63] Further, on a close reading of the majority opinions of Ray and Mathew he concluded that they had utilized basic structure values like representative democracy and judicial review to assess the validity of the challenged legislation in any case. Beg fails to distinguish the *Election* case holding and his efforts are directed at playing down the express and strident refusal of the bench in that case to subject ordinary legislation to basic structure review.

The analysis in this section clearly suggests that Beg's analytical approach to the basic structure doctrine in the *Inquiries* case was more precise and persuasive than that adopted by the bench in the *Election* case. Moreover, the *Inquiries* case was before a 7-judge bench while the *Election* case came before a 5-judge bench. Technically this means that Beg's majority opinion in the *Inquiries* case should overrule the

---

[63] Ibid. (Beg, CJ).

Election case on the applicability of basic structure review to ordinary legislation. However, the presence of plural opinions in the *Inquiries* case does not allow us to assert the proposition on basic structure review and ordinary legislation unequivocally. Beg does not expressly overrule the *Election* case and concludes that the basic feature of 'federalism' does not impose a further limit on the Union's power to legislate on inquiries in the States. Hence, this leaves some ambiguity on the impact of the *Inquiries* case. Given the diametrically opposite conclusions arrived at by the two benches on the applicability of basic structure review with respect to ordinary legislation, it was left to the subsequent cases to establish which of these arguments were to succeed. I will turn to this in the next section and then conclude on the constitutional basis of basic structure review as it applies to ordinary legislation and executive action.

The *Rajya Sabha* Case

The basic structure doctrine has been applied to test the constitutionality of legislation and executive action in several cases after the *Inquiries* case. However, most of these cases failed to reconcile the conflicting views of the judges in the *Election* and *Inquiries* cases on the constitutional basis for extending basic structure review to ordinary legislation and executive action. Significantly, in *Ismail Faruqui* v. *Union of India*,[64] the basic structure doctrine was used to invalidate an ordinary legislation, namely Ayodhya (Acquisition of Certain Areas) Act, 1993. In several other cases, the basic structure doctrine has been used to validate legislations and executive action. I turn to these cases in Chapter 4 as they assist in refining the type and standards of review for the basic structure doctrine.

Raju Ramachandran complains that these decisions do not distinguish the 'authoritative view laid down in *Indira Gandhi*'[65] but he ignores the impact of the *Inquiries* case. Moreover he argues that that these cases '... illustrate the danger of an easy resort to the basic structure mantra when the Court could have invalidated the

[64] (1994) 6 SCC 360. See also *G.C. Kanungo* v. *State of Orissa* (1995) 5 SCC 96, where the court used basic structure review to invalidate a state arbitration law.

[65] Raju Ramachandran, 'The Supreme Court and the Basic Structure Doctrine', in B.N. Kirpal *et al.* (eds) *Supreme but not Infallible*, New Delhi: Oxford University Press, 2004 (n) 124.

concerned legislation on other well-recognized grounds'. This is an argument about the nature of basic structure review and its relationship with existing models of judicial review which I will consider in greater detail in Chapter 4.

The ambiguity around the constitutional basis for basic structure review of ordinary legislation and executive action was sought to be settled decisively in a recent 5-judge bench in *Kuldip Nayar* v. *Union of India*.[66] Kuldip Nayar challenged amendments to the Representation of People Act, 1951 on two grounds, both of which relied on the basic structure doctrine. First, he challenged the amendment which dispensed with the requirement of a candidate for a Rajya Sabha election to be domiciled in the State he seeks to represent. He argued that this principle of representation was central to the composition of the Rajya Sabha as a Council of States and its removal damaged the basic feature of federalism which dispensed with the requirement of a secret ballot in Rajya Sabha elections as it irreparably damaged the feature of 'democracy' which entails a free and fair election by secret ballot.

Sabharwal, speaking for the majority, upheld both amendments and held that the 'doctrine of basic feature in the context of our Constitution..., does not apply to ordinary legislation...'.[67] He reached this conclusion by relying extensively on the opinions of several judges in the *Election* case where the court categorically ruled that basic structure review does not apply to ordinary legislation.[68] While considering the impact of the *Inquiries* case Sabharwal cited from portions of Beg's opinion where he pointed out that the basic structure doctrine 'must be justified by references to the express provisions of the Constitution'[69] but surprisingly did not cite his conclusion that limits arising out of the express provisions of the constitution, basic structure review applied in full measure to ordinary legislation.[70] Sabharwal then goes on to cite Untwalia's concurring

---

[66] *Kuldip Nayar* v. *Union of India*, (2006) 7 SCC 1.

[67] Ibid. (Sabharwal, CJ).

[68] *Kuldip Nayar*, supra n. 67, pp. 62–6 (Sabharwal, CJ).

[69] *State of Karnataka* v. *Union of India*, supra n. 56 cited at *Kuldip Nayar* (n. 67) p. 66 (Sabharwal, CJ).

[70] Ibid., p. 679 (Beg, CJ).

opinion in the *Inquiries* case where he rejects the application of basic structure review to ordinary legislation.[71]

The Supreme Court passed over on the opportunity in the *Rajya Sabha* case to reconcile the conflicting positions in the *Election* and *Inquiries* cases. While the court's ruling that basic structure review does not apply to ordinary legislation is likely to be treated as the current position of law, this proposition should be reconsidered and revised at the next available opportunity. In this section I have argued that Beg's opinion in the *Inquiries* case offers us the best rationale for applying basic structure review to ordinary legislation and executive action. As we have shown above, the implied limitations which sustain basic structure review are readily accommodated by the language of Articles 245 and 246 which requires that all powers must be exercised 'subject to the provisions of the constitution'.

CONCLUSION

We conclude this chapter by responding to some of the recent work by Sathe who is one of the few scholars who have seriously tracked the evolution of the basic structure doctrine beyond the review of constitutional amendments. He concludes his review of the *Bommai* case by posing a critical question: 'Do we conclude that the basic structure doctrine could now be pressed into service for challenging the validity of an executive act?'[72] In this chapter I have argued that the answer to this precisely framed question has to be an unambiguous yes. Although Sathe construes the political impact of the *Bommai* case to be a warning the political right which sought to put in place a majoritarian Hindu state, I have attempted to articulate a general constitutional basis for the application of basic structure review to higher executive action or the exercise of prerogative powers. He then observes that while the court refers to the basic structure in other cases where ordinary legislative and executive action is challenged, it seems to use the words 'basic structure' in a different sense from which they are used in determining the validity of a constitutional amendment.[73] This is the topic I turn to in the next chapter where I

[71] *Kuldip Nayar*, supra n. 67, p. 67 (Sabharwal, CJ).

[72] S.P. Sathe, *Judicial Activism in India*, New Delhi: Oxford University Press, 2002, p. 97.

[73] Ibid., p. 98.

outline the type and standards of basic structure review as it applies to these various forms of state action. I conclude this chapter with a final endorsement of Sathe's prognosis on the evolution of the basic structure doctrine:

So it seems that while the horizon of the basic structure doctrine may expand to include legislative as well as executive actions, its use for considering the validity of a constitutional amendment may become rare.[74]

[74] Ibid.

3

Applying Basic Structure Review
The Limits of State Action and the Standard of Review

In Kesavananda Bharati's case... this Court had not worked out the implications of the basic structure doctrine in all its applications. It could, therefore, be said, with utmost respect, that it was perhaps left there in an amorphous state which could give rise to possible misunderstandings as to whether it is not too vaguely stated or too loosely and variously formulated without attempting a basic uniformity of its meanings or implications.[1]

Beg in the quotation above observes the need for the doctrine of basic structure to be rigorously developed in the cases following *Kesavananda*. This task of formulating the doctrine cannot proceed unless the tendency, in the court and academic literature, to criticize and deal with the doctrine in an undifferentiated fashion is abandoned. By utilizing the analytical distinction between different aspects of a doctrine of judicial review I find that the judicial output on the doctrine may be reorganized along discrete themes. These thematic enquiries allow us to analyse the judicial output critically and to assess strengths and weaknesses of parts of the doctrine as it presently stands and to respond to criticisms of excessive and careless use.

In this work I argue that basic structure review has evolved into a fully developed independent doctrine of judicial review. In Chapters 1 and 2 I investigated the constitutional basis of the basic structure doctrine

[1] *State of Karnataka* v. *Union of India*, AIR 1978 4 SC 68 (Beg, CJ) 119.

for the judicial review of constitutional amendments, the proclamation of emergency power, as well as ordinary legislative, and executive power. In this chapter I investigate the application of the doctrine—the type of review and standard of scrutiny—to varied forms of state action. After the conception of the basic structure doctrine in *Kesavananda*, a clear type of basic structure review of constitutional amendments emerges in *Indira Gandhi* v. *Raj Narain*.[2] In this case, the court identifies different types of basic structure review of constitutional amendments: namely, an extension of Article 13-type judicial review for compliance with fundamental rights to constitutional amendments, or an independent new form of judicial review. I argue that basic structure review as developed by the courts in *Indira Gandhi* and subsequent cases is best understood as an independent type of judicial review of constitutional amendments.

Where basic structure review is applied to proclamations of emergency as well as ordinary executive action, the court has to consider whether the doctrine applies as an independent competence criterion against which the vires of the executive action may be assessed or whether basic structure review is to be accommodated with the existing administrative law model of judicial review of executive action. In *Bommai* the court characterized the emergency proclamation power as a prerogative power which was not subject to ordinary jurisdictional limits of executive action. Instead, the court ruled that such an action may be reviewed only on the Wednesbury unreasonableness standard into which it combined basic structure review in order to conclude that the proclamation of emergency was unconstitutional. I will argue that the court's approach to basic structure review of executive action fails to articulate the relationship between basic structure review and administrative law review of executive action. Irrespective of the executive action being reviewed—higher executive action or ordinary executive action—basic structure review must operate as a substantive limit on the action which circumscribes the sphere of valid authority of the executive branch of government.

I conclude the first part of this chapter by evaluating basic structure review of ordinary legislation which has been applied by the courts in an unsophisticated manner. Even if ordinary legislative action

[2] AIR 1975 SC 2299.

complies with judicial review for competence and fundamental rights, the court has recognized that basic structure review may still be applied to find such legislation unconstitutional. Hence with ordinary legislation, basic structure review is supplementary to other models of constitutional judicial review[3] and operates as a substantive limit on the boundaries of permissible legislation.

In the second part of this chapter I critically examine the standard of scrutiny which the court applies to state action under basic structure review. Unlike the type of basic structure review considered in the previous part of the chapter, the arguments relating to the standard of scrutiny remain the same irrespective of the type of state action being challenged. Notably the standard of scrutiny is unevenly developed in the cases dealing with different types of state action. So in some sections though I may only consider one type of state action the conclusions apply to all types of state action. The phrase which best captures the standard of review applied is whether the state action 'destroys or damages the basic features or basic structure of the Constitution'.[4] The phrase 'destroys or damages' indicates the high threshold of constitutional injury, or conversely the low standard of judicial scrutiny, employed by the courts in reviewing constitutional amendments. In other words, basic structure review does not employ the intense scrutiny, associated with Article 13 judicial review for compliance with fundamental rights or Articles 245 and 246 judicial review for competence where any minor violation of the provisions may lead to the court striking down the state action as unconstitutional. Instead, a constitutional amendment may be struck down only where there is substantial evidence that there is change in the 'form, character, and content'[5] of the constitution so that it may be said that the 'identity' of the constitution is irrevocably altered.

I then briefly consider three issues related to the level at which courts scrutinize state action under the basic structure doctrine: first, it has been suggested that basic structure review ensures compliance with principles and not rules and I show that this distinction is not useful or sustainable. Second, I examine whether basic structure

---

[3] *Ismail Faruqui* v. *Union of India*, (1994) 6 SCC 360.

[4] *Indira Gandhi*, supra n. 2, p. 2314 (Ray, CJ).

[5] *Ganpathrao* v. *Union of India*, AIR 1993 SC 1267, 1291 (Pandian, J).

review may be characterized as a soft incompatibility review and not a hard unconstitutionality review. The evidence on this is mixed as it seems that the court uses basic structure review in both these ways. I argue that this accommodates the dual normative force of basic features as implied limits on state action and as aids to constitutional interpretation. Third, I conclude this section, and the chapter, by assessing whether judicial deference has any role to play in basic structure review and conclude that the identification of the type and standard of basic structure review with precision renders the language of judicial deference to be of no further assistance and should be abandoned.

TYPE OF BASIC STRUCTURE REVIEW

In the 'Introduction' I outlined the types of judicial review jurisdictions enjoyed by the Supreme Court and High Courts in India. These are review for jurisdictional competence of legislative and executive actions and review for compliance with fundamental rights. Besides jurisdictional competence and rights compliance review the courts have continued to develop administrative law review by building on, and at times going beyond, their common law inheritance. The introduction of basic structure review in *Kesavananda* requires the court to articulate whether such review will adopt and mould pre-existing types of review employed by the courts or develop a novel and distinctive model of review. The application of basic structure review has developed independently for each type of state action and I will consider them separately in this part of the chapter.

Where the challenged state action is constitutional amendments or executive action by high constitutional authorities, basic structure review may be the only available model of review. Nevertheless, there has been considerable confusion about whether basic structure review would be integrated with fundamental rights review or administrative law review for these respective state actions. However, where ordinary legislative and executive power is challenged, the presence of other types of judicial review for such actions may result in basic structure review being suitably modified to supplement rather than supplant other types of judicial review. With this general introduction I now examine the application of basic structure review to different forms of state action. The discussion in the rest of this part of the chapter will consider basic structure review of constitutional amendments, ordinary legislation, and executive action in that order.

Constitutional Amendments

In *Kesavananda*, the court developed the constitutional basis of the basic structure doctrine extensively but did not pay much attention to the type and standard of review. While a majority of judges found that the Constitution (25th Amendment) Act, 1971 which inserted Article 31-C into the constitution damaged the basic structure of the constitution, they expressed the basic structure review test in different terms. Sikri concluded that Parliament's amending power could not 'completely change the fundamental features of the constitution so as to destroy its identity'.[6] Khanna proposed that the basic structure doctrine limited amending power insofar as it did not 'include the power to abrogate the Constitution nor does it include the power to alter the basic structure or framework of the Constitution'.[7] Likewise, Hegde and Mukherjea found that the amending power does not include 'the power to destroy or emasculate the basic elements or the fundamental features of the Constitution'.[8] All three opinions phrase the basic structure test in negative terms as a form of judicial review where the court will determine the outward boundaries of amending power. The opinions describe these boundaries in three ways: first, when a constitutional amendment abrogates the entire constitution; second, when a constitutional amendment damages or destroys a basic feature of the constitution; and third, where the challenged amendment, in Sikri's words, threatens the very 'identity' of the Constitution.[9] As the application of these various tests to the challenged constitutional amendment in *Kesavananda* was not very illuminating it fell to subsequent judgments to clarify the normative force of the doctrine and distinguish it from the other forms of constitutional judicial review.

[6] *Kesavananda Bharati* v. *State of Kerala*, (1973) 4 SCC 225 (Sikri, CJ) 405.

[7] Ibid., p. 824 (Khanna, J).

[8] Ibid., p. 512 (Hegde and Mukherjea, JJ).

[9] R. Dhavan, *Supreme Court and Parliamentary Sovereignty*, New Delhi: Sterling Publishers, 1976, pp. 191–230 for a similar distinction on the implied limits on amending power.

It was in *Indira Gandhi*[10] that the court applied basic structure review to constitutional amendments and ordinary legislation. As significant disagreements about the type of judicial review that the court should undertake under basic structure review arose in this case, it deserves careful attention. The High Court of Allahabad had found the (then) recently elected prime minister guilty of corrupt election practices under the Representation of People Act, 1951 and disqualified her from public office and from contesting elections for a period of six years. Parliament enacted the Constitution (39th Amendment) Act, 1975 to overcome the decision of the Allahabad High Court using three distinct devices. Article 71 was amended to allow Parliament to regulate the election of the president and vice-president by law, including the grounds on which such an election may be challenged before the courts. A new Article 329-A was introduced which allowed Parliament to enact laws to regulate the election of the prime minister and the speaker to either House of Parliament. Clauses 4 and 5 of Article 329-A provided that all previous laws, pending legal proceedings, including orders passed under such pre-existing laws were void. The third means of overcoming the decision of the Allahabad High Court was to insert the amended Representation of People Act, 1951, the Election Law (Amendment) Act, 1975, and the Representation of People (Amendment) Act, 1974 into the 9th Schedule thereby protecting them from judicial review for violation of fundamental rights.[11]

Several legal and constitutional issues were raised before the court, but I will confine myself in this section to those arguments related to the application of the basic structure doctrine to review constitutional amendments. It was argued that the basic features affected by the 39th constitutional amendment included the separation of powers, democracy, equality, republicanism, rule of law, and the sanctity of judicial review itself. I am not concerned for the moment with this list of basic features as the problems related to the identification of basic features are dealt with in Chapter 4. In this section I examine why the plural opinions in the *Indira Gandhi* took differing views about the relationship between basic structure review and other

[10] *Indira Gandhi*, supra n. 2.
[11] Article 31-B read with the 9th Schedule, Constitution of India, 1950.

types of constitutional judicial review and then conclude the section by evaluating the development of these views in subsequent cases.

The majority opinions in *Kesavananda* had proposed a form of judicial review which had the potential to limit the amending power of Parliament. Two distinct approaches emerge in *Indira Gandhi*. The first was to construe basic structure review to be an extension of existing models of constitutional judicial review to constitutional amendments. The second approach to develop a novel form of judicial review distinct from existing models of judicial review hitherto applied by the court. I will consider each of these in turn.

Extension of Article 13 Judicial Review

In *Indira Gandhi*, the clearest illustration of the extension of Article 13 judicial review is Chandrachud's opinion. He assesses whether Clauses (4) of (5) to Article 329-A satisfied the guarantee of equality which he had earlier identified to be a 'basic postulate of our constitution'.[12] He argued that since *Anwar Ali Sarkar* v. *State of West Bengal*[13] the court has in Article 14 cases investigated whether the classification adopted by the law or executive action was founded on an intelligible differentia which has a rational relation to the object sought to be achieved by such law or action. Applying the same test to the 39th Amendment, he concluded that the differential treatment of the elections to high constitutional office, including that of the prime minister, from elections of other ordinary members of Parliament would fail this rationality standard.[14] It is surprising that Chandrachud took the basic structure test to be an extension of the Article 14 doctrine, developed under Article 13 constitutional judicial review of ordinary legislative and executive action, to constitutional amendments. Notably, he did not apply the same model of analysis to determine whether the 39th Amendment destroys other basic features like democracy, judicial review, separation of powers, or the rule of law; as unlike equality, these basic features are not traceable to a single provision of the Constitution around which constitutional doctrine has been developed.

---

[12] *Indira Gandhi*, supra n. 2, p. 2469.
[13] AIR 1952 SC 75.
[14] *Indira Gandhi*, supra n. 2, p. 2469.

Chandrachud's inconsistency in *Indira Gandhi* is amplified by his approach to the constitutional validity of the Constitution (42nd Amendment) Act, 1976 in his majority opinion in *Minerva Mills* v. *Union of India*.[15] The 42nd Amendment introduced Article 31-C which immunized legislation, which advanced directive principles set out in Part IV of the Constitution, from being challenged for violation of Articles 14 and 19 fundamental rights. Reviewing the constitutionality of this amendment, Chandrachud observes:[16]

The answer to this question must necessarily depend on whether Arts 14 and 19, which must now give way to laws passed in order to effectuate the policy of the State towards securing all or any of the principles of Directive Policy, are essential features of the basic structure of the Constitution. It is only if the rights conferred by these two articles are not a part of the basic structure that they can be allowed to be abrogated by a constitutional amendment.

He then found that as Articles 14 and 19 were basic features of the Constitution they had been abrogated by Article 31-C. He concludes that the 42nd Amendment, by giving absolute primacy to the directive principles over fundamental rights, violated the 'harmony and balance between fundamental rights and directive principles' which is 'an essential feature of the basic structure of the Constitution'.[17]

Chandrachud's opinion in these cases raises two connected issues: first, he identifies the basic structure of the Constitution by isolating important individual provisions which are made immune from amendment. This is an issue related to the identification of basic features considered in Chapter 4. Second, he understands basic structure review to be an assessment of whether the challenged constitutional amendment violates these important provisions of the constitution. This second issue is about the character of basic structure review as Chandrachud extends the court's existing Article 13 judicial review analysis to constitutional amendments with two additional features. First, basic features may include other provisions of the constitution besides the rights included in Part III which are protected by Article 13 judicial review. Second, the challenged constitutional amendments must damage or destroy the

---

[15] *Minerva Mills* v. *Union of India*, AIR 1980 SC 1789.
[16] Ibid., p. 1803 (Chandrachud, CJ).
[17] *Minerva Mills*, supra n. 15, p. 1806 (Chandrachud, CJ).

constitutional provision and not merely 'abridge' fundamental rights to be declared unconstitutional.

In *R.C. Poudyal* v. *Union of India*,[18] Sharma's dissenting opinion adopts a similar approach to basic structure review. He enquires into whether the reservation of a legislative seat for the Buddhist Sangha violates 'Article 15 as also several other provisions of the Constitution; and further whether these constitutional provisions are unalterable by amendment'.[19] He then goes on to consider whether the reservation of the seat violates Article 15 which prohibits discrimination on the basis of religion. In both these enquiries, basic structure review enables the court to apply judicial review for human rights compliance under Article 13 to constitutional amendments.

In two recent decisions of the Supreme Court, the conflation of basic structure review and Article 13 fundamental rights review has intensified. In *M. Nagaraj* v. *Union of India*[20] four constitutional amendments which introduced new provisions regarding reservations in public employment were challenged on two basic structure grounds: first, that Parliament had amended the constitution to overcome judicial decisions and hence damaged the basic feature of judicial review and second, that these constitutional amendments which enlarged the scope for reservation damaged the basic feature of equality. While responding to the second challenge, Kapadia, speaking unanimously for the 5-judge bench, suggests that he is conscious of the distinction between equality as a fundamental right and equality as a basic feature of the constitution,[21] but he does not apply this distinction to the constitutional validity of these amendments. He proposes that basic structure review is made up of two tests which apply disjunctively: namely, the 'width test' and the 'identity test'.[22] The 'width test' extends Article 13 judicial review to constitutional amendments for compliance with fundamental rights but such amendments must cause greater damage to rights than other forms of state action under Article 13 judicial review. He concludes that the challenged constitutional amendments are valid as they do not

---

[18] AIR 1993 SC 1804.

[19] *R.C. Poudyal* v. *Union of India*, AIR 1993 SC 1804.

[20] *M. Nagaraj* v. *Union of India*, (2006) 8 SCC 212.

[21] Ibid., pp. 242–6 (Kapadia, J).

[22] Ibid., p. 268 (Kapadia, J).

damage the basic structure of the constitution. These amendments do away with 'the concept of the "catch-up" rule and "consequential seniority" [which] are not constitutional requirements. They are not constitutional limitations. They are concepts derived from service jurisprudence... Obliteration of these concepts or insertion of these concepts does not change the equality code indicated by Articles 14, 15, and 16 of the constitution.'[23] One may infer that where a constitutional amendment obliterates a fundamental rights provision then the constitutional amendment would be unconstitutional under basic structure review.

I.R. Coelho v. State of Tamil Nadu[24] is the latest judgment which follows through on this line of reasoning about the type of basic structure review. Article 31-B was inserted into the Constitution by the Constitution (1st Amendment) Act, 1950 to protect Union and State laws from Article 13 fundamental rights review for violation of Articles 14, 19, and 21. To be protected under Article 31-B these laws had to be inserted into the 9th Schedule of the constitution by a constitutional amendment. Alhough Article 31-B was introduced to protect land reform legislation from judicial review, it eventually cast a protective umbrella over laws covering varied subject matter. As the constitutional amendments inserting laws inserted into the 9th Schedule were challenged on basic structure grounds, 'the extent and nature of immunity that Article 31-B can validly provide'[25] was the central issue in the case. Sabharwal, speaking for a unanimous 5-judge bench, concluded that basic structure test would examine 'the nature and extent of infraction of a Fundamental Right by a statute, sought to be constitutionally protected, and on the touchstone of the basic structure doctrine *as reflected in Article 21 read with Article 14 and Article 19* by application of the "rights test" and the "essence of the right" test...'.[26] It is not clear from this passage, or from the rest of the judgment, whether Sabharwal had one or two tests in mind. In any event it is abundantly clear that in either case he is concerned with 'the actual effect and impact of the law on the rights guaranteed under Part III... for determining whether or

---

[23] *M. Nagaraj*, supra n. 20, p. 268 (Kapadia, J).
[24] *I.R. Coelho* v. *State of Tamil Nadu*, (2007) 1 Supreme Court Almanac 197.
[25] Ibid., p. 222 (Sabharwal, CJ).
[26] Ibid., p. 240.

not it destroys the basic structure. The impact test would determine the validity of the challenge.'[27]

These recent cases develop Chandrachud's opinion in *Indira Gandhi* which views basic structure review as a text-based limit on amending power which prevents the abrogation or obliteration of important provisions of the constitution. As all these cases deal with threats to fundamental rights provisions, the court developed basic structure review as an extension of Article 13 fundamental rights review but with the additional requirement of having to show a more intense level of constitutional injury. Before I evaluate the merits of an approach to basic structure review modelled on judicial review for fundamental rights compliance, I will turn to alternative approaches to basic structure review developed in *Indira Gandhi* and other subsequent cases.

Independent Substantive Judicial Review

The court's application of basic structure review to evaluate the 39th Amendment for damage to the basic features of democracy and judicial review in *Indira Gandhi* is a useful starting point for our investigation into an alternative approach to basic structure review. Chandrachud and Mathew assessed whether the 39th Amendment Act damaged the basic feature of democracy but reached opposite conclusions.[28] The preliminary task while assessing whether a particular amendment damages the basic feature of democracy is to work out what the constitutional principle of democracy requires in the particular context which the constitutional amendment operates. To do this the court must ascertain how the constitution entrenches the principles of democracy and its political practice in India and distinguish it from the various versions adopted by different countries.[29] Neither opinion sought to identify an abstract set of principles which constitute the core of the concept of democracy and instead confined themselves to the principles of democracy adopted by the Constitution. They equated democracy as set out in the Constitution with the 'representation of the people in Parliament

---

[27] *I.R. Coelho*, supra n. 24, pp. 239–40 (Sabharwal, CJ).

[28] Ray took the view that democracy did not count as one of the basic features of the constitution: *Indira Gandhi*, supra n. 2, p. 2320.

[29] *Indira Gandhi*, supra n. 2, p. 2467 (Chandrachud, J).

and State Legislature by the method of election'.[30] That such an election should be free and fair follows from the principles of democracy as adopted in the Constitution. The 39th Amendment Act was tested against this derived principle of free and fair election.

Mathew found that a commitment to the principle of free and fair elections entailed that all election disputes were to be resolved in a judicial manner. As the 39th Amendment gave Parliament the power to resolve election disputes, he concluded that this damaged the principle of free and fair elections and in turn the basic feature of democracy.[31] Chandrachud took a different view. He accepted that democracy was a basic feature and that free and fair elections are an essential requirement of democracy. However, he reasoned that the 39th Amendment did not 'destroy the democratic structure of the government'[32] as even after the amendment the rule is 'still the rule of the majority' and the amendment has 'not abrogated the electoral process'. [33] Chandrachud explained that it was 'hard to generalize from a single instance that such an isolated act of immunity has destroyed or threatens to destroy the democratic framework of our government. One swallow does not make a summer.'[34] Mathew and Chandrachud use a similar model of basic structure review of constitutional amendments for compliance with constitutional principles or basic features—as distinguished from constitutional provisions—but their application of different standards of review leads them to different conclusions.

Bhagwati's opinion in *Minerva Mills* v. *Union of India*[35] develops the distinctive character of basic structure review in a sharper fashion. He carefully analyses the opinions in *Kesavananda* and *Indira Gandhi* and points out that the majority holdings in these cases show that 'fundamental rights are not part of the basic structure of the constitution and therefore…they could be abrogated or taken away by Parliament by an amendment under Article 368'.[36] Although

---

[30] Ibid., p. 2372 (Mathew, J).
[31] Ibid., pp. 2373–4.
[32] Ibid., p. 2468 (Chandrachud, J).
[33] *Indira Gandhi*, supra n. 2.
[34] Ibid.
[35] AIR 1980 SC 1789 (Bhagwati, J) p. 1811.
[36] *Minerva Mills*, supra n. 15, p. 1818 (Bhagwati, J).

I argue in Chapter 4 that fundamental rights should be considered while identifying basic features of the constitution, I am concerned in this section with Bhagwati's clear articulation of a version of basic structure review which is distinct from Article 13 judicial review for violation of fundamental rights. This distinction is borne out in his analysis of the challenge to the constitutionality of Article 31-C.

Article 31-C provides that legislation giving effect to the equitable redistribution of the material resources of society, a principle set out in Article 39 (b) and (c), was not to be declared unconstitutional on the grounds that it violated Articles 14 and 19. As Article 31-C grants 'primacy to Directive Principles over Fundamental Rights in case of conflict between them'[37] the question posed is whether the constitutional amendments which inserted Article 31-C into the constitution would damage or destroy the basic structure of the constitution. He proceeds to answer this question by tracing the drafting history of these two parts of the Constitution in great detail[38] and concludes that 'socio-economic rights embodied in the Directive Principles are as much a part of human rights as the Fundamental Rights'.[39] Hence he argues that the 'amendment in Article 31-C far from damaging the basic structure of the Constitution strengthens and reinforces it'. Interestingly, he distinguishes between 'equality before the law in the narrow and formalistic sense'[40] in Article 14 and the egalitarian principle which is an 'essential element of social and economic justice'[41] sought to be achieved by the Directive Principles. Basic structure review for Bhagwati required the courts to apply the equality principles and not the constitutional doctrine developed by the court interpreting Article 14.

Bhagwati's analysis in *Minerva Mills* clearly distinguishes between Article 13 fundamental rights judicial review and basic structure review. When a court engages in basic structure review it is not interested in whether fundamental rights in the constitution are affected even where the basic feature which is the ground for the constitutional challenge is expressed in the constitution in fundamental rights terms. The court

---

[37] *Minerva Mills*, supra n. 15, pp. 1842–3 (Bhagwati, J).
[38] Ibid., pp. 1842–53 (Bhagwati, J).
[39] Ibid., p. 1845 (Bhagwati, J).
[40] Ibid., p. 1847 (Bhagwati, J).
[41] Ibid.

must evaluate whether the challenged amendments damage the basic features to the extent that it can be claimed that the constitutional identity has been irrevocably altered. Put this way, basic structure review is a novel and independent model of judicial review where the courts engage in a substantive analysis of whether the challenged constitutional amendments damage or destroy the basic structure of the Constitution. In the rest of this section, I will carefully unpack the character of this substantive review of compliance with basic features as it has developed in subsequent cases.

The substantive character of basic structure review requires potentially wide-ranging types of analyses. Bhagwati's approach in *Minerva Mills* opens up three lines of enquiry: first, whether the policy objectives sought to be achieved by the challenged constitutional amendment damages basic features of the constitution; second, the proposed constitutional amendments may be subjected to a historical analysis to assess if they are compatible with the intentions of the framers of the constitution; third, we examine if the challenged amendments may be reconciled with the basic features of the constitution in a principled fashion so that the identity of the constitution remains intact. I look to each of these in turn.

In *Indira Gandhi* substantive review for the wisdom of the policy choices made by the legislature was rejected as the appropriate model basic structure review of constitutioal amendments. Beg, responding to the argument that disputes surrounding the election of a private individual could not be the appropriate subject matter for constitutional amendments observed: 'The subject-matter of constitutional amendments is a question of high policy and Courts are concerned with the implementation of laws, not with the wisdom of the policy underlying them'.[42] By circumscribing the range of analysis appropriate to basic structure review the court signals a critical self-imposed limit on this model of review. In *Kihoto Hollohan* v. *Zachilhu*,[43] Venkatachaliah speaking for the majority endorsed the view that where there 'is the legislative determination through experimental constitutional processes to combat'[44] the 'legislatively

[42] *Indira Gandhi*, supra n. 2, (Beg, J) 2464.
[43] *Kihoto Hollohan* v. *Zachilhu*, 1992 (Supp) 2 SCC 651.
[44] Ibid., p. 679 (Venkatachaliah, J).

perceived political evil of unprincipled defections induced by the lure of office and monetary inducements'[45] the court is not required to assess the 'plus and minus of all areas of experimental legislation' and must distinguish between what is constitutionally permissible and what is outside'.[46] Having categorically ruled out a substantive policy analysis as the thrust of basic structure review, I will now proceed to consider how the court should assess compatibility with basic features.

The second method of substantive basic structure review is the historical method. This distinctive method of applying basic structure review was developed by Chandrachud in *Waman Rao* and *Minerva Mills*. In *Waman Rao* Articles 31-A, 31-B, and 31-C which had been introduced to advance the land reform programmes were challenged as violations of the basic structure of the Constitution. He observed that these 'questions have a historical slant and content: and history can furnish a safe and certain clue to their answer'.[47] He then went on to review the legislative history of the Constitution (1st Amendment) Act, 1950 and noted that: 'Looking back over the past thirty years of constitutional history of our country, we as lawyers and Judges, must endorse the claim made…that if Article 31-A were not enacted, some of the main purposes of the Constitution would have been delayed and eventually defeated…'.[48] Despite this heavy reliance on political history, he also advanced an independent justification for the amendments as implementing the constitutional purposes as outlined in Article 39(b) and (c), namely 'that the ownership and control of the material resources of the community are so distributed as best to subserve the common good'.[49] This historical mode of assessing compatibility with basic features adopts a crude form of 'originalism'. The court first seeks to establish the framer's intentions with respect to the particular provisions being amended or constitutional objectives more generally. Then the court may analyse whether the challenged amendment was in accordance with such intentions.

[45] Ibid., p. 678.
[46] Ibid.
[47] AIR 1981 SC 271 (Chandrachud, CJ) 280.
[48] *Waman Rao*, supra n. 48 (Chandrachud, CJ) 283.
[49] Ibid., p. 284.

However, at other points in his judgment, Chandrachud criticizes the historical approach and observes that 'conscious as we are that … extraneous aids to constitutional interpretation are permissible the views of the mover of a Bill are not conclusive on the question of its objects and purposes, we will consider for ourselves the question, independently…'.[50] Further, one may add that the observations above, though strictly about the intentions of the framers of a constitutional amendment, apply equally to the intentions of the framers of the Constitution. Perhaps these intentions may be relevant insofar as they clarify the historical contexts which give rise to the general normative principles adopted by the freedom movement and thereafter enshrined in the Constitution. In this sense, the task of basic structure review requires the court to review the political history of the Constitution and identify the normative commitments therein, while paying careful attention to the particular form of their adoption in the Constitutional text. Thereafter, one has to evaluate whether the challenged constitutional amendments damage or destroy these constitutional principles embodied in the provisions of the constitution.

The role of historical analysis in basic structure review came to be settled further in *Ganpatrao*. Articles 291, 362, and 366(22) were omitted by the Constitution (26th Amendment) Act, 1971. The effect of these amendments was to do away with the privy purses and privileges granted to the former Indian Rulers of the pre-Independence princely states. The articles which were omitted by this constitutional amendment had inserted into the constitution the terms and conditions of the pre-constitutional Instruments of Accession, the Merger Agreements, and the covenants entered into by the Indian Union with the rulers of the princely states. The petitioners argued that these amended provisions were as a matter of historical fact the political basis for the integration of the princely states and the formation of the Indian Union. In that sense, these constitutional provisions were, as a matter of political history, 'integral' and basic to the constitution and their removal destroyed the basic structure of the constitution.

Ratnavel Pandian, speaking for a majority in this case, rejected such a political–historical approach to basic structure review in

[50] Chandrachud on use of history.

favour of an alternate 'socio-economic and political philosophy'[51] perspective. He concluded that the amendment being challenged was compatible with the sovereign and republican forms of government adopted by the Constitution and advanced the egalitarian principles in the Constitution. Therefore the fact that the provisions omitted were crucial to the political arrangement which formed the Union as a historical matter was not decisive in basic structure review in this case. Basic structure review sought to ensure compatibility and coherence of constitutional amendments with constitutional principles. Basic structure review in this sense is a form of substantive review which seeks to preserve the normative identity of the constitution by ensuring that amendments do not make 'any change in the personality of the constitution either in its scheme or in its basic features'.[52]

At this point I may summarise the discussion on the type of review. The alternative to a version of basic structure review which is an extension of Article 13 fundamental rights judicial review is an independent substantive judicial review that evaluates whether constitutional amendments damage or destroy overarching constitutional principles central to the identity of the constitution. The court may analyse the policy objectives or historical background of the challenged constitutional amendments or the constitutional provisions sought to be amended but the overriding concern in basic structure review is to preserve the integrity of the constitution as a statement of key constitutional principles. This 'identity test' has been reaffirmed in slightly different ways in several opinions[53] on the basic structure doctrine. By confining the courts to arguments of constitutional principle this model gives basic structure review a clear focus.

Conclusion

In the section above, the contrasting versions of basic structure review advanced by the courts was discussed. I argue that the

---

[51] *Ganpatrao* v. *Union of India*, AIR 1993 SC 1267 (R. Pandian, J) 1287. Venkatachaliah's opinion in *Kihoto Hollohan* v. *Zachillhu*, 1992 Supp (2) SCC 651 endorses such a view.

[52] *Ganpatrao*, supra n. 49, p. 1291.

[53] *Minerva Mills*, supra n. 15, p. 1824; *I.R. Coelho*, supra n. 24, p. 232 (Sabharwal, CJ); G.J. Jacobsohn, 'Constitutional Identity', 68 *The Review of Politics* 361–97 (2006) considers the basic structure doctrine to be an effort to protect constitutional identity.

character and type of basic structure review is best conceived as an independent and novel form of judicial review which seeks to protect a body of core constitutional principles central to our constitutional identity for the following reasons. Firstly, the extension of existing Article 13 fundamental rights judicial review to constitutional amendments is a legal proposition which was accepted in *Golaknath* and expressly overruled in *Kesavananda*. The reintroduction of rights-based review to constitutional amendments as an element of basic structure review subverts the holding of the court in *Kesavananda* which is binding on all subsequent cases.

Secondly, such an approach misunderstands the character and type of review necessary for the doctrine of judicial review to impose substantive limits on the amending power of the constitution. The discussion of *Golaknath* in Chapter 2 illustrates the futility of imposing text-based limits on the amending power as such limitations are easily overcome by Parliament. For example, in *Minerva Mills* the court was confronted with the Constitution (42nd Amendment) Act, 1976 which sought to amend Article 368 and conferred unlimited constituent power on Parliament and excluded judicial review of constitutional amendments. This amendment sought to displace the textual basis for the *Keshavananda* opinion. Any useful model of judicial review of constitutional amendments has to necessarily be for compliance with substantive constitutional principles traceable to the constitution, taken as a coherent whole, and not tied to the particular phrasing of any article.

Finally, the conflation of Article 13 fundamental rights judicial review with basic structure review invariably results in the mistaken identification of basic features with constitutional provisions, and more particularly with fundamental rights in the constitution. Arguably as I will show in Chapter 4, no basic feature of the constitution is embodied in a single article of the constitution. For example, the idea of equality finds expression in Articles 14, 15, 16, 17, 18, 25–8, besides the Preamble to the Constitution. It is not clear whether an amendment which violates the basic feature of equality should satisfy some or all of these articles. Arguably the amendment may omit or modify some of these articles and still satisfy basic structure review as it may preserve the constitutional principle of equality in some other textual format. Hence, a model of basic structure review which is focussed on the text of the constitution will fail to preserve constitutional principles as it is both under inclusive and over inclusive in its scope of protection.

In this section I have advanced an independent substantive model of basic structure review as an approach which will overcome these defects and successfully review challenged constitutional amendments for compliance with constitutional principles. Like Article 13 fundamental rights judicial review, this independent model of review imposes substantive limits on the scope of constitutional amendment. However, these limits or basic features are identified as constitutional principles which are distinct from the constitutional provisions which embody these principles. Moreover, as a legitimate form of basic structure[54] review must mark out the distinction between ordinary democratic law making and higher level democratic law making, it must rightly identify the different limits on these two forms of law making. Only an independent model of basic structure review which ensures that constitutional amendments do not destroy core constitutional principles can fulfil this requirement.

Executive Power

The Governor is a functionary under the Constitution and is sworn to 'preserve, protect and defend the Constitution and the laws'. The Governor cannot, in the exercise of his discretion or otherwise, do anything that is contrary to the Constitution and law...[55]

We had noted in Chapter 2 that basic structure review of executive power includes the review of two types of executive power: ordinary executive power exercised by the Union and State governments and executive power exercised by high constitutional authorities like the President of the Union and the Governors of states. This distinction relies on the different phrasing of constitutional provisions authorizing these powers. The court has applied this distinction in administrative law review and basic structure review. The categorization of executive power into lower and higher executive power allows the court to limit the scope of administrative law review to lower executive power and exempt higher executive power from the full rigours of such review. This distinction mirrors

---

[54] Compare Chapter 5.
[55] B.R. Kapur v. State of Tamil Nadu, AIR 2001 SC 3435 (Bharucha, J) 3455.

the English administrative law review to statutory executive power and prerogative powers such as power to grant mercy and the power to select a Prime Minister where there is no clear majority in the House. For the purposes of this section the distinction is relevant insofar as the court articulates a different approach to basic structure review to each type of executive power.

The key issue in cases where executive action is challenged on basic structure grounds is to identify the type and character of review that the court should employ. Bharucha's observation excerpted above indicates that the court will use basic structure review, as is the case with the review of constitutional amendments, to impose substantive limits on the exercise of executive power. However, the court has on other occasions found it difficult to accommodate basic structure review with conventional models of administrative law review on the one hand and with rights compliance and jurisdictional competence review of administrative action on the other. Therefore, in the rest of this section I will consider each of these problems for the application of basic structure review to the review of executive action, at each point paying attention to the type of executive power being reviewed and the constitutional provisions authorizing that power.

Executive Action by High Constitutional Authorities

Although administrative law judicial review of executive action has not been expressly provided for in the constitution, in the last five decades the High Courts and Supreme Court have woven this into their interpretation of several constitutional provisions. The rights to equality and life in Articles 14 and 21 together with the powers of judicial review in Articles 32, 226, and 142 have carried much of this interpretive burden. The first issue to be resolved by the court is whether its rather well developed administrative law doctrine of judicial review should apply with full force to executive action by 'high constitutional authorities'. Next, the court has to analyse whether basic structure review should apply to such actions and if so, whether it will be accommodated within administrative law review or operate as an independent type of substantive review.

In the early cases where executive proclamations of emergencies were challenged, objections were raised against the extension of administrative law review doctrine to executive action by 'high constitutional authorities'.[56] In these cases the court articulated a limited basis for judicial review of such action which was reiterated by Bhagwati in *Minerva Mills* where a proclamation of national emergency was challenged in these words:

A Proclamation of Emergency is undoubtedly amenable to judicial review though on the limited ground that no satisfaction as required by Art. 352 was arrived at by the President in law or that the satisfaction was absurd or perverse or mala fide or based on an extraneous or irrelevant ground.[57]

Although Bhagwati did not consider whether basic structure review could apply to the exercise of the executive power of proclamation, he did apply it to read down Clause 5 of Article 352 introduced by the Constitution (38th Amendment) Act, 1975 which sought to exclude judicial review of the proclamation by declaring the Proclamation to be final and conclusive. He applied basic structure review and also preserved two grounds of administrative law review—the *mala fides* and irrelevant considerations—to review executive action by high constitutional authorities.

In *S.R. Bommai* v. *Union of India* the court considered the extent to which basic structure review and administrative law review should apply to proclamations of regional emergency. The Union of India proposed that the scope of judicial review in constitutional law is limited to cases where there is an infringement of rights or a transgression of the scheme of division of power between the three branches of government. It was argued that it was a mistake to extend the rules and principles in the field of administrative law where the court reviews the action of public authorities to prevent excesses and irregular exercise of executive power under constitutional law judicial review.

This broad and incisive argument invited the court to locate and develop a coherent framework for judicial review of executive action by high constitutional authorities. The plurality opinions in the case endorsed the limited application of common law judicial review articulated in the early cases discussed above. Sawant's [58] lead

---

[56] *State of Rajasthan* v. *Union of India*, AIR 1977 SC 1361.

[57] *Minerva Mills*, supra n. 15, p. 1839 (Bhagwati, J).

[58] *S.R. Bommai* v. *Union of India*, AIR 1994 SC 1918 (Verma, J). In a brief concurring opinion Verma equates the scope of judicial review of executive

opinion distinguished between the nature and scope of the power of judicial review in administrative law and constitutional law. He found the argument that administrative law review had no place in the review of constitutionally conferred executive power 'too broad to be accepted' and concluded that 'many of the parameters of judicial review developed in the field of administrative law are not antithetical to the field of constitutional law, and they could equally apply to the domain covered by the constitutional law'.[59] He reasoned that where the constitution provides preconditions for the exercise of power by constitutional authorities or identifies the purposes for which a power is entrusted to such authorities, the court should exercise power to ensure that these conditions are satisfied and improper purposes avoided. He relied on the court's role as the guardian and ultimate interpreter of the constitution in support of these conclusions. The challenge before Sawant was to articulate the role of basic structure review in this context where administrative law review of executive proclamations of emergency also applies.

Basic structure review, which had already been applied to constitutional amendments, could potentially be re-formulated to apply to the judicial review of executive action. Sawant seems to embrace such a possibility when he notes that 'provisions such as Article 356 have a potentiality to unsettle and subvert the entire constitutional scheme'.[60] He is aware that the 'exercise of power vested under such provisions needs...to be circumscribed to maintain the fundamental constitutional balance lest the Constitution is defaced and destroyed'[61] and recognizes the need to 'scrutinize the material on the basis of which advise is given and the President forms his satisfaction'[62] to ensure that basic features are preserved. Surprisingly these observations do not lead him to the conclusion that basic structure review should hereafter apply to executive action of this sort and instead he concludes that this 'can be done by the courts while

---

proclamation of emergency under the Indian Constitution with the scope of judicial review of prerogative powers in English common law. See pp. 1956–7.

[59] Ibid., p. 1963 (Sawant, J).

[60] *Bommai*, supra n. 57, p. 1976.

[61] Ibid.

[62] Ibid.

confining themselves to the acknowledged parameters of the judicial review ... illegality, irrationality, and mala fides.'[63]

His effort to accommodate basic structure review by modifying administrative law review rather than supplementing it with an independent substantive model of review is similar to the development of basic structure review with respect to amendments as traced in the section above. While reviewing the existing models of constitutional judicial review, Sawant fails to account for basic structure review as an independent substantive model of judicial review distinct from competence and fundamental rights compliance review. This failure to appreciate the distinctive type and character of basic structure review prompted him to accommodate basic structure concerns by grafting these on to existing administrative law grounds of review. Moreover, he seems to be concerned that the 'scrutiny of the material ...' should 'be within the judicially discoverable and manageable standards'.[64]

As there is no further case law on basic structure review of executive action by high constitutional authorities, it is still not settled whether such a modified administrative law review model will persist or whether basic structure review will emerge as an independent substantive model of review. This is an argument that I will return to below after discussing how basic structure review has developed vis-à-vis other forms of executive action.

Ordinary Executive Action

Basic structure review of executive powers has developed more rapidly in cases unrelated to the proclamation of emergency. These include cases where executive power is conferred by statute or directly by constitutional provisions. In the section above I noted that constitutionally conferred executive powers should properly belong to the category of executive action by 'high constitutional authorities'.

However, for no clear reason, the Supreme Court has treated these categories of executive power as being distinct and of different status. I observed that the distinction between ordinary executive action and executive action by high constitutional authorities may be

[63] Ibid.
[64] *Bommai*, supra n. 57, p. 1976.

based on two criteria: first, the source of executive power and second, the extent of judicial review of the power. Neither criterion supports a further distinction between executive power exercised by higher constitutional authorities and constitutional executive power.

However, the application of administrative law review and constitutional judicial review for competence and fundamental rights compliance to ordinary executive power, but a lesser level of judicial review to other types of constitutional executive power generates an unsustainable distinction between these types of executive power. On closer scrutiny I find that the court does not deal consistently with the latter executive action by constitutional authorities as it has been reluctant to apply constitutional judicial review and administrative law review to executive proclamations of emergency but has applied such review with full rigour to other forms of constitutional executive action. For the purposes of this section I will ignore this inconsistency in the court's approach to constitutional executive action, and discuss the recent cases on constitutional executive action and ordinary executive action together in this section. I will begin with a recent case on the exercise of a constitutional executive power before I turn to cases involving the review of ordinary executive power.

In *B.R. Kapur* v. *State of Tamil Nadu*[65] the court was called on to determine whether a person who is not elected to the legislature and has been convicted of a criminal offence, but whose conviction has not been suspended on appeal, may be sworn in and continue to function as the chief minister of a state. Article 164(1) provides that the 'Chief Minister shall be appointed by the Governor.'[66] and provides for a non-legislator to be appointed chief minister provided she gets herself elected to the legislature in a period of six months. Article 173 which provides for the qualifications and disqualifications for membership in any State legislature set out in clause (c) that Parliament may by law 'prescribe other qualifications as it deems fit'. The Representation of Peoples Act, 1950 is law made under Article 173 prescribing qualifications and it provides that those convicted of the offences listed in the statute and other corrupt practices are disqualified from membership of any legislature.

[65] AIR 2001 SC 3435.
[66] Article 164(1).

The petitioners argued that the Governor had exceeded his discretion by inviting a person who is convicted of a criminal offence to be chief minister and pressed the court to issue a direction in the nature of a writ of quo warranto against the chief minister. Two key arguments were raised in this case: first, whether the discretion of the Governor under Article 164 was limited by the other provisions of the constitution and second, whether it is constitutionally impermissible for the court to judicially review the governor's action in appointing a chief minister who had secured an overwhelming popular mandate.

Bharucha relied on the holdings in *Keshavananda* and *Minerva Mills* and concluded: 'Nothing can better demonstrate that it is permissible for the Court to read limitations into the Constitution based on its language and scheme and its basic structure.'[67] He found that the Governor's discretion to appoint a chief minister under Article 164 should be understood in the context of his role as a functionary under the constitution and observed that the 'Constitution prevailed over the will of the people as expressed through the majority party...The Governor is a functionary under the Constitution and is sworn to preserve, protect, and defend the Constitution and the laws.'[68] These obligations which arose out of his constitutional role meant that the Court could judicially review the Governor's action as the 'Governor cannot, in the exercise of his discretion or otherwise, do anything that is contrary to the Constitution and the laws...'.[69] In the instant case, Bharucha concluded that the Governor had overstepped his discretion under the relevant constitutional provisions and laws in appointing as Chief Minister a person who was otherwise disqualified, to be a legislator.

In *B.R. Kapur* the court developed the doctrine of basic structure review to apply to executive action independently of administrative law review. Where two interpretations of Article 164 were possible, one which accommodated the basic structure of the Constitution and another which did not, the court emphatically chose the former. Thereby, basic structure review imposes substantive limits on the ways

[67] *B.R. Kapur*, supra n. 64 (Bharucha, J) 2449.
[68] Ibid., p. 3455.
[69] *B.R. Kapur*, supra n. 64, p. 3455 (Bharucha, J).

in which executive discretion was exercised. Unfortunately Bharucha did not articulate the basic features at stake in this case and provide reasons why they support his conclusion in the case. He could have reasoned that 'democracy' which has repeatedly been articulated as a basic feature of the Constitution, would require a representative government led by qualified and properly elected leaders, which the Governor's action failed to uphold.

Now I examine how the court accommodates basic structure review with administrative law review of ordinary executive action. Three recent cases have provided the court with an opportunity to develop the type and character of such review to ordinary executive action. As the court already possesses the power of administrative law review under common law doctrine and competence and fundamental rights compliance review under the constitution over such executive action I need to clarify the need for basic structure review and ascertain whether it performs a different function. In all three cases considered below, the basic feature of 'secularism' was invoked in support of, or to challenge, the executive action but in slightly different ways.

In *Aruna Roy* v. *Union of India*[70] and *P.M. Bhargava* v. *University Grants Commission*,[71] changes to education curriculum and policy were challenged using administrative law review and basic structure review grounds. I will examine each case in turn. In *Aruna Roy*, the National Curriculum for School Education published by the National Council of Education, Research and Technology was challenged for being anti-secular and for not following the established practice of consultation with an interstate body called the Central Advisory Board of Education. The Central Advisory Board of Education is a non-statutory board constituted by resolutions of the Ministry of Human Resource Development which supervises education policy. Despite its expertise in education policy and its significant role as a body aiding centre–state coordination of education policy there was little evidence of a legal requirement for such prior consultation. Surprisingly, no argument relying on a procedurally legitimate expectation to consult the Board was raised in this case. The court con-

[70] *Aruna Roy* v. *Union of India*, AIR 2002 Supreme Court 3176.
[71] (2004) 6 SCC 661.

cludes that while consultation was a good process to follow it was not essential for the formulation of policy and that it would not strike down the education policy for the failure to consult.[72]

The second challenge to the new National Curriculum was on the ground that it was anti-secular and therefore failed fundamental rights review and basic structure review. The petitioners argued that the inclusion of Hindu religious values into the school curriculum under the rubric of value-based education offended the right to freedom of speech and information,[73] the right to education,[74] and the constitutional prohibitions against religious instruction or religious worship in state-aided educational institutions.[75] Besides these fundamental rights violations, it was argued that the executive orders implementing this modified curriculum damaged the constitutional principle of secularism, which is a part of the basic structure of the constitution.

The lead majority opinion by Shah, as well as the concurring opinions by Dharmadhikari and Sema, failed to distinguish the two different types of judicial review in this case. The opinions focused on the Article 28 bar on religious instruction in institutions maintained wholly out of state funds and the case law on this provision concluding that there was a distinction between religious education and instruction 'inculcating the tenets, the rituals, the observances, ceremonies, and modes of worship of a particular sect or denomination'[76] and education about religions as 'an academic or philosophical study'.[77] While the latter form of value-based education was constitutionally permissible, the former was not.

If the constitutional challenge to the new curriculum could be decided on an interpretation of Article 28 alone, the references to 'secularism' as a part of the basic structure of the Constitution were redundant or superfluous. Shah's lead opinion takes the Indian constitutional principle of secularism to require the state to be neutral

---

[72] *Aruna Roy*, supra n. 69, p. 3184 (Shah, J).

[73] Constitution of India, Article 19(1)(a).

[74] *Unnikrishnan* v. *State of Andhra Pradesh* AIR 1993 SC 2178 held that the right to education was a part of Article 21 Constitution of India 1950.

[75] Constitution of India, Article 28.

[76] *Aruna Roy*, supra n. 70, p. 3186 (Shah, J).

[77] Ibid.

in matters of religion and its tolerance of religious practice does not make it a religious or theocratic state. This distinction between secularism in the Indian constitutional tradition and other constitutional traditions has been explored rigorously elsewhere and is not the central issue in this section.[78] Shah goes on to enunciate the requirements of secularism using almost exclusively Hindu religious sources and idiom. He drew support from the S.B. Chavan report on which the Union government claimed the curriculum revision was based, which itself endorsed value-based education using language that was almost exclusively reliant on Hindu scriptures. Dharmadhikari draws on a more diverse range of religious resources in support of the proposition that religious pluralism was at the heart of the principle of secularism and that any curriculum devised must respect these constitutional principles. Neither opinion articulates whether basic structure review would operate independently of judicial review for compliance with the fundamental right in Article 28. Hence it is difficult to decipher the impact of the lengthy discussions on secularism as a basic feature on the outcome in this case. I will now turn to other recent basic structure challenges to executive action to examine whether they develop a better response to this issue.

In *P.M. Bhargava* v. *Union of India*,[79] the petitioner approached the Supreme Court to issue a writ of mandamus directing the University Grants Commission not to start, or grant any funds for, Graduate and Post-Graduate Courses in 'Jyotir Vigyan' or Vedic astrology. Petitioners argued that the course in Vedic astrology cannot be termed as a course of scientific study as astrology had never practised the rigours of scientific method or engaged serious scientific research. It was also argued that the proposal to 'introduce Jyotir Vigyan is a clear attempt on the part of the respondents to saffronize education and of thrusting their hidden agenda of imposing Hindu values in higher education'.[80] This is the argument I am concerned with in this section.

As the petitioners did not allege the 'breach of any statutory provision, rule, or regulation', G.P. Mathur concluded that it was

[78] G.J. Jacobsohn, *The Wheel of Law*, New Delhi, Oxford University Press, 2003, pp. 91–119.

[79] *P.M. Bhargava* v. *Union of India*, 2004 (6) SCC 661.

[80] *P.M. Bhargava*, supra n. 79.

imprudent for the court to interfere in a policy arena where the 'decision to start the course has been taken by an expert body... The courts are not expert in academic matters and it is not for them to decide as to what course should be taught in university and what should be their curriculum.'[81] This conclusion is plausible if the court was only applying common law rules and principles in administrative law review. However, when the petitioners 'urged that the attempt of the respondents to introduce courses of Vedic astrology in the universities is malafide and it amounts to saffronizing education'[82] which offends the principle of secularism which 'is part of the basic structure of the Constitution and is essential for the governance of the country'[83] the court was no longer confronted with an administrative law review challenge.

This is the first case in which basic structure review has been clearly identified as providing a basis for the substantive review of ordinary executive action in such a clear manner. As the executive action challenged in the case satisfies constitutional judicial review for fundamental rights compliance and competence and as the petitioners were unable to establish a serious common law administrative challenge, basic structure review comes to the forefront. The court responded to this challenge in a tepid fashion. While it did acknowledge that basic structure review of executive action is possible, it concluded that the executive action did not damage secularism as the judges did not agree with the petitioner's argument that Vedic astrology is 'something peculiar to Hindus and associated with Hindu religion.'[84] The weaknesses in the court's conclusions are not confined to its sociological analysis of Vedic astrology but extend to its application of basic structure review.

Critically, the court did not articulate the type of substantive analysis or the extent of damage that such executive action must inflict before it is struck down under basic structure review. A fuller response would require that the courts elaborate what the basic feature of secularism requires of state policy in the funding and establishment of new courses by state-funded and supported institutions.

---

[81] Ibid., (G.P. Mathur, J)

[82] Ibid.

[83] Ibid.

[84] *P.M. Bhargava*, supra n. 78.

I noted in our discussions of *Aruna Roy* above that the Indian constitution embodied a constitutional principle of secularism that did not mandate a church–state separation but required principled distance from all religions. The court may well have instructed the University Grants Commission to introduce astrology into higher education curriculum only if it drew on the plural religious and cultural approaches to the subject of astrology and does not embrace a Hindu worldview. This may not have satisfied the petitioners who argued that astrology should be dropped altogether as it was a pseudo science, but it would have kept the executive action within the framework of the basic features of the Constitution.

The third and final case I will consider in this section is *State of Karnataka* v. *Thogadia*[85] where the Additional District Magistrate of Dakshina Kannada district in the State of Karnataka barred the respondent from taking part in any public meeting in the district for a period of 15 days. This order under section 144 of the Criminal Procedure Code, 1975 was made on the grounds that the respondent had on previous occasions made communally provocative speeches and incited violence and that the district had become communally sensitive with a history of communal clashes starting from 1988 resulting in several deaths and damage to public and private properties. Two arguments were made against this action: first, that the Additional District Magistrate was not empowered to make such an order and second, that the respondent was merely engaging in political debates of national importance and hence that the order was politically motivated and bad in law. The court dismissed the first contention easily and spent some time on the latter issue.

Arijit Pasayat speaking for the court ruled that given the antecedents of the respondent the order was justified. He observed that 'whenever the concerned authorities in charge of law and order find that a person's speeches or actions are likely to trigger communal antagonism and hatred resulting in fissiparous tendencies gaining foothold undermining and affecting communal harmony, prohibitory orders need necessarily to be passed, to effectively avert such untoward happenings'.[86] This conclusion was supported

[85] *State of Karnataka* v. *Thogadia*, AIR 2004 SC 2081.
[86] Ibid., (A. Pasayat, J).

by an elaborate discussion on the principles of secularism as a basic feature of the Constitution. Pasayat did not clarify how basic structure review may impact on the legality of the executive action to issue prohibitory orders under section 144. Though in this case the executive action drew support from the principles of secularism, one may easily anticipate that the refusal to take preventive measures against communal violence may damage the principles of secularism and for this reason executive action may fail basic structure review. In order to work out precisely how basic structure review would operate as a substantive review on ordinary action we need to examine the standards of review that the court should apply. This is considered in the section below in our discussion on the intensity of review.

So far in this section, I have considered the varied circumstances in which basic structure review has been applied to executive action. The court's distinction between executive action by high constitutional authorities and ordinary executive action is designed to restrict the scope and intensity of review of these actions under common law administrative review grounds. This distinction is neither well supported by constitutional argument nor consistently applied in the case law. In *B.R. Kapur*, the Governor's invitation to the leader of the majority party to be chief minister was an executive action by the highest officer in a State using powers granted under Article 164. If the distinction developed by the court pays attention to the source of the power—constitutional or statutory—or whether the power is historically regarded as a prerogative power to be exercised independently by the Governor, an invitation to form the government should be classified as one by a high constitutional authority. Arguably, the distinction has a sound basis if it distinguishes between constitutionally conferred and statutorily conferred executive power, but the court erred in *B.R. Kapur* in not applying the distinction consistently. This classificatory dispute on the type of executive action does have a direct bearing on the applicability of basic structure review to executive power if basic structure review applies differently to each type of executive action. However, if basic structure review is to apply as an independent substantive limit on the exercise of executive power, there is no need for a distinction based on the source of executive power.

I had noted in Chapter 2 that the court has failed to articulate a sound constitutional basis for the extension of basic structure review to executive power. In this section I show that the court has been unable to clarify the type and extent of basic structure review of executive action. A first step would be to establish how basic structure review relates to common law administrative review. In *Bommai* the court grafted basic structure review onto pre-existing common law administrative review by using basic features of secularism and democracy to circumscribe the proper purposes to which executive action may be directed. So in this case, administrative law review of executive action is modified to accommodate basic features of the constitution into pre-existing grounds of review, particularly illegality. In *B.R. Kapur* the court tentatively set out an independent and significant role for basic structure review by suggesting that basic features may impose substantive limits on the exercise of executive discretion. In this case basic structure review operates as an independent substantive review to ensure that executive action does not damage or destroy basic features of the constitution. If applied in this manner, the type of review carried out under basic structure review of executive action would be similar to that of constitutional amendments discussed in the earlier section.

However, this type of basic structure review has been poorly developed in subsequent cases reviewing ordinary executive action where the court considered the applicability of basic structure review in this fashion. In none of the cases disucssed in this part has the court gone so far as to strike down executive action on the grounds of damaging and destroying the basic structure of the constitution. This is maybe, in part due to the facts and circumstances of the cases brought before the court. Moreover, the court has failed to develop the contours of a substantive model of review with a nuanced standard of review which pays attention to the subject matter of the executive action and the intensity of review. In the next part of this chapter I consider the arguments relevant to the development of the appropriate intensity for basic structure review to operate as an independent model of substantive review for all types of state action. But first, I consider the application of basic structure review to legislation in the next section.

Legislative Power

In most cases where legislation is challenged on basic structure review grounds, this challenge is often intricately intertwined with challenges to executive action sanctioned by such legislation or constitutional amendments which cast a protective umbrella over such legislation. Hence, it is not always possible to state with precision the type and force of the basic structure challenge to legislation in such cases. In the discussion below I will examine the possibility and utility of basic structure review of legislation. As the courts apply fundamental rights compliance and competence judicial review to ordinary legislation, I have to ascertain whether basic structure review plays any useful role with respect to such state action. This section will show that basic structure review plays a very useful role in grounding challenges to the constitutional validity of legislation which clearly damage basic features of the constitution, but satisfy other doctrines of judicial review.

In early cases like *Indira Gandhi, Waman Rao,* and *Minerva Mills,* the challenged legislations were protected under the rubric of constitutional amendments which were subject to a basic structure review challenge. The constitutional amendments which inserted Articles 31-A, 31-B, and 31-C into the constitution were challenged as these amendments exempted ordinary legislations of a certain description from fundamental rights judicial review for abridging Articles 14, 19, and 31 and other rights. Articles 31-A and 31-B provided for the inclusion of all protected legislation into a Schedule of the constitution. Therefore, in these cases the constitutionality of the protected legislation was contingent on the constitutionality of the constitutional amendment which inserted them into the Schedule and this led to the court applying the basic structure doctrine to such legislation. In *Waman Rao* the court clarified that the inclusion of various Acts and Regulations into the 9th Schedule 'are open to challenge on the ground that they, or any one or more of them, are beyond the constituent power of the Parliament since they damage the basic or essential features of the Constitution or its basic structure'.[87] This holding has been reaffirmed recently in *I.R. Coelho* v.

---

[87] *Waman Rao* (Chandrachud, CJ), supra n. 35.

State of Tamil Nadu[88] though the challenge has been rephrased to be a challenge to the constitutional amendment which inserts an Act in to the 9th Schedule and not to the legislation itself. Nevertheless, the enquiry in such cases is into the 'actual effect and impact of the law on the rights guaranteed…' and 'whether or not it destroys the basic structure'[89] of the constitution. Hence, it is the statutory 'provisions' which 'would be open to attack on the ground that they destroy or damage the basic structure'[90] of the constitution.

In *Bhim Singhji* v. *Union of India*, it was argued that the Urban Land (Ceiling and Regulation) Act, 1976 destroyed the basic feature of equality. Krishna Iyer in his majority opinion took the view that the 'question of basic structure being breached cannot arise when we examine the vires of an ordinary legislation as distinguished from a constitutional amendment'. He continued by noting that not 'every breach of equality spells disaster as a lethal violation of the basic structure… Therefore what is a betrayal of the basic feature is not a mere violation of Article 14 but a shocking, unconscionable, or unscrupulous travesty of the quintessence of equal justice. If a legislation does go that far then it shakes the democratic foundation and must suffer the death penalty'.[91] Iyer's observations in this case are difficult to reconcile as he first denies that basic structure review should apply to legislation but then insists that legislation which offend core constitutional principles should be declared unconstitutional. The most accurate aspect of his observations are with respect to the distinction between a violation of Article 14 and the constitutional principle of equality recognized as a basic feature of the Constitution. Further, he accurately indicates the different standards which apply to judicial review for fundamental rights violations and for damage to basic features of the constitution. However, I will need to look elsewhere for clarity on the application of basic structure review to legislation.

It was in *Ismail Faruqui* v. *Union of India*[92] where the Acquisition of Certain Area at Ayodhya Act, 1993 was challenged on basic structure

---

[88] *I.R. Coelho*, supra n. 24.
[89] Ibid., p. 239.
[90] Ibid., p. 240.
[91] *Bhim Singhji* v. *Union of India*, AIR 1981 SC 234 (Krishna Iyer, J) 242.
[92] *Ismail Faruqui* v. *Union of India* (1994) 6 SCC 360.

grounds and there was no constitutional amendment involved in the case. Thus, the court had the opportunity to consider the applicability of basic structure review to a statute independently of its application to a constitutional amendment. In order to appreciate the nature of the challenge I need to pay some attention to the factual background to the case. The Ram Janma Bhumi agitation, led by a coalition of right wing Hindu political organizations including the Bharatiya Janata Party, claimed that the site on which the Babri Masjid was located was the birth place of the Hindu god, Ram. The nationwide agitation led to widespread communal violence and resulted in a large number of deaths and culminated in the destruction of the Babri Masjid in Ayodhya which shook the political stability and viability of the state and federal governments at the time.

The Union government enacted the Ayodhya Act, 1993 to acquire the disputed property and thereby stymie the dispute. The Statement of Objects and Reasons of the statute provides perspective on the goals pursued by the Union Congress government: 'As it is necessary to maintain communal harmony and the spirit of common brotherhood amongst the people of India, it was considered necessary to acquire the site of the disputed structure and suitable adjacent land for setting up a complex which could be developed in a planned manner wherein a Ram temple, a mosque, amenities for pilgrims, a library, museum, and other suitable facilities can be set up.'[93] Soon after passing the Act the Central Government utilized the power to make a Presidential Reference under Article 143 of the Constitution and referred the core of the dispute to the Supreme Court in these terms: 'Whether a Hindu temple or any Hindu religious structure existed prior to the construction of the Ram Janma Bhumi-Babri Masjid (including the premises of the inner and outer courtyards of such structure) in the area on which the structure stood?'[94]

The petitioners challenged the validity of the Ayodhya Act and the executive's act of referring the dispute to the Supreme Court on basic structure grounds. The challenge paid particular attention to the purposes and effect of the reference and legislation and it was

[93] *Ismail Faruqui*, supra note 92 (Verma, J) 384.

[94] Special Reference under Article 143, signed by Shanker Dayal Sharma, President of India, on 7 January 1993 excerpted in *Ismail Faruqui*, supra n. 92, p. 384 (Verma, J).

argued that 'the real object and purpose of the Reference is to take away a place of worship of the Muslims and give it away to the Hindus offending the basic feature of Secularism'.[95] Other challenges included the violation of the right to equality guaranteed in Article 14 and the rights guaranteed under Articles 25 and 26 to the practice of religion by the acquisition of a mosque which was a place of religious worship. For the purposes of this section I will focus my attention on the basic structure review argument that 'the statute... is a mere veiled concealment of a device adopted by the Central Government to perpetuate the consequences of the demolition of the mosque ...'.[96] This is the first case where this argument was pressed independently of other challenges to the validity of the statute.

Unfortunately the court divided on religious lines with the minority community judges[97] concluding that the statute failed basic structure review while the majority[98] accepted the state's argument that the statute promoted secularism. However, both opinions approached basic structure review in a similar fashion. They considered what the basic feature of secularism and the rule of law required of law makers in this area and evaluated whether the enacted statute satisfied these requirements. Both opinions agreed that section 4(3) which provided for the abatement of all suits, appeals, or other proceedings related to the acquired property was unconstitutional. This conclusion rested on a violation of the basic feature of the rule of law as the special reference under Article 143(1) could not be construed as 'an effective alternate dispute-resolution mechanism to permit substitution of the pending suits and legal proceedings'.[99] The disagreement arose with the application of the basic feature of secularism.

The core of the disagreement was not about what secularism entailed for state action. Both opinions coalesced around a principle of secularism where the state has no officially sanctioned religion and guarantees equality in the matter of religion to all individuals and groups. Agreement could not be reached on the factual basis

[95] Ibid., p. 389.

[96] *Ismail Faruqui*, supra n. 92, p. 391 (Verma, J).

[97] Ibid., (Bharucha, J).

[98] Ibid., p. 378 (Verma, J, for Venkatachaliah, CJ and G.N. Ray, J).

[99] *Indira Gandhi*, supra n. 2, held that the Legislature failed to comply with the Rule of Law by legislating a solution to a legal dispute before the courts.

for making an assessment whether this principle was honoured or breached and on the standard of review the court must apply. As I am concerned with the type of basic structure review in this section I will confine myself to the first question and return to questions regarding the intensity of review in the next part of this chapter.

Taking into account the undisputed fact that the Muslim Waqf Board owned and managed the Babri Masjid till its demolition by Hindu right wing groups, Bharucha found it 'impermissible ... for the State to acquire that place of worship to preserve public order ...' as it would 'efface the principle of secularism from the Constitution.'[100] Bharucha understood such an acquisition to merely compound the failure of the State to protect the property interests of the minority community and not repair the damage caused. The majority took a different view of the historical circumstances in which this acquisition took place. Given the communal riots unleashed in the country immediately after the Babri Masjid demolition they were satisfied that 'any step taken to arrest escalation of communal tension and to achieve communal accord and harmony can, by no stretch of argumentation, be termed non-secular much less anti-secular or against the concept of secularism ...'.[101] Moreover, they came to the conclusion that the acquisition was neither complete[102] nor permanent and by preserving the prior community interests in the property albeit in an attenuated form, the state was doing the best it could in difficult circumstances.

A similar disagreement between the majority and minority judgments in the case is evident in the analysis of sections 6 and 7 of the Act. These sections imposed a mandate on the state to maintain status quo in the management of the area over which the disputed structure stood, as it existed at the time of acquisition. Bharucha was of the view that by imposing a status quo order on the date of acquisition rather than the date of demolition of the pre-existing mosque the statute effectively conferred legitimacy on the demolition of the mosque and installation of Hindu idols on the site. As this legislation disproportionately affects the interests of the minority community he concluded that the effect of the Act is to 'favour

---

[100] *Ismail Faruqui*, supra n. 92, p. 438 (Bharucha, J).

[101] Ibid., p. 407 (Verma, J).

[102] Ibid., p. 405.

one religious community and disfavour another' thereby violating the principle of secularism. Verma considered the circumstances in which the legislation was enacted carefully and then concluded that 'the comparative significance of the disputed site to the two communities and also the impact of the acquisition is equally on the right and interest of the Hindu community'.[103] He went further to find that by freezing the scope of the Hindu community's right to worship on the date of acquisition, the Act imposed a punitive sanction that the 'Hindu community, must... bear on its chest, for the misdeed of the miscreants reasonably suspected to belong to their religious fold.'[104] Hence, the legislation protects the basic feature of secularism rather than damage it.

The discussion above vividly illustrates the application of basic structure as an independent substantive model of judicial review to test the constitutionality of legislation. The challenge to the constitutionality of the statute in this case cannot be traced to particular provisions of the constitution but to the constitutional principles that the court identifies to be basic features of the Constitution. First, the court has to identify the substantive limits imposed by the constitutional principle, or basic feature, on this area of state action. In this case, the principle of secularism was tested in exceptional circumstances where the demolition of the Babri Masjid by Hindu right wing activists generated a national crisis of seismic proportions. The court then carefully considered the motivations for, and the effects of, the challenged provisions of the acquisition statute. In this case, the majority and minority judges disagreed about the results of this substantive analysis primarily as they applied different historical and normative frameworks to evaluate the statute. The application of constitutional principles to test the constitutionality of legislation will allow for a greater scope for disagreement about precisely what the constitutional principle requires which is an issue I return to in the next part of the chapter.

This form of basic structure review of ordinary legislation has been reiterated recently in *Indra Sawhney* v. *Union of India*.[105] The State

---

[103] *Ismail Faruqui*, supra n. 92, p. 408 (Verma, J).

[104] Ibid., p. 409.

[105] *Indra Sawhney* v. *Union of India*, (2000) 1 SCC 168.

of Kerala enacted the Kerala State Backward Classes (Reservation of Appointments or Posts) Act, 1995 to overcome the effect of the *Indra Sawhney (I)*[106] decision on the constitutionality of reservation for the other backward classes in public employment. This statute sought to overcome the court's ruling requiring the State to exclude elite sections of backward classes from the benefits of affirmative action policy by declaring that 'there are no socially advanced sections in any backward classes who have acquired capacity to compete with forward classes'.[107] Jagannadha Rao speaking for the court, pointed out that 'Parliament... cannot transgress the basic feature of the Constitution, namely, the principle of equality enshrined in Article 14 of which Article 16(1) is a facet... What even Parliament cannot do, the Kerala Legislature cannot achieve'.[108] However, the application of basic structure review in this case failed to appreciate key issues relating to the identity of basic features and the intensity of review in such cases. These are the important questions considered in the next part of the chapter.

The decision of the court in *Kuldip Nayar* v. *Union of India*[109] where amendments to the Representation of Peoples Act, 1951 were challenged on the grounds of basic structure review are a sharp break in the development of basic structure review to test the constitutionality of legislation. In our discussion in Chapter 2 I observed that the court erred in concluding that basic structure review does not apply to legislation. For the purposes of our discussion in this section it is useful to briefly analyse the court's view on the type of substantive review required under the basic structure doctrine and its independence of other forms of constitutional judicial review. Sabharwal spent considerable effort responding to the petitioner's arguments on the impact of the amendments on the basic features of federalism[110] and democracy.[111] In doing so, he effectively engages in the substantive analysis of the limits imposed by constitutional principles on this area of legislation and inadvertently demonstrates

---

[106] *Indra Sawhney* v. *Union of India*, AIR 1993 SC 477.
[107] Kerala State Backward Classes Act, 1995 Section 3.
[108] *Indra Sawhney*, supra n. 105, p. 202 (Jagannadha Rao, J).
[109] *Kuldip Nayyar* v. *Union of India* (2006) 7 SCC 1.
[110] Ibid., pp. 49–56 (Sabharwal, CJ).
[111] Ibid., pp. 109–39 (Sabharwal, CJ).

that the legislation challenged in this case would survive basic structure review. Second, the existence of basic structure review as an independent model of substantive judicial review is not affected by the use of basic features, or core constitutional principles, as aids in the interpretation of the provisions of the constitution. Thus, if I disregard Sabharwal's express rejection of basic structure review to legislation, the extensive analysis of federalism and democracy in this decision are good indicators of the type of substantive analysis which basic structure review of legislation must engage in.

In the first part of the chapter I identified the type of judicial review required under basic structure review and its relationship with existing models of constitutional judicial review. The court has adopted different approaches to basic structure review depending on the state action being challenged before it—constitutional amendments, executive action, and legislation. I have argued that irrespective of the kind of state action challenged before the courts, basic structure review operates as an independent substantive limit on constitutionally permissible state action. If used in this way basic structure review may be coherently developed to apply independently of other models of constitutional judicial review and require a distinct analysis of core constitutional principles to delimit the constitutional scope of permissible state action. To the extent that the court allows the normative force of basic features of the Constitution to have a bearing on the pre-existing models of judicial review by remoulding existing models of judicial review or as an interpretive aid, it should do so without confusing these types of judicial review with basic structure review. In the discussion above at several points there were cross-cutting issues relating to the level and intensity of scrutiny required under basic structure which I did not resolve. I take up this important aspect of basic structure review in the next part of the chapter.

INTENSITY OF BASIC STRUCTURE REVIEW

Having developed the constitutional basis for basic structure review in *Kesavananda*, the court was yet to articulate the impact that such a doctrine would have on the review of amending, legislative, and executive power. In the previous section I examined the nature of review that the court applies to these types of powers and its relationship with the other models of constitutional judicial review. I argued that basic structure review is an independent substantive type of review for compliance with constitutional principles identified as basic features of the Constitution. In this section I critically analyse the extent and type of compliance with basic features that basic structure review requires. This enquiry into the standards of scrutiny that the court develops must pay attention to two key factors. First, the court must consider the relevant consequences of applying general constitutional rules as opposed to specific rules in the constitutional text. Basic features are articulated at a level of abstraction which requires courts to articulate working rules which mediate between basic features and the facts and circumstances of each case. Moreover, there are cases where relevant applicable basic features may lend support to opposing conclusions.

The second aspect of scrutiny that courts must pay attention is to ensure that it respects the relationships between the legislature, judiciary, and the executive. The court may assume guardianship of the constitutional principles to the exclusion of the legislature and executive and enforce strict compliance with such principles. Alternatively, the court may choose to be dialogic in its relationship with other institutions and may defer in certain circumstances to versions of basic structure values advanced by other institutions. In the latter approach, the court will adopt a standard of review which is reflective of this institutional arrangement and require that a high threshold be met before basic structure principles may be said to be damaged or destroyed. Keeping these general concerns in mind I turn to a discussion on the level of scrutiny that the court must adopt in basic structure review.

Level of Scrutiny

The first issue I consider in this section is the level of scrutiny that courts must employ when exercising basic structure review. I argue that basic structure review calls for a very low level of scrutiny as only the most egregious types of state action are likely to 'damage or destroy' the basic structure of the constitution. The court must appreciate the particularly low level of scrutiny involved in basic structure review as it is in sharp contrast to the higher levels of scrutiny employed in other types of constitutional judicial review employed by the court.

Moreover, the level of scrutiny employed by the court is intimately connected to arguments about the legitimacy of the basic structure doctrine and hence deserves close attention. As discussions about the levels of judicial scrutiny are not common in Indian constitutional law I begin this section by briefly examining the practice of the court in pre-existing models of constitutional judicial review.

Article 13 provides that the 'State shall not make any law which takes away or abridges'[112] fundamental rights in the Constitution and any law shall be void to the extent of such contravention. The courts have interpreted Article 245 which provides that the Parliament and State legislatures may make laws in their respective territorial domains 'subject to the provisions of this Constitution'[113] to grant the Supreme Court power to judicially review legislation to declare them unconstitutional and void to the extent of such violation.[114] The Supreme Court has construed these constitutional provisions to provide for fundamental rights compliance judicial review and competence judicial review to be activated as soon as a petitioner can demonstrate any violation of these provisions. While applying fundamental rights review, the court enquires into whether 'the direct consequence and effect'[115] of the state action is to abridge the fundamental right. In jurisdictional competence review the court investigates whether the legislation or executive action is in 'pith and substance'[116] within the scope of the legislative entry in the Seventh Schedule. Hence, the level of scrutiny under both these types of constitutional judicial review is very high and the legislature and executive branches of government are given a limited scope for action in these spheres. By contrast, basic structure review adopts a very different approach to the level of scrutiny.

In *Kesavananda*, Khanna set out the clearest statement of the standard to be applied in basic structure review cases and deserves to be quoted in full. He noted that:

---

[112] Constitution of India, Article 13(2).

[113] Ibid., Article 245(1).

[114] *A.K. Gopalan* v. *State of Madras*, AIR 1950 SC 27 held that legislative powers were subject to the constitutional provisions, particularly fundamental rights.

[115] *R.C. Cooper* v. *Union of India*, AIR 1970, SC 564 (Shah J).

[116] *Prafulla* v. *Bank of Commerce*, AIR 1946 Privy Council 60.

The word 'amendment' postulates that the old constitution survives without loss of identity despite the change and continues even though it has been subjected to alterations...the old Constitution cannot be destroyed and done away with...a mere retention of some provisions even though the basic structure or framework of the Constitution has been destroyed would not amount to the retention of the old constitution. The words 'amendment of the Constitution' with all their wide sweep and amplitude cannot have the effect of destroying or abrogating the basic structure or framework of the constitution.[117]

This passage identifies several key features which distinguish the level of scrutiny in basic structure review from that applied by the court in other forms of constitutional judicial review. It recognizes that there may be several amendments which may alter important parts of the Constitution but do not fail basic structure review. Further, basic structure review is not a quantitative assessment of the number of articles which may have been amended or conversely the number of articles which remain in the constitution. Instead, the court engages in a qualitative substantive assessment of whether the effect of the amendment is to 'destroy or abrogate' the Constitution or, in other words, whether the identity of the Constitution is altered.

For example, where an amendment is challenged on the grounds that it destroys the basic feature of democracy, the court should not be concerned with the number of constitutional provisions which have been amended. Instead, the court may usefully ask whether the effect of these amendments, individually or cumulatively, is that the constitution may no longer be characterized as being democratic in any sense of that term. Unlike other forms of constitutional judicial review, the court does not enquire into whether the amendment merely 'violates' the basic feature of democracy but requires a greater level of constitutional injury before it will interfere under basic structure review. Subsequent courts have come to characterize this level of scrutiny with the phrase 'damage or destroy the basic structure of the Constitution' and apply this test to review constitutional amendments and legislative and executive actions. In the rest of this section I will carefully examine a few significant examples of how courts have applied this level of review.

---

[117] [1973] 4 Supreme Court Cases 225 (Khanna J) 767.

In *Indira Gandhi* v. *Raj Narain*,[118] the disagreement between Mathew who found that the 39th Amendment violated the basic structure doctrine by providing that election disputes were no longer to be resolved in a judicial fashion, and Chandrachud who did not, presents us with a useful starting point. Both opinions agreed that democracy was a basic feature of the Constitution and that the 39th Amendment threatened this basic feature. They disagreed about what the basic feature, or constitutional principle, of democracy required with respect to the conduct of elections and the extent to which the courts must regulate state action under basic structure review. Mathew understood the basic feature of democracy to require that the representation of people in Assemblies was secured by a method of election which possessed three features: first, that elections are governed by pre-announced laws and regulations; second, that an executive body is charged with conducting these elections fairly; and finally, that a judicial tribunal should resolve all disputes.[119] He concluded that the 39th Amendment damaged the basic feature of democracy as Parliament usurped the power to decide certain election disputes and did not follow due judicial process to settle these disputes which arose in the case.[120]

Chandrachud agreed that democracy was a basic feature of the Constitution but for him this only required that the rule of the majority was ascertained through some fair electoral process.[121] Though Mathew proposed a more elaborate conception of democracy, as noted above, their disagreement extends to the level of scrutiny that they consider necessary in such a case. Chandrachud went on to investigate the 'kind and form of democracy [that] constitutes a part of our basic structure…'.[122] He rejected the view that 'the form of government' must 'strictly comport with some classical definition of the concept'[123] or that one must compare versions of democracy in other parts of the world.[124] Instead he contrasted 'the pre 39th Amendment period and

---

[118] AIR 1975 SC 2299.
[119] *Indira Gandhi*, supra n. 118, pp. 2372–3 (Mathew, J).
[120] *Indira Gandhi*, supra n. 118, p. 2378 (Mathew, J).
[121] Ibid., p. 2468.
[122] Ibid., p. 2467 (Chandrachud, J).
[123] Ibid.
[124] Ibid., p. 2468.

the post 39th Amendment period in the context of our Constitution'[125] to find that the 'rule is still of the majority … and no law or amendment of the fundamental instrument has provided for the abrogation of the electoral process.'[126] He elaborated that 'it is hard to generalize from a single instance…' that the legislation or amendment 'has destroyed or threatens to destroy the democratic framework of our government. One swallow does not make a summer'.[127]

The core of the disagreement in the two opinions discussed above may be traced to the different election mechanisms they considered to be required by the basic feature of democracy and the different levels of scrutiny they applied. As Mathew was of the view that judicial resolution of election disputes was a necessary element of the basic feature of democracy, he concluded that the 39th Amendment destroyed democracy by allowing Parliament to settle electoral disputes through a non-judicial process. Chandrachud tested the 39th Amendment for its effect on the principle of majority rule and a well-ordered election process and found that both these arrangements survived the amendment. As basic structure review requires judges to engage in a substantive analysis to utilize general constitutional principles to evaluate the particular state action challenged in every case, there will no doubt be some room for disagreement on what these principles require in a particular case. I will examine whether there is a greater likelihood of such disagreement in basic structure review in the next section below.

The second source of disagreement between the judges in *Indira Gandhi* arose as they took a different view of the intensity of review required under basic structure review. Chandrachud was right in clarifying that basic structure review evaluated the effect of the constitutional amendment on the basic feature of democracy, not in any general theoretical sense, but by having due regard to the particular expression of the democratic principle in the constitution and its practice in the Indian context. Moreover, he grasped the temporal dimensions of such review by comparing the effect of the state action on the basic feature as it stood before the challenged

[125] Ibid.
[126] Ibid., pp. 2468–9.
[127] Ibid., p. 2468.

state action and after it. Lastly, he emphasized that for a challenged state action to be struck down under basic structure review it must erase the basic feature from the constitution—a significant constitutional injury which is difficult to demonstrate in any case. Mathew's application of basic structure review agrees with that of Chandrachud on all of the above.

However, their disagreement emerges from the use of the last phrase used in the quotation excerpted above—one swallow does not make a summer. Mathew concludes that the challenged constitutional amendment damages the basic feature of democracy sufficiently to be declared unconstitutional while Chandrachud seems to suggest that the amendment would be unconstitutional only if Parliament had substantively altered the election framework set up by the Constitution so that it may no longer be called free and fair. The metaphor employed by Chadrachud suggests that the substantive analysis in basic structure review requires a qualitative element as distinct from a quantitative analysis of whether the basic features of the constitution are damaged. It is this aspect of the level of scrutiny in basic structure review that I examine below.

In *R.C. Poudyal* v. *Union of India*[128] the reservation of a seat for a representative of the Buddhist Sangha in the Sikkim Legislative Assembly was challenged on the grounds that it violates the basic features of democracy and secularism. I have considered the details of the legal challenge and reasoning of the court earlier in this chapter. In this section I will confine my analysis to the court's approach to the quantitative or qualitative aspect of the level of scrutiny in basic structure review. Sharma dissenting in the case observed that 'only one seat has been reserved today for the Monasteries in Sikkim is the thin edge of the wedge which has the potentiality, to tear apart, in the course of time, the very foundation, which the democratic republic is built upon'.[129] Venkatachaliah, speaking for the majority, gave some weight to the argument that reservation of a single seat when understood in a historical context would not destroy secularism. No doubt his conclusion in the case rested partially on the empirically unsubstantiated claim that as Buddhist monasteries were a religious

---

[128] *R.C. Poudyal* v. *Union of India*, AIR 1993 SC 1804.
[129] *R.C. Poudyal*, supra n. 128, pp. 1822–3 (Sharma, CJ).

and social organization, such reservation was not based entirely on religious considerations and did not offend secularism.

This case is a useful example to illustrate that the 'the damage or destroy basic features' level of scrutiny requires qualitative and not quantitative analysis. In other words, not much would turn on the reservation of one or ten seats for religious bodies in the local legislative assembly. The enquiry is whether there is damage or destruction to the constitutional principle of secularism in this case. In order to succeed the petitioners will need to show that the challenged state action damages or destroys the constitutional principle of secularism to such an extent that the constitution may no longer be said to enshrine any reasonable version of the secularism principle. The reiteration of Chandrachud's axiom about the qualitative character of basic structure in *R.C. Poudyal* is the last occasion on which the Supreme Court has considered the application of basic structure review in a quantitative or qualitative manner.

So far in this section I have considered the level of scrutiny which the court must apply under basic structure review of constitutional amendments. I observed that the level of scrutiny of the court under basic structure review is expressed in two ways: first, to ensure that basic features of the constitution are not damaged or destroyed and second, to ensure that the identity of the constitution is preserved. I will now assess whether both these expressions require the court to exercise the same level of scrutiny under both these tests and to all forms of state action. Further, while it is plausible that the above discussion on the 'damage or destroy' standard may apply equally when the court reviews legislation or executive action, the requirement that the state action must alter the identity of the Constitution may not always be easy to translate when the state action does not alter any provision of the constitution. I will conclude this section by briefly exploring the relationship between the 'damage or destroy' standard and 'preserve the identity of the constitution' standard and propose that these tests may be applied to other forms of state action with little or no modification.

Nani Palkhivala suggests that '[l]ogically speaking, the limit to the amending power should be that the Constitution cannot be made to suffer a loss of identity through the amending process. The identity of the Constitution is the sum of its essential features. If the

Constitution is not to suffer a loss of identity, each of its essential features has to be preserved.'[130] Although this clarifies that the identity of the Constitution may be lost even if a single basic feature is eliminated, and that it is not a defence in basic structure review to assert that other basic features are preserved, it is difficult to ascertain whether the court's application of the identity-preserving element of the basic structure scrutiny is independent of, or complementary to, the 'damage or destroy' enquiry.

In *Ganpatrao* v. *Union of India*[131] the Constitution (26th Amendment) Act, 1971 which abolished the privy purses and other privileges guaranteed to pre-Independence princely rulers of India was challenged on the grounds that it destroyed the basic features of equality and other provisions which 'facilitate stabilization of the new order and ensure organic unity of India.'[132] In this case, the court uses the 'damage or destroy' and 'identity change' tests to scrutinize the challenged constitutional amendment. Pandian observes that 'on a deep consideration of the entire scheme and content of the Constitution…the removal of Articles 291 and 362 has not made any change in the personality of the Constitution either in its scheme or its basic features, nor in its basic form or character. The question of identity will arise only when there is a change in the form, character and content of the Constitution'.[133] He concluded that the challenged amendments reaffirmed the basic feature of the republican form of government and that they sought to achieve political, social, and economic justice. By eliminating the special privileges which had accrued to erstwhile princely rulers, Parliament had taken some steps to achieve 'fraternity and the unity of the nation'.[134]

In *Ganpatrao* the identity-preserving aspect of the basic structure scrutiny appears to be aligned with the 'damage or destroy' enquiry. In both enquiries basic structure scrutiny assesses the impact of the challenged state action on the basic features of the constitution. In *Ganpatrao* it was argued that the 26th Constitution Amendment

---

[130] Nani Palkhivala, *Our Constitution: Defaced and Defiled*, Delhi: Macmillan Co. of India, 1974, p. 150.

[131] AIR 1993 SC 1267.

[132] *Ganpatrao*, supra n. 49, p. 1274 (Pandian, J).

[133] *Ganpatrao* v. *Union of India*, Supra n. 131, p. 1291 (Pandian, J).

[134] Ibid., p. 1292.

Act omitted the provisions of the constitution which were historically essential to the formation of the Indian Union and in that sense, are crucial to the identity of the Constitution. Pandian rejected such an approach and suggested that basic structure review sought to preserve the basic feature of equality and fraternity. This rejection of the historical argument about the identity of the Constitution is best understood as a reiteration of the normative character of basic structure review. While in a historical sense many particular events and provisions of the Constitution may be thought to be essential aspects of the Constitution, from the perspective of basic structure review the analysis is a normative and not historical one. I return to this case in greater detail when I consider the nature of basic features and how they are identified in Chapter 5. The analysis above leads to the conclusion that the identity of the constitution which basic structure review preserves is the normative identity of the Constitution, supported by a coherent interpretation of its core constitutional principles or basic features. An amendment, and for that matter, any other form of state action may be said to threaten this identity where the effect of such action is to damage or destroy any of these principles even where they are not completely erased from the constitution. In this sense, the constitutional identity–preserving aspect and the enquiry into damage to the basic features of the Constitution require the same normative constitutional enquiry expressed through different phrases. I now examine how this test may be applied to forms of state action other than constitutional amendment.

When the court subjects ordinary legislation and executive action to basic structure review as there is no change to the form or content of the constitution, it has been suggested that the core basic structure review enquiry into whether basic features have been 'damaged or destroyed' or whether there has been a constitutional identity requires some modification. This suggestion misunderstands the type of review the courts undertake under basic structure review. In this section I have tried to show that basic structure review, even where it applies to constitutional amendment, is not concerned with the quantitative analysis of the degree of textual effacement of constitutional provisions. The core concern in basic structure review is the maintenance of the normative identity of the constitution by ensuring that the core constitutional principles are not damaged or destroyed, this test may be applied to all forms of state action without modification. In such cases the court is concerned with the consequences or impact of the challenged state action and not the manner and form in which it is advanced. However, there is greater diversity in the use of basic structure review in cases where ordinary legislation and executive action is challenged. I assess these cases in greater detail in the section below and show that this diversity relates more to the wider range of remedies available where state action other than constitutional amendments are challenged and does not affect the type of review that the court carries out under basic structure review.

Hard or Soft Review

In this section I briefly examine the normative character of basic structure review. I am concerned here with the extent and nature of compliance with basic features that the court requires and the remedies granted by the court in cases where the state action fails the review. In *Indira Gandhi* a majority in the court found the challenged amendments to be 'unconstitutional' and therefore void. Several other courts have granted such a remedy thereby modelling basic structure remedies along the lines of the other types of ultra vires review in the Constitution. While retaining the option to invalidate amendments later, courts have been willing to apply a bouquet of remedies by reading down amendments,[135] applying the doctrine of severability to excise the offending portions of the amendment,[136] and to give their decisions prospective effect where there is likely to be a substantial disturbance to settled interests.[137] This brief survey clearly establishes that with respect to constitutional amendments basic structure review operates as a hard edged model of ultra vires review where courts may declare a constitutional amendment invalid in full or in part

[135] *Minerva Mills* v. *Union of India*, AIR 1980 SC 1789 (Bhagwati, J) 1809. Bhagwati's partial dissenting opinion in this case reading down Article 31-C which he otherwise found to be constitutional. Chandrachud's majority opinion struck down the entire amendment as unconstitutional.

[136] *Kihoto Hollohan*, supra n. 41, p. 693 (Venkatachaliah, J).

[137] In *Waman Rao* v. *Union of India*, AIR 1981 SC 271 Chief Justice Chandrachud applied the *Kesavananda* holding prospectively to the Acts inserted into the 9th Schedule, p. 290.

but are likely to fashion a wide range of remedies which respond to the facts and circumstances of the case.

In cases where other other forms of state action are challenged, the courts apply basic structure review in various ways: in some cases they modify the normative character of basic structure review so that basic features or principles of the Constitution—are utilized as interpretive aids to assist the court in applying existing types of judicial review;[138] in other cases courts use basic structure review to impose substantive limits on amending, legislative, and executive power. While arguably, the normative force that basic features of the constitution exert on state action may depend in part on the type of action being reviewed as the court has to mould basic structure review depending on the action being reviewed, there is no reason to conclude that basic structure review should be soft judicial review in all other cases of state action apart from constitutional amendments.

The Indian constitution provides for both soft and hard judicial review. While Articles 13 and 246 set out a model of hard judicial review for competence and compliance with fundamental rights respectively, Article 37 provides for a soft model of judicial review for compliance with directive principles which allows for judicial cognizance but expressly bars judicial enforcement of these principles. Having developed the constitutional basis for basic structure review in *Kesavananda*, the court had to choose between these two alternative models of judicial review when applying the doctrine to review amending, legislative, and executive power. In this section I have examined whether basic structure review is best understood as a hard or soft model of judicial review. The brief survey of the relevant case law in this section suggests that the court has developed basic structure review along the lines of hard judicial review which in appropriate cases can lead to orders striking down the offending state action. There are other cases where the offending state action is not struck down and the court uses a range of remedies. Though this aspect of the doctrine is underdeveloped and it is possible that these hypotheses may be premature, basic structure review must on the present evidence be categorized as hard judicial review.

[138] *Ismail Faruqui*, supra n. 3.

Rules and Principles

A significant unresolved aspect of basic structure review is whether such review allows the court sufficient textual or normative resources to resolve concrete constitutional problems that come before it. There are two ingredients to this argument about the ambiguity of basic structure review: First, the identity of basic feature of the constitution which I discuss in Chapter 4. The second source of ambiguity is rooted in the difficulty in applying these general constitutional rules to resolve particular problems that come before the court. I will address this second ingredient in this section and argue that whenever the court is confronted with generally phrased rules it must develop mediating working rules to allow it to resolve concrete problems in an intelligible and rational fashion.[139]

Where the court undertakes rights compliance and competence review for violations of the textual provisions of the constitution, the petitioner has to convince it that a provision of the constitution is violated and then it will step in to provide a remedy. Basic structure review requires the court to consider what the basic feature requires in the area of state action, and to evaluate the effect of the challenged action on these general constitutional rules. The task before the court is not merely a result of the linguistic determinacy of constitutional rules as distinguished from the more abstract, general terms in which a basic feature is expressed. Constitutional provisions are often expressed in terms which give rise to considerable doubts as to what they require in concrete cases. The Indian courts interpretation of the right to life in Article 21 is adequate evidence for the open-textured character of some constitutional provisions. By clarifying the character of normative guidance that basic features provide, I will eliminate a significant confusion that plagues the approach of the court in basic structure review cases. This aspect of basic structure review has received almost no attention in the judicial decisions of the Supreme Court. While potentially the distinction has application in almost every case that has come before the court, I will examine three cases as illustrations of how this distinction would clarify the scope of basic structure review.

---

[139] O Fiss 'Groups and the Equal Protection Clause', 5 *Philosophy & Public Affairs* 107 (1976) 107–8.

I begin by briefly returning to a case discussed in the section above. In *Indira Gandhi* and *Minerva Mills* I noted that Chandrachud confuses basic structure review and rights compliance review. This confusion has three sources: first, a lack of clarity about the character of basic structure review; second, confusion about the identity of basic features as text-emergent constitutional principles or simply key provisions of the constitution; and finally, a failure to distinguish between review for compliance with constitutional provisions and constitutional principles under basic structure review. In this section, I focus on this third confusion as it arises in subsequent basic structure cases.

In *Kihoto Hollohan* v. *Zachilhu*[140] the constitutionality of the Tenth Schedule introduced by the Constitution (52nd Amendment) Act, 1985 was challenged on the grounds that it violated the freedom of speech of members of elected assemblies, the basic features of democracy, and judicial review by curtailing the jurisdiction of the court. Parliament inserted the Tenth Schedule into the Constitution to 'curb the evil of political defections motivated by the lure of office or other similar considerations which endanger the foundation of … democracy. The remedy proposed is to disqualify the member of either House of Parliament or of the State Legislature who is found to have defected from continuing as a member of the House.'[141] This drastic attempt to regulate unprincipled defections by reinforcing internal party discipline was bolstered by providing that the Speaker's decision on whether the grounds provided in the Tenth Schedule have been satisfied is final and beyond the scrutiny of the court.

Of the two basic features which grounded the challenge, the majority and minority opinions agreed that the basic feature of judicial review was violated by the exclusion of the court's jurisdiction to review the decision of the Speaker. The court was divided on whether this part of the amendment was severable in order to save the rest of the amendment from being struck down.[142] In this section I am more concerned with the court's analysis of whether

---

[140] *Kihoto Hollohan* v. *Zachilher*, [1992] (Supplementary) 2 SCC 651.
[141] *Kihoto*, supra n. 41, p. 670 (Venkatachaliah, J).
[142] Ibid., pp. 718–9 (Verma, J).

anti-defection measures adopted by the amendment were detrimental to democracy as a basic feature.

Petitioners argued that the Tenth Schedule, by ignoring the freedom of speech, the right to dissent, and the freedom of conscience of the elected members of the legislatures, undermined the foundations of Parliamentary democracy. The court did not find that freedom of speech within the house was a part of the basic structure of the constitution.[143] Venkatachaliah, speaking for the majority, took the view that as 'there is a real and imminent threat to the very fabric of Indian democracy by their utter and total disregard of well recognized political proprieties and morality'[144] Parliament's response may be said to promote democratic values. He acknowledged that elected representatives are to represent the concerns of their constituents, but this representative function in the Parliamentary system of democracy was attenuated by the need to maintain internal political party structures. Given that democracy as a basic feature or constitutional principle supported arguments on both sides of the argument on the constitutional validity of the Tenth Schedule the court needs to develop mediating rules to allow it to decide whether the amendment damaged the basic feature of democracy. In other words the court would have to specify what democracy requires in such a case.

The decision of the court in this case to hold the amendment constitutionally valid has been criticized. Sathe argues that the majority decision in this case was wrong for two reasons: first, it mistakes the interest being protected as being those of the member while the 'primary interest' sought to be protected by Article 105 and 194 'is of ... society' as a whole.[145] Second, he urges that ' ... this was the most deserving case for using the basic structure doctrine and the judicial restraint was misplaced'.[146] Sathe's criticisms are misdirected as the contention that the freedom of speech is a basic feature was

---

[143] In *P.V. Narasimha Rao* v. *State*, (1998) 4 SCC 626 the court's obiter observation that freedom of speech of a member of Parliament was a part of the basic structure of the constitution.

[144] *Kihoto Hollohan*, supra n. 140, 679 (Venkatachaliah, J).

[145] Sathe, *Judicial Activism in India*, New Delhi: Oxford University Press, 2002, p. 91.

[146] S.P. Sathe, supra n. 145, p. 93.

considered and rejected. Further, this criticism fails to account for the necessity for the courts to develop mediating rules that allow it to articulate an intelligible basis for decision making in basic structure review cases.

In *Kihoto Hollohan*, the court considered whether, and to what extent, freedom of speech could be considered to flow from the basic feature of democracy. It concluded that the preservation of the basic feature of democracy does not require the preservation of free speech interests of elected representatives in the assembly at all costs to the exclusion of all other concerns. The court emphasized the institutional mechanisms of the political party which are central to the realization of the democratic principle in almost all liberal democracies. It recognized the complexity of political practice in contemporary democracies and took the view that compliance with the basic feature of democracy could be achieved through a variety of institutional mechanisms. In *Kihoto Hollohan* the basic feature of democracy may be preserved with or without the anti-defection provisions of the Tenth Schedule. Unlike a specific constitutional rule which may be formulated in terms that allow a court to assess compliance in an either-or fashion, a general constitutional requirement such as preservation of democracy provides the court with a range of constitutionally permissible options, of which the Tenth Schedule may be one.

Sathe's second objection to the 'judicial restraint' in the case fails to recognize the significance of the argument made above regarding judicial review for compliance with general constitutional rules. Unlike cases of judicial review where compliance with specific constitutional rules is called for, basic structure review requires that the court develop mediating rules that translate the general requirement into specific requirements in the case before it. The court while interpreting general constitutional rules will inevitably permit other state institutions sufficient scope to innovate while preserving these basic features of the constitution. These are not instances of the court adopting a posture of 'judicial restraint' but a necessary consequence of basic structure type review for compliance with general constitutional rules.

The next illustration of the confusion that arises from the failure to distinguish between basic structure review for preserving general constitutional rules and other forms of judicial review that secure compliance with specific constitutional rules is the recent affirmative action cases. In *Indra Sawhney* v. *Union of India*[147] the attempt by the Kerala state government was to overcome the creamy layer test evolved by the Court in *Indra Sawhney* v. *Union of India (I)*[148] and *Ashoka Kumar Thakur* v. *State of Bihar*.[149] In *Indra Sawhney (I)* and *Ashoka Kumar Thakur* the court had evolved the creamy layer test to filter out members of the Backward Classes who belonged to an economic class or educational status which disentitled them from belonging to the beneficiary category for affirmative action programmes. This body of constitutional doctrine was developed by the courts in these cases when called on to interpret the equality guarantee in Article 14 and the affirmative action provisions in Article 16. In these cases the court had noted that equality is a basic feature of the Constitution and supported the conclusions reached.

In *Indra Sawhney (II)* the Kerala State Backward Classes (Reservation of Appointments or Posts in the Services under the State) Act, 1995 provided that 'having regard to known facts in existence in the State of Kerala, there are no socially advanced sections in any Backward Classes who have acquired capacity to compete with forward classes'[150] and that the Backward Classes in the State were not 'adequately represented' in the services under the State and hence that they would continue to be entitled to reservation under Clause (4) of Article 16 of the Constitution.[151] These provisions were challenged on the grounds of violating Articles 14 and 16 of the Constitution and damaging the basic feature of equality.

This basic structure argument is not critical to the outcome in this case as the court was dealing with ordinary legislation which could have been declared unconstitutional for non-compliance with constitutional doctrine developed by the court on Articles 14 and 16. Nevertheless, the court held that where 'the creamy layer is not excluded there will be a breach, not only of Article 14 but of the basic structure of the Constitution.'[152] Rather unhelpfully the

[147] *Indra Sawhney* v. *Union of India*, (2000) 1 SCC 168.

[148] (1992) Supp (3) SCC 217.

[149] (1995) 5 SCC 403.

[150] Kerala State Backward Classes (Reservation of Appointments or Posts in the Services under the State) Act, 1995 Section 3.

[151] Ibid.

[152] *Indra Sawhney* (II) (n) 202 (Jagannadha Rao, J).

court continued that such 'an illegality offending the root of the Constitution of India cannot be allowed to be perpetuated even by constitutional amendment'.[153] This ruling confuses both the character of basic structure review and the nature of basic features as general constitutional rules as distinguished from specific constitutional provisions. I distinguished between the types of constitutional judicial review earlier in this chapter and in the following paragraphs I will illustrate why the court failed to appreciate the nature of review for compliance with general constitutional rules.

In *Indra Sawhney (I)*, besides the creamy layer test discussed in *Indra Sawhney (II)* above, the court also held that reservation quotas in public employment could not exceed 50 per cent of the available seats and that there should be no reservation for seats to be filled up through promotions. The Constitution (76th Amendment) Act, 1994 inserted a Tamil Nadu statute which provides for more than 50 per cent reservation into the 9th Schedule to immunize it from constitutional challenges under Articles 14, 19, and 21. The Constitution (77th Amendment) Act, 1995 added clause 4-A to Article 16 which provides for reservation in favour of Schedule Castes and Scheduled Tribes even where public jobs are filled up by promotions. Further, the Constitution (85th Amendment) Act, 2001 amended Article 16(4-A) to protect consequential seniority of those who benefit from affirmative action in promotions. The Constitution (82nd Amendment) Act amended Article 335 to introduce a proviso to overcome the justification for the *Indra Sawhney (I)* judgment. The Constitution (81st Amendment) Act, 2000 added Article 16(4-B) which overcame the 50 per cent limit to reservation quotas. These amendments taken together overcome the holding of *Indra Sawhney (I)* which had justified its conclusions by pointing out that equality was a basic feature of the constitution.

Sathe anticipates a basic structure challenge to these constitutional amendments and suggests that the court is unlikely to do so as these amendments were enacted with bi-partisan support and in a sense constitute 'political limitations on the basic structure doctrine'.[154] He

---

[153] Ibid., Section 4.

[154] Sathe, *Judicial Activism in India*, New Delhi: Oxford University Press, 2003, p. 94.

sagely recommends that the court must read the amendments 'strictly' and require the state to provide more empirical evidence in support of its policy.[155]

Indra Sawhney (II) and Sathe's discussion on the 76th and 78th amendments, makes similar mistakes in their understanding of basic structure review. These arguments proceed on the mistaken view that all the propositions upheld in *Indra Sawhney (I)* are basic features of the Constitution. While there are obiter dicta in Jeevan Reddy's majority opinion in *Indra Sawhney (I)* which support such a view, this is surely a mistake as these propositions are interpretations of the detailed constitutional provisions which seek to work out what these provisions entail for the resolution of the disputes before the court. Basic features are those general constitutional principles identified at a level of generality which make them less able to resolve disputes about service rules in public employment. If there is a basic feature at stake in these cases, it is the principle of equality stated in these broad terms which will guide the court in assessing these constitutional amendments. Far from being a political limit on the operation of the basic structure doctrine, these amendments are merely political means of overcoming particular interpretations of constitutional provisions. For basic structure review to be useful in these cases, one must be able to show that state action does not advance any version of the principle of equality. A sceptic may suggest that basic structure review for constitutional principles at such a level of abstraction is far from useful in a wide majority of cases likely to come before the court, to which our reply must be that this is an inevitable consequence of the nature and standard of basic structure review.

The court had the opportunity to consider these suggestions in a recent case of *M. Nagaraj* v. *Union of India*[156] where all the above amendments were challenged on the grounds that they destroyed the basic feature of equality. Justice Kapadia speaking for the unanimous court applied a 'width test' and 'identity test'[157] and found that the constitutional amendments did not alter constitutional principles like 'secularism or federalism...' which led him to conclude that as

---

[155] Sathe, supra n. 154, p. 96.

[156] AIR 2007 SC 71.

[157] *M. Nagaraj*, supra n. 156, 67 (Kapadia, J).

the constitutional amendments did not alter the equality code in the constitution set out in Articles 14, 15, and 16 and that they satisfied basic structure review. Justice Kapadia expresses his conclusions in his own inimitable style which pays too little attention to the language in which the basic structure doctrine was previously expressed, but nevertheless does capture the essence of basic structure review.

I conclude our discussion of the distinction between judicial review on the basis of specific and general rules with a discussion of *Bommai*, a case I considered more elaborately in our discussion above on the nature of basic structure review of executive action. Briefly, in *Bommai* the court held that where the President was satisfied that a state government has already acted or is likely to act contrary to the basic features of the Constitution, then he is justified in dismissing such a government under Article 356. While I endorsed the reasoning of the court in the discussion above, I explore some other complexities that may arise in the near future. Executive action proclaiming a regional emergency under Article 356, and in some circumstances the proclamation of a national emergency under Article 352, involve the suspension or dismissal of a democratically elected government. Almost by definition then in any case where such proclamations are challenged under the basic structure doctrine, the basic feature of democracy is at stake. So in a case like *Bommai*, the court must carefully consider the circumstances under which the proclamation power has been exercised to evaluate whether the defence of the basic feature of secularism outweighs the negative effects on democracy that necessarily result from such an action. In all such cases, basic structure review on the basis of general constitutional rules may result in basic features pointing to opposite conclusions. Such a possibility of conflict is inherent in the character of basic features as general constitutional rules. In such an event the court has no easy options and must explore the precise factual circumstances of the challenge in each case to assess the extent of damage to each basic feature and reach a conclusion in the particular case.

In this section, I have considered the distinct character of basic structure review which assesses damage to 'general' constitutional rules or basic features of the constitution. I have shown that the court applying basic structure review must appreciate that the character of basic features as general constitutional rules which require the court to develop mediating rules which allow it resolve concrete disputes that come before it. The choice of mediating rules and the variety of institutional arrangements that satisfy a particular basic feature of the constitution has given rise to the suggestion that the court must exercise judicial restraint or judicial deference in such cases. I turn to this argument and conclude the discussion in this chapter.

CONCLUSION

Since *Kesavananda*, the Supreme Court has invoked the basic structure doctrine to strike down constitutional amendments five times, legislation just once, and never invalidated executive action. Several other constitutional amendments, emergency proclamations, and ordinary legislative and executive actions have been challenged on the grounds of violating the basic structure doctrine but have either satisfied basic structure review, or have been struck down on other grounds. Since the judgment in *Kihoto Hollohan*, when portions of the Constitution (52nd Amendment) Act, 1985 was struck down, 42 constitutional amendments have been enacted. Some of these amendments are significant in their scope and effect.

The Constitution (73rd Amendment) Act, 1992 and the Constitution (74th Amendment) Act, 1992 introduce a third tier of local government at urban municipalities and rural–panchayats. Moreover these amendments extended quota based representation on elected bodies for Scheduled Caste/Scheduled Tribe communities and introduced new quotas for women. The validity of these amendments has not been challenged. I noted in our discussions in the section above that some aspects of the *Indra Sawhney (I)* decision overcome by constitutional amendments which have been upheld in *Nagaraj*. Are these statistics and trends an outcome of the nature and standard of basic structure review or a sign of judicial deference to other branches of government?

Sathe suggests the latter and observes that 'it is only through a judicial policy of giving maximum deference to the will of the legislature that the basic structure doctrine can be sustained without impairing democracy'.[158] A similar view has been advanced by Venkatachaliah in *Kihoto Hollohan* who observes that the amendments challenged

---

[158] Sathe, supra n. 154, p. 85.

are 'pre-eminently an area where Judges should defer to legislative perception of and reaction to the pervasive dangers of unprincipled defections to protect the community'.[159] Unfortunately, he offers no description of the area in which deference might be due or the reasons for such an attitude of deference.

An extensive body of critical commentary on the question of judicial deference in constitutional and administrative law review offers us guidance on how such an approach may be adopted in basic structure review. However, it is the argument in this chapter, and the work more broadly, that analytical clarity about the constitutional basis, nature and standards of basic structure review together with the identification of basic features of the Constitution will allow us to overcome many misconceptions and criticisms of the basic structure doctrine. The argument for deference may play some role in constitutional judicial review for rights compliance and competence where any violation of constitutional provisions and constitutional doctrine will result in invalidity. In this chapter I have tried to show that in the ordinary course, the nature of basic structure review for general constitutional rules and moreover the 'damage or destroy' or 'identity preserving' standards will ensure that if it were at all possible to accommodate state action within the normative boundaries of the basic features of the Constitution, the doctrine will not strike down such action. Such an outcome need not be contrived by an ill-thought out attitude of judicial deference where it is already woven into the warp and weft of the doctrine. However, the discussion on judicial deference alerts us to the critical need to identify the normative character of the basic features of the Constitution with precision. It is to this problem that I now turn.

[159] *Kihoto*, supra n. 41, p. 680 (Venkatachaliah, J).

4

Grounds of Review
Basic Features of the Constitution

The very nature of these lists suggests that the court has not quite thought through the constitutional principle behind the basic structure doctrine. Rather, they picked out items from the text of the constitution without specifying why. It is almost as if the Supreme Court takes the view that we recognize the basic structure when we see it.[1]

In *Kesavananda*, the Supreme Court announced the basic structure doctrine, but it fell to later decisions to elaborate on the nature and character of basic features and to specify the mode by which they may be identified. At various points the court has suggested that democracy, secularism, rule of law, federalism, judicial review, separation of powers, among others, are basic features of the constitution. A first step to clarify the identity of basic features of the Constitution is to scrutinize the important judicial opinions in *Indira Gandhi*, *Waman Rao*, *Minerva Mills*, *Bommai*, and *Ganpatrao*, as well as the early speculations in *Kesavananda* in order to identify the main arguments and concerns about the basic features of the Constitution. Next, I filter out unsupported and unfounded claims and criticisms of the courts attempts to identify basic features and then critically evaluate the remaining few substantive issues. Pratap Mehta, in the quotation above, emphatically concludes that the Supreme Court has failed to adopt a principled approach to the task of identifying the basic features of the constitution. In the rest of this chapter I will show that the court has indeed developed a distinct method

[1] P.B. Mehta, 'The Inner Conflict of Constitutionalism' in Zoya Hasan (ed.) *India's Living Constitution*, New Delhi: Permanent Black, 2002, p. 201.

for identifying basic features and though the set of basic features so identified may not constitute a coherent set captured by a single principle of constitutional or political morality, this failure may not be as fatal to the doctrine as the quotation above suggests.

In the 'Introduction', I proposed that the basic structure doctrine has evolved into a full-fledged doctrine of constitutional judicial review. Such a doctrine may be understood as possessing a sound constitutional basis, and a distinct and discrete type and standard of review to assess compliance with identifiable grounds or bases of review. By structuring our assessment of the doctrine in this fashion I am able to better focus the analysis and criticism of the doctrine, on its core ingredients and avoiding the broad-brush generalizations which plague the existing secondary literature. In this chapter I address the third aspect of any doctrine of constitutional judicial review identified above; the grounds or bases of review.

This chapter may be usefully divided into two parts: first, I will examine the nature and character of the basic features of the Constitution and second, isolate the judicial technique employed to identify these features. I argue that the basic structure doctrine seeks to identify 'basic features' of the Constitution, as distinguished from core articles[2] or 'integral'[3] parts of it. These features are general constitutional rules which are foundational to the identity and character of the Indian Constitution and include principles of institutional design as well as substantive values which together frame decision-making under it. I argue that the court is right to refuse to provide an exhaustive catalogue of basic features in a legislative mode. I will show that the court has committed itself to a common-law, case-by-case technique to discover basic features of the constitution.[4] In each case the court considers, in the circumstances before it, whether

[2] *Indira Gandhi* v. *Raj Narain*, AIR 1975 Supreme Court 2299. Chandrachud identifies basic features with the core articles in the constitution, while Mathew correctly points out that such an approach is misguided as all articles of the constitution are important and a structural interpretation would require basic features to be etched out in a broader range of provisions.

[3] *Ganpatrao* v. *Union of India*, AIR 1993 SC 1267.

[4] This constraint of the development of the doctrine is necessarily entailed by the constraints on a court developing a doctrine by interpreting the text of the constitution and resolving the case before it. See generally Adam Steinman, 'A Constitution for Judicial Law Making', 65 *Univ of Pittsburg L Rev* 545, (2004).

the basic feature claimed to be damaged in the case is adequately supported by the textual provisions of the constitution. Where such a feature is thus supported by the constitutional text taken as whole, the court evaluates arguments from the constitution's underlying moral or political philosophy, the political history of the freedom movement, and more particularly speeches in the Constituent Assembly Debates, to assess whether such features are 'basic' or foundational to the normative identity of the constitution.

The level of abstraction at which a basic feature is identified as critical to basic structure review as the general character of basic features has a bearing on the level of scrutiny at which basic structure review takes place, an issue I consider more fully in Chapter 3. I suggest in the discussion below that there has been much confusion about the basic feature identified and the derivative reasons, which emerge from these features and assist the court to decide the case before it. For example, different opinions have identified democracy,[5] parliamentary democracy,[6] and free and fair elections[7] as being basic features in the Constitution. When one considers that presidential democracy has been the focus of many constitutional reform proposals, the precision with which basic features are identified affects the nature of basic structure review. For example, a constitutional amendment introducing presidential democracy may survive basic structure review for damaging democracy so long as it ensures free and fair elections. However, if parliamentary democracy is itself taken to be a basic feature, the very prospect of substituting the parliamentary executive with a presidential executive would violate this basic feature. I will suggest that basic features are best understood as constitutional values identified at a level of abstraction, as values expressed in the preamble, in order to preserve basic structure review as a distinct and novel form of constitutional judicial review with an appropriate standard of scrutiny.

THE NATURE OF BASIC FEATURES

In *Golaknath* v. *State of Punjab* the Supreme Court held that the permitted scope of Parliament's amending power did not extend

---

[5] *Indira Gandhi*, v. *Raj Narain*, supra n. 2 (Mathew, J).
[6] *Kesavananda Bharati* v. *State of Kerala*, (1973) 4 SCC 225 (Jaganmohan, J)
[7] *Indira Gandhi*, supra n. 2 (Chandrachud, J).

to the fundamental rights set out in Part III of the Constitution. I considered and rejected the approach of the court in this case for several reasons explored more fully in Chapter 1. Further, this proposition was roundly rejected by the court in *Kesavananda*. However, the *Golaknath* court articulated a clear and unambiguous basis for judicial review and the unamendable core features of the Constitution were easily identified—rights in Part III of the Constitution. By contrast, in *Kesavananda* the court articulated a sounder constitutional basis for the basic structure doctrine but was imprecise about the grounds on which judicial review of constitutional amendments should proceed. This imprecision provoked a great deal of criticism about the character and source of basic features in the Constitution and the method by which they were to be identified.

The court was challenged to provide a complete catalogue of these basic features without which, it was argued, Parliament would not get sufficient guidance on the scope of its amending power.[8] Tripathi goes further to suggest that *Kesavananda* failed to articulate a common basis for judicial review and that the 'six Judges led by the Chief Justice very nearly hold that the power of amendment under Article 368 is subject to reasonable restrictions, and has to be scrutinized like an ordinary statute challenged on the ground of violation of the rights guaranteed in Article 19'.[9] Such 'reasonableness' type judicial review does not, in his view, require the identification of basic features of the Constitution. The development of the basic structure doctrine over the last three decades shows that Tripathi was wrong in his early assessment about the nature of basic structure review and the need to identify basic features of the Constitution. The courts have developed basic structure review as a distinct type of judicial review which shares little with 'reasonableness' analysis under Article 19. To sustain the distinctiveness of basic structure review, I consider and respond to the criticisms about the nature and character of basic features which operate as the grounds of review. This is the task I undertake in this section of the chapter.

[8] R. Dhavan, *Supreme Court and Parliamentary Sovereignty*, New Delhi: Sterling Publishers, 1976.

[9] P.K. Tripathi, '*Kesavananda Bharati* v. *State of Kerala*: Who Wins?' (1977) 3 SCC (Journal) p. 3.33.

In order to make any progress in identifying basic features of the Constitution there is a need for a clarification of terms. In *Kesavananda*, the plural opinions delivered by the court allowed for considerable doubt about the target of the doctrine. It has been suggested that while Sikri, and five other judges who concurred with him, spoke in terms of 'basic features' and 'essential elements', Khanna formulated the doctrine in terms of 'the basic structure or framework' of the Constitution.[10] So I must first clarify whether this characterization of the *Kesavananda* opinion is accurate and if so, whether these terms are synonymous and if not, which of these views is correct.

Basic Structure or Essential Features

Raju Ramachandran suggests that Khanna's concept of basic structure was clearly different from the 'basic features' view of the other judges. He suggests that the other majority judges viewed certain features, embedded in particular provisions of the Constitution, to be unamendable. Khanna was concerned with the power to amend the constitution as a whole. He understood amending power to not include the power to abrogate the entire constitution and replace it with an entirely new one. It is from this perspective that he observed that the basic structure or framework of the Constitution could not be destroyed.[11] This argument gives weight to the particular phrasing used by the judges in their opinions—'basic structure' or 'basic features'—to suggest that there were two distinct versions of the basic structure doctrine announced in *Kesavananda*. In this section I examine this argument at greater length and find that while it is crucial to bring clarity to the language in which the basic structure doctrine is expressed, far too much is made of the early dissonances in *Kesavananda*.

Sikri, in the concluding part of his *Kesavananda* opinion, held that the amending power under Article 368 did not extend to the abrogation of fundamental rights or 'to completely change the fundamental

---

[10] *Minerva Mills* v. *Union of India*, AIR 1980 SC 1789 (Bhagwati J) 1817–18. P.K. Tripathi supra n. 9. Compare D.G. Morgan, 'The Indian Essential Features Case 30 ICLQ 307 (1981).

[11] R. Ramachandran, 'The Supreme Court and the Basic Structure Doctrine', in *Supreme But Not Infallible*, New Delhi: Oxford University Press, 2000, p. 115.

features of the constitution so as to destroy its identity'.[12] Earlier in the opinion he suggests that while every provision of the Constitution was essential, they could be amended 'provided in the result the basic foundation and structure of the constitution remains the same'.

The basic structure may be said to consist of the following features:

1. Supremacy of the Constitution
2. Republican and Democratic form of Government
3. Secular character of the Constitution
4. Separation of powers
5. Federal character of the Constitution

The above structure is built on the basic foundation, that is, the dignity and freedom of the individual.[13]

These excerpts make clear that Sikri did not envisage basic features to be equivalent to, or reside exclusively in, individual articles of the constitution. Instead he outlines a doctrine which operates at a considerable degree of abstraction from the constitutional text by identifying constitutional principles which are rooted in, and exemplified by, several provisions of the Constitution simultaneously. Later in this chapter I will assess whether Sikri provides us with an adequate account of how these features may be identified. At this point it is sufficient to note that when he speaks of basic features, he is referring to constitutional rules residing in the constitution and not the constitutional provisions themselves.

Khanna, in his partly concurring opinion in *Kesavananda* held that the only limits on amending power under Article 368 was that it could not 'touch the foundation or alter the basic institutional pattern'[14] of the constitution. He identified 'democratic government' and the 'secular character' of the constitution to be among the features of the constitution which are unamendable. His reference to 'the basic institutional pattern' promises a refinement of the possible scope of basic features to be identified and that basic structure review

---

[12] *Kesavananda* (Sikri, CJ), supra n. 6, p. 405.

[13] *Kesavananda Bharati* v. *Kerala* (Sikri, CJ), supra n. 6, n. 366. Compare W.F. Murphy, 'An Ordering of Constitutional Values', 53 *Southern California L Review* 704–60 (1979–80) for a similar argument that all constitutional values are rooted in the dignity of the individual.

[14] *Kesavananda*, supra n. 6, p. 767.

may be geared to ensure broad participation in the processes of government and the benefits of this process by guarding against the undue restriction of the channels of political change.[15] However, this phrase has attracted very little attention in subsequent cases and the secondary literature discussing these issues. Though Khanna did not employ the language of basic features or constitutional principles and spoke in terms of the basic structure, it is clear from the principles he identified that his understanding of the nature of basic features and the level of abstraction at which basic structure judicial review took place was identical to that of Sikri.

Though Sikri and Khanna certainly advanced different interpretative justifications for the doctrine, the suggestion that the lead majority opinions in *Kesavananda* had two different versions of the doctrine in mind is misplaced. In both opinions, the 'basic structure doctrine' protects the identity of the constitution, by ensuring that important constitutional principles or basic features are immune from amendment. Though I have distinguished between the 'basic structure' doctrine and 'basic features' of the Constitution consistently in this work as a whole, this clarity about the character of basic features which forms the basis of constitutional judicial review under the basic structure doctrine is not sustained in subsequent decisions of the court. The most significant of these confusions is between basic features as constitutional principles or individual articles in the Constitution and it is to this that I turn to in the next section.

Individual Articles or Constitutional Features

The *Golaknath* court, by making amendments subject to fundamental rights, had identified specific articles which operated as limits on Parliament's amending power. Even after the court overruled the *Golaknath* holding in *Kesavananda*, there remained a residual tendency to identify basic features as individual articles, particularly fundamental rights, in the Constitution. The question was partially settled by Khanna's holding in *Kesavananda* that the right to property, a fundamental right set out in Article 31, was not a basic feature and therefore amendable by Parliament. But this ruling, even

---

[15] *United States* v. *Carolene Products Co.* 304 US 144(1938). Compare J.H. Ely, 'Foreword: On Discovering Fundamental Values', 92 *Harvard L Rev.* 5–55 (1978–79).

if correct, still left open the possibility that other fundamental rights or other important constitutional articles could be a part of the basic features protected by the basic structure doctrine.

The argument that fundamental rights are the basic features of the Constitution was considered in two subsequent cases where substantially different arguments were raised. In *Indira Gandhi* it was argued that Khanna had categorically ruled out the possibility that fundamental rights could be a part of the basic structure of the Constitution. As Khanna was part of the bench in *Indira Gandhi* he had the opportunity to clarify expressly that this was not what he had in mind when he ruled that Parliament's amending power allowed it to amend the right to property. He went on to hold that secularism was a basic feature of the Constitution, which as Seervai correctly points out,[16] is a constitutional value exclusively set out in the various rights guaranteed to citizens in the fundamental rights chapter in the Constitution. This clarification allows us to assert that fundamental rights are vital ingredients in any assessment of what are basic features of the Constitution and are not categorically excluded from the basic feature enquiry. However, I am yet to specify whether fundamental rights may themselves be considered as basic features of the Constitution.

In *Indira Gandhi*, the petitioners claimed that the amendments challenged violated a range of basic features: judicial review, rule of law, separation of power, equality guaranteed under Article 14, democracy, and free and fair elections. A cursory look at this wide array of basic features suggests several confusions about the character of basic features at various levels. Unlike in *Kesavananda* where the lead opinions were reasonably clear about the nature of basic features, the petitioners in *Indira Gandhi* confuse basic features of the constitutions with particular articles of the Constitution as well as derivative principles like free and fair elections which emerge from the basic feature of democracy. Faced with these diverse contentions the court needs to articulate the level of abstraction at which basic features should be identified, distinguishing them from specific

---

[16] H.M. Seervai, *Constitutional Law of India* (Universal Law Publishing, 4th edn, Vol. 3, Rep. 2004) p. 3138. Seervai concludes that Khanna's views on the constitutionality of Article 31-B and Schedule IX in *Kesavananda* are no longer tenable after this clarification.

constitutional provisions or rules of the constitution on the one hand, and intermediate principles derived from more general constitutional rules on the other.

Mathew's opinion in *Indira Gandhi* dealt with the question of whether equality guaranteed by Article 14 was a basic feature of the constitution. It was argued by the petitioner that some articles, like Article 14, protect core values such as equality which are, by virtue of their importance for any theory of justice, themselves basic features of the constitution. Surprisingly, Mathew dismissed this argument on a narrow application of *Kesavananda* as precedent for the proposition that Article 14 was not a part of the basic structure.[17] Though, as I noted above, there is no doubt that the *Kesavananda* majority opinions identify basic features as general constitutional rules, I should offer more reasons to reject the argument that basic features are simply the important articles of the Constitution.

Mathew engaged with other reasons why equality may not be suitable to be a part of the basic structure of the constitution. He advanced two arguments in support of his conclusion that equality was not a part of the basic structure. First, he suggested that as equality 'is a multi-coloured concept incapable of a single definition' which is 'capable of many shades and connotations' and hence it is unlikely to provide 'a solid foundation'.[18] Second, he suggests that as the concept of equality is 'subsumed under specific articles of the Constitution like Articles 14, 15, 16, 17, and 25'[19] there is no other principle of equality behind these articles which is an essential feature. When one considers that Mathew went on to identify democracy and the rule of law as basic features, these arguments against equality as a basic feature seem all the more tenuous.

There may well be other reasons which motivated the court to deny the petitioners' arguments that Article 14 was beyond the amending power or that equality was a basic feature. However, the first reason offered: that equality is a complex or contested concept subject to extensive theoretical disputations is true of the basic features of the 'rule of law' and 'democracy' identified by Mathew. Moreover, the reason offered by Mathew reveals that he misunderstands the type

[17] *Indira Gandhi*, supra n. 2, p. 2383 (Mathew, J).
[18] Ibid.
[19] Ibid.

and standard of basic structure review as applied to constitutional amendments as well as the nature and character of basic features of the Constitution. I had noted in Chapter 3 that when it is argued that an amendment damages or destroys the basic feature of equality, if the respondent can support the amendment under any reasonable and constitutionally defensible version of equality, the court will allow the amendment to stand. In other words, the level of scrutiny at which basic structure review takes place allows for the court to accommodate state action which may draw support from several, often contesting, versions of equality. If our argument about the type and standard of basic structure review is correct then basic features of the Constitution will admit of various conceptions and versions and the complexity of basic features should be understood to be an integral aspect of the character of basic structure review.

The second reason offered by Mathew to reject equality as a basic feature of the constitution is also unconvincing. While it is correct to assert that the principle of equality is well etched out in several constitutional provisions, there is no force to the view that the principle may somehow be exhausted by such a detailed exposition in the constitution. To the contrary, the presence of equality in various provisions of the Constitution lends support to the view that it is a feature which is central to our constitutional design. It may be that Mathew's discomfort with recognizing equality as a basic feature of the constitution arose from concerns which he failed to articulate in his opinion. One possible concern is whether the basic features of the constitution are meant to include commitments to substantive normative values like equality and free speech or only to such features which maintain the 'institutional arrangements' set up by the constitution. This is a theme which will be explored in greater detail in the next section.

The second source of confusion in the identification of basic features is the level of abstraction at which such constitutional principles should be expressed. I noted earlier in this section that identifying basic features as the important articles of the Constitution is far too specific and detailed, and confuses the character of basic structure review with other forms of constitutional judicial review. On the other hand, identifying basic features as constitutional principles of an intermediate character which may be seen to be properly derived from other basic features ignores how various constitutional principles are inter related and the nature of judicial reasoning by which abstract constitutional values are used by courts to decide particular cases. I will illustrate this second problem by examining an example of such confusion.

In *Indira Gandhi* the court had identified several basic features including democracy and free and fair elections. Most opinions in the case treated both of these as constituting separate basic features of the Constitution. As free and fair elections are a part of democratic practice it is useful to see the former to be entailed by the latter. Khanna's opinion in *Indira Gandhi* exhibited clarity and pointed out that democracy, which was part of the basic structure of the constitution, entailed free and fair elections. Hence he concluded that amended Article 329-A (4) violates the principles of free and fair election by extinguishing the dispute relating to the election of the Prime Minister, and such an amendment would damage or destroy the basic feature of democracy.

The argument about the appropriate level of abstraction may seem a semantic quibble. It may be that it makes no difference to the outcome in *Indira Gandhi* whether free and fair elections is taken to be a basic feature by itself or it to be seen as being entailed by democracy as a basic feature. However, two reasons may be offered to support the argument that basic features should be identified at an appropriate level of abstraction. First, it allows the court to manage a small set of basic features and prevent the proliferation of disparate principles as basic features of the Constitution. By recognizing basic features as those constitutional principles supported by several articles of the Constitution and integral to its design, the court maintains a distinct technique of identifying such principles. The Constitution says nothing about elections, an area of law almost entirely regulated by statute, subordinate legislation, and the Election Commission. So identifying free and fair elections to be a basic feature is not supported by adequate evidence. Free and fair elections are a necessary component of the practice of liberal democracy as it is conceived today, and hence it may be seen to be entailed by democracy as a basic feature of the Constitution and therefore play an important role in the court's conclusion in *Indira Gandhi*. Though democracy and free fair elections may be inter-related in this fashion and both play a significant role in the decision, it is crucial to the basic structure doctrine that there is clarity about the character of basic features of the Constitution and the subordinate principles which may be derived from it.

Second, the identification of derivative constitutional principles as basic features carries the risk that the court will end up conducting a far too intensive standard of scrutiny under basic structure review. Let us examine this difficulty with a hypothetical example. The courts have identified both 'democracy'[20] and 'parliamentary democracy'[21] as basic features of the Constitution. One of the persistent proposals for constitutional amendment over the last few decades has been the proposed change from a parliamentary to a presidential democracy. If such a proposal is carried out there is no doubt that it will be subject to basic structure review. In such a case, if the court takes the view that parliamentary democracy is a basic feature of the Constitution then the proposal for a presidential democracy is bound to fail basic structure review. However, if the court were to find that 'democracy' is a basic feature of the Constitution then the proposal for presidential democracy may be assessed in detail to ensure that it is essentially democratic in character. This hypothetical example suggests that the generality at which basic features are identified is crucial to sustain the nature and character of basic structure review as an independent and distinct form of constitutional judicial review.

In the next chapter, I will argue why the court should carry out basic structure review to preserve basic constitutional values at a level of generality sufficient to allow the amending power of Parliament the scope to make substantial changes to the Constitution. In this section it is sufficient for me to show that the court must consecrate as basic features only general constitutional rules which are not to be confused with the important articles of the Constitution or the intermediate and derivative principles which provide reasons for decisions in particular cases.

'Integral Parts' but not Basic Features

In the sections above I have considered the character of basic features of the Constitution as general constitutional rules. In this section I

---

[20] *Indira Gandhi*, supra n. 2 and more recently in *Kihoto Hollohan* v. *Zachilhu*, AIR 1993 SC 412.

[21] *P.V. Narasimha Rao* v. *State*, AIR 1998 SC 2120 (S.C. Agarwal, J).

consider whether basic features are general constitutional rules which emerge from historically contingent political arrangements or compacts which make up the political foundation for the constitution or the moral principles which lie at the core of the normative identity of the constitution. This question is best explored by examining the court's approach to this task in *R. Ganpatrao* v. *Union of India*[22] where the Constitution (26th Amendment) Act, 1971 was challenged on the grounds that it damages or destroys the basic structure of the constitution and was beyond the powers of Parliament under Article 368.

The petitioner was the co-ruler of the princely state of Kurundwad Jr, a sovereign state in treaty relationship and under the suzerainty of the British Crown. The petitioner's co-ruler executed an instrument of accession[23] and a merger agreement, on behalf of both rulers, thereby committing the princely state to being a part of the Dominion of India. As a condition for the signing of these agreements, the rulers were entitled to receive annually from the revenues of the State his privy purse, as specified in the Merger Agreement free of taxes, besides preserving his other personal rights, privileges, and dignities. These entitlements were subsequently recognized by Articles 291 and 362 of the Constitution of India, 1950. The Constitution (26th Amendment) Act repealed these articles and inserted a new Article 363-A depriving the rulers of their recognition and declaring the abolition of the Privy Purse. This Amendment Act was challenged on the grounds that it violated the fundamental rights of the petitioner and damaged and destroyed the basic structure and essential features of the constitution. I will confine my analysis in this chapter to the basic structure review challenge.

The petitioner claimed that it was only on the basis of the Constituent Assembly's acceptance of the provisions of Articles 291, 362, and clause 22 of Article 366 that the Rulers adopted the Constitution of India in relation to the States. The Privy Purse settlements were in the nature of consideration for the surrender by the Rulers of all their ruling powers and the dissolution of the

[22] AIR 1993 SC 1267.
[23] This instrument of accession was executed under Section 5 of the Government of India Act, 1935 as adopted under the Indian Independence Act, 1947.

States as separate units. For these reasons, counsel for the petitioner argued that these articles were an 'integral part of the constitutional scheme'[24] and formed a part of the 'basic structure'.[25] As these articles were the key to achieving 'the unity of India' their deletion would damage and destroy the basic structure. This argument was supported by the claim that 'there can be no basic structure of a Constitution divorced from the historical evolution of the precepts and principles on which the Constitution is founded'.[26] Other petitioners urged that the Constitution (26th Amendment) Act, 1971 damaged other essential features. While one identified the damaged basic features to be equality—in Article 14—and to property—in Article 19(1)(f) as it then was—another suggested that the principle violated was the 'principle of prohibition against impairment of contract obligations' which was incorporated into Articles 362 and 291.[27]

Of the arguments advanced in this case, I will pay particular attention to the argument that contractual commitments made to princely rulers during the formation of the India Union, now reflected in various provisions of the Constitution, were basic features of the Constitution. This challenge to the 26th Amendment was expressed in the terms that 'the privileges of Rulers are made an integral part of the constitutional scheme'[28] by the historical nature of the Instruments of Accession and its subsequent incorporation into the Constitution. In its strongest form, it is argued that the present geographical shape and political form of the Indian Union could not have been achieved without the concessions and privileges conceded by these treaties of accession. In this sense, these treaties constitute an 'integral' part of the structure of the Union which ensured the organic unity of India. For these reasons, the petitioners argued that Articles 291, 362, and 366(22) are beyond the amending powers of Parliament under Article 368.

This argument encourages the court to analyse the evolution of the provisions of the Constitution against the background of the

[24] *Ganpatrao*, supra n. 22, p. 1274.

[25] Ibid.

[26] Ibid., p. 1275.

[27] Ibid., p. 1276.

[28] *Ganpatrao*, supra n. 22, p. 1287 citing Shah's observations in *Madhav Rao Scindia* v. *Union of India*, AIR 1971 SC 530.

political history of the Indian nation. It suggests that some articles of the Constitution originate in certain political events that were so critical to constituting India[29] that such articles acquire sanctity and immunity from amendment. Hence, the task of identifying basic features is to identify such historically salient articles.

The alternative view conceives of basic features as general constitutional rules or values that are discerned by reading the Constitution as comprising moral and political principles expressed in various provisions of the Constitution. When read in this fashion the courts identify basic features as those principles which are integral to the constitutional design without which the 1950 Constitution loses its normative identity. This is the approach that Pandian adopts in *Ganpatrao*.

Pandian contended with this argument at two levels. First, he marshalled historical evidence to argue that far from being a principled bargain, the treaties of accession were agreed upon by the rulers of the princely states under popular pressure in their territories from a large majority of subjects who were keen to be a part of the Indian Union. Even if this historical argument is open to doubt, he offered a second independent and far more compelling argument. He took the view that in order to identify basic features one must read the Constitution as an integrated document which incorporates a 'particular socio-economic and political phlosophy'.[30] Pandian suggests that the 'permanent retention of the privy purses and privileges would be incompatible with the sovereign and republican form of Government'[31] instituted by the Constitution. Further, he suggested that as these provisions were incompatible with the 'egalitarian form' of our constitution, their deletion advanced the principles of economic, political, and social justice embodied in the Constitution.

In *Ganpatrao* the court had to choose between the historical and normative arguments about the nature and character of basic features of the Constitution. Pandian concludes that the basic

---

[29] Compare S. Sen, *Popular Sovereignty* and *Democratic Transformations: The Constitution of India* (New Delhi: Oxford University Press, 2007) pp. 3–5.

[30] *Ganpatrao*, supra n. 22, p. 1287.

[31] *Ganpatrao*, supra n. 22, p. 1288.

features protected are not embodied in the concrete language of particular articles or in the historically contingent political events that go to make up the Indian Union today. Instead he identifies as basic features those political, moral, and legal principles, which are reflected in several articles in the Constitution, which together make the core normative identity of the Constitution. In this case, the court's denial of the status of basic features to the articles protecting the treaties of accession, suggests that the identity of basic features are not historically contingent provisions of the Constitution precommitted to during the founding of constitution. Instead the court identifies basic features as those moral, legal, and political principles which are the foundational normative core on which the rest of the Constitution is built.

I should be careful here not to overstate this point. The court is surely concerned with the textual provisions of the Constitution adopted by the Constituent Assembly and the values they express. History is relevant insofar as it allows the court to isolate the moral and political principles which ground the Constitution of India, 1950 as adopted by the constituent assembly. Hence, identifying basic features of the constitution is not an exercise in abstract moral or political philosophy to identify the 'best' constitutional principles for all time. It is an attempt to synthesize those core normative principles which may be understood to be central to our constitutional design.

In this part of the chapter I have analysed the nature of basic features of the Constitution. I began by clarifying that the grounds of review under the 'basic structure' doctrine are 'basic features' of the Constitution. By eliminating the inconsistency in the use of the phrases 'basic structure', 'basic feature', and 'essential feature' I clear the ground for a more sustained enquiry into the nature of basic features. Next I clarified that basic features are not simply those 'articles' of the Constitution which may be considered to be pre-eminent by any chosen method of ranking. Instead the court looks for 'features' of the Constitution expressed in several provisions of the Constitution which may be considered to be moral and political principles at the normative core of our constitution. In the next part of this chapter I examine the various techniques and resources used to identify the basic features of the Constitution.

FINDING BASIC FEATURES

The majority decision in *Kesavananda Bharathi* case no doubt evolved the doctrine of basic structure or framework, but did not lay down that any particular named features of the constitution formed part of its basic structure or framework.[32]

Bhagwati, as reflected by the quotation above, took the view that *Kesavananda* was not binding authority on the question of what the basic features of the constitution are. One may support such a view for several reasons of which two are particularly important: first, the basic features identified by several judges in that case did not represent the majority opinion of the court. Second, and more importantly, these observations about the basic features of the constitution were *obiter* as the court did not apply any of these features to decide the challenges before them in *Kesavananda*.

Since *Kesavananda*, the court has unfortunately not addressed the method of identifying basic features of the Constitution in a forthright and consistent manner. I may at best gather some general indications of how the court approaches the problem of identifying basic features. The rest of this part of the chapter identifies these general approaches, critically analyses them, and develops them to the extent possible.

An Open-Ended Catalogue of Basic Features?

It is often suggested that the Court should enumerate what constitutes the basic structure of the Constitution. In our submission such enumeration must come in the form of a policy statement.[33]

The most persistent and harsh criticism of the basic structure doctrine over the many years of its existence has been directed at the open-ended nature of the basic feature catalogue. Most recently, R.K.P. Shankardass criticizes the court for expanding the basic feature catalogue and observes that 'the open-ended nature of the doctrine is beginning to lead to an irrational and confusing situation'.[34] Sathe,

[32] *Minerva Mills*, supra n. 10, p. 1820 (Bhagwati, J).

[33] S.P. Sathe, *Judicial Activism in India*, New Delhi: Oxford University Press, 2002, p. 97.

[34] R.K.P. Shankardass, 'The Anomalies of the Doctrine' in Pran Chopra (ed.), *The Supreme Court versus the Constitution*, New Delhi: Sage Publications, 2006, p. 137.

in the quotation above, takes the view that the basic features of the Constitution should be consolidated in a single statement which exhaustively lists the basic features of the Constitution. In the rest of this section I evaluate the court's approach to the task of identifying basic features and then conclude by setting out some general features of constitutional adjudication which constrain the modes through which the court can go about this task.

Sikri, in his lead opinion in *Kesavananda* boldly set out to provide a catalogue of basic features which rest on the foundation of 'the dignity and freedom of the individual'.[35] He was joined by the other judges on the bench who took the liberty to list their preferred constitutional values as basic features of the Constitution. In *Kesavananda* various features were identified in the plural opinions delivered: these include features such as democracy, secularism, and federalism which subsequent decisions have reaffirmed as basic features and others such as republicanism, sovereignty, and the mandate to build a welfare state which have received less attention. I am not particularly concerned with the features identified in this case, as I am with the method by which this is done.

The *Kesavananda* approach to basic features is the closest that the Indian courts have got to meeting the demand for a catalogue of basic features that Sathe makes in the quotation at the start of this section. He does not elaborate whether he conceives of a basic feature 'policy statement' as being one delivered in the course of a judicial opinion or to one to be made extra-judicially. An extra judicial statement is bound to be controversial much like the summary of the *Kesavananda* judgment which was signed by nine judges.[35] Moreover, even if the courts were to list a catalogue of basic features exhaustively while deciding a case before it, the court would be going beyond its judicial role as an 'interpreter' of the Constitution. A theoretical perspective on constitutional adjudication sympathetic to the court's approach in basic structure review would concede only a limited law making power to resolve the dispute before it. The rules of *ratio decidendi* and *obiter dicta* when applied to ascertain the binding legal rule which emerges from a decided case ensures that the court cannot make law in a legislative fashion. Clarity about the law making power of

---

[35] *Kesavananda*, supra n. 6, p. 366.

a court allows us to better understand the appropriate method by which the Indian court identifies basic features of the Constitution. Before I conclude this theoretical enquiry into the judicial role as an interpreter of the Constitution I will examine the court's approach to this problem after *Kesavananda*.

In *Indira Gandhi*, Chandrachud correctly observed that the ratio in *Kesavananda* 'is not that some named features of the Constitution are a part of its basic structure but that the power of amendment cannot be exercised so as to damage or destroy the essential elements or the basic structure of the Constitution.'[36] Having circumscribed the *Kesavananda* ratio not to extend to the basic features identified therein, he then set out a different approach to identifying basic features in these terms: 'one has perforce to examine in each individual case the place of the particular feature in the scheme of our Constitution, its object and purpose, and the consequences of its denial on the integrity of the Constitution as a fundamental instrument of country's governance'.[37] Bhagwati in *Minerva Mills* emphatically reiterates Chandrachud's approach to identifying basic features of the Constitution[38] but unfortunately subsequent cases have not built on this approach. There are several reasons why this approach is appropriate to the task of identifying basic features of the constitution as best adopted by the courts.

There are two key elements to Chandrachud's proposal for identifying basic features of the Constitution. First, basic features must be identified 'in each individual case' and secondly, basic features are those constitutional principles which are central to the 'integrity of the Constitution'. The Supreme Court interprets the Constitution in every case, apart from presidential references under Article 143, to resolve the dispute before it. In common law jurisdictions it is generally understood that 'the Courts can never promulgate a code governing a whole area of law. They are basically limited to playing down single rules or principles. If they pronounce a view in favour of a whole set of principles this view is *obiter* except insofar as it concerns the principle on which the actual decision in the case rests'.[39]

[36] *Indira Gandhi*, supra n. 2, p. 2465.

[37] Ibid.

[38] *Minerva Mills*, supra n. 11, p. 1821 (Bhagwati, J).

[39] J. Raz, *Authority of Law*, Oxford: Clarendon Press, 1979, p. 196.

The failure to recognize this fundamental limitation to judicial law making which distinguishes it from legislation has muddled the debate about identifying basic features of the Constitution. As long as the identification of basic features of the Indian constitution is judicially managed it will develop as constitutional common law rather than through any codifying technique. Such an approach will allow the court to continuously develop new basic features of the constitution as and when they are raised in specific cases before it. When one considers that the Supreme Court's expertise lies in resolving specific disputes rather than abstract moral questions about the core values which should guide our political society then the case-by-case approach to identifying basic features recommends itself. The versatility of common law adjudication technique does allow for modifications and alterations to the basic features of the Constitution by the techniques of overruling and distinguishing precedents, which will require the court to exercise great care in handling this body of law. However, this method when rigorously applied allows the court to adopt a calibrated and nuanced approach to identifying basic features of the constitution which organically responds to contemporary constitutional politics and political morality.

The second element which Chandrachud points to in *Indira Gandhi* relates to a substantive restriction on the general constitutional rules which may be identified as basic features of the Constitution. Basic features are those principles which are central to the 'integrity of the Constitution.' This restriction, unlike the institutional features of common law adjudication considered above, constrains the 'justifying reasons'[40] which may be advanced in support of the argument that a particular principle is a basic feature of the constitution. So when a court considers whether a particular feature of the Constitution—the balance between Part III and Part IV[41]—is central to the Constitution, it must assess whether the normative identity of the Constitution survives even if this feature is excised or modified. By reducing the range of justifying

[40] Compare Aileen Kavanagh, 'The Elusive Divide between Interpretation and Legislation under the Human Rights Act 1998', 24 *Oxford Journal of Legal Studies*, pp. 259–85, (2004).

[41] The balance between Parts III and IV was accepted as a basic feature by Chandrachud in *Minerva Mills*.

reasons which may be offered in support of a basic feature argument, Chandrachud qualifies the basic feature enquiry in a significant manner.

I began this section by considering a plea for a closed catalogue of basic features so that basic structure review may be predictable and to provide normative guidance to the other branches of government. I considered the attempt by the court to provide such a catalogue in *Kesavananda* and concluded that a closed catalogue of basic features cannot result from the common law adjudication techniques that our Supreme Court adopts while interpreting the Constitution. In any event, this approach has been abandoned subsequently in *Indira Gandhi* and *Minerva Mills*. The approach of the Court in the latter cases rightly recognizes the constraints the judicial law making involved in identifying basic features by proceeding on a case–by–case basis and narrowing the range of justifying reasons for accepting a basic feature to normative reasons central to the integrity of the Constitution. It may cynically be said that such a restriction does not amount to much. However, such cynicism would be a general argument directed at the nature of normative restraints on human conduct and not specifically focused on the identification of the basic features of the Constitution.[42] A careful survey of the case law in the last three decades of basic structure review suggests that barring a few extravagant excesses the basic features of the constitution identified by the court have been relatively consistent which suggests that such restraints have been reasonably effective.

Basic Features and the Constitutional Text

The concept of a basic structure as brooding omnipresence in the sky apart from the specific provisions of the Constitution constituting it is too vague and indefinite to provide a yardstick to determine the validity of an ordinary law.[43]

In *Kesavananda*, Sikri took the lead in pronouncing a catalogue of basic features at the end of a survey of the various parts of the

[42] Quentin Skinner 'Some Problems in the Analysis of Political Thought and Action', in J. Tully (ed.) *Meaning and Context: Quentin Skinner and his Critics*, (Princeton 1988) pp. 97–118.

[43] *Indira Gandhi*, supra n. 2, pp. 2388–9 (Mathew, J).

Constitution. This approach does not reveal the factors one considers to identify features of the constitution to be 'basic' and the extent to which these features are set out in the constitutional text. This ruling prompted arguments in subsequent cases that basic features were essentially the 'spirit' of the constitution to be divined by learned judges paying attention to our constitutional history, the aspirations stated in the Preamble or the teachings of moral philosophy. This section analyses the court's development of a distinctive approach to the identification of basic features focusing particularly on its relationship to the textual provisions of the Constitution.

In *Indira Gandhi*, Mathew responded to this issue in an analytically incisive opinion. He pointed out that for a principle to be part of the 'basic structure it must be a terrestrial concept having its habitat within the four corners of the Constitution'.[44] In other words what constitutes the basic structure is not like a 'twinkling star up above the constitution.'[45] He rejected conceptions of the basic structure as a 'brooding omnipresence', and grounded the basic feature enquiry squarely within the judge's role as interpreters of the text of the constitution.

Once it is established that basic features of the Constitution must be supported by the constitutional text there are further questions which remain: what is the extent and kind of textual support that is necessary for a basic feature to exist? How does the court derive general constitutional rules from the detailed constitutional provisions? Are there any parts of the Constitution which enjoy a normative priority over others in the basic features enquiry? Before I engage with any of these questions in the following section, I take note of the approaches which Mathew rejected and assess whether he was right in doing so. First, I examine approaches which use the preamble as a repository of basic features; then consider whether basic features of the Constitution are those features which are pre–eminent in a historical sense and finally whether basic features are pre-constitutional common law principles or natural law values in a different garb.

In *Sajjan Singh*, a decade before the basic structure doctrine was announced in *Kesavananda*, Mudholkar suggested that if there

[44] *Indira Gandhi*, supra n. 2.
[45] Ibid.

are to be limits on amending power then it is the 'preamble which appears to be an epitome of the basic features of the Constitution. Can it not be said that these are the indicia of the intention of the Constituent Assembly to give a permanency to the basic features of the Constitution?'[46] Hegde and Mukherjea reiterated this approach in *Kesavananda* and observed that '[U]nlike in most of the other constitutions, it is comparatively easy in the case of our constitution to discern and determine the basic elements or the fundamental features of our Constitution: for doing so, one has only to look to the Preamble'.[47]

The Preamble to the Indian constitution is an elaborate list of political and moral aspirations proclaimed by 'We, the People' in attractive verse. The preamble proclaims India to be a sovereign, socialist, secular, democratic, republic which secures to its citizens justice, liberty, and equality of various hues and complexions. At first glance, using the preamble as a catalogue of basic features is an attractive option as constitutional values in this part of the Constitution are expressed at a level of generality suitable for basic structure adjudication. On closer scrutiny serious problems arise.

First, the court has consistently held that the preamble is neither a source nor a limit on power.[48] By treating the preamble to be the storehouse of basic features of the Constitution they are invested with an extraordinary status in constitutional adjudication and this does not square up with the court's precedents on the legal authority of the preamble. Second, the question of whether the Preamble was a limit on amending power was expressly considered and rejected in *Kesavananda*. The court considered the historical evidence to establish the sanctity and high regard for the preamble to the Indian Constitution and rejected this argument that the preamble could operate as a limit on Parliamentary power. Hence, it would be inappropriate to resuscitate the preamble through the backdoor by treating these as basic features as this legal proposition has been considered and expressly rejected.

[46] *Sajjan Singh* v. *State of Rajasthan*, AIR 1965 SC 845.
[47] *Kesavananda*, supra n. 6.
[48] This position was stated in *Re Berubari Union*, AIR 1960 SC 845 and has been reiterated ever since including in *Kesavananda*, supra n. 6.

Finally, and most crucially, the preamble is both under and over-inclusive of the basic features of the Constitution. Federalism and the separation of powers are constitutional principles which are fundamental to our constitutional design but find no mention in the preamble. Fraternity is a virtue that the Preamble aspires to achieve but there are few constitutional provisions which meaningfully pursue this proclaimed value. By contrast, equality is a virtue. Other values such as equality are firmly entrenched in the constitutional provisions and enjoy a significant place in the preamble. This brief survey suggests that the preamble is an uncertain guide to the task of identifying the basic features of the Constitution. One would do better to pay closer attention to the values etched out in the detailed provisions of the Constitution rather than use the preamble as a shortcut to achieve this task.

I now examine whether basic features may be identified by relying on the salience of certain values when viewed through the prism of events of political and academic constitutional histories. Earlier in this chapter[49] I had considered whether the basic features of the Constitution are those historically necessary and sufficient political principles without which the Constitution and the Indian Union would not have come into existence. I found that the court had rightly concluded that basic features are those important political and moral principles which come together to make up the normative core of the Indian constitution and hence are not essentially historical in character. In this section I consider the role that our constitutional history plays as an extra-textual source which aids the court in identifying basic features.

The use of constitutional history is best assessed by analysing the court's approach in *Minerva Mills*. Section 4 of the 42nd Constitution (Amendment) Act, 1976 amended Article 31-C to provide that no law giving effect to the policy of securing 'all or any of the principles laid down in Part IV' shall be deemed to be void if it takes away or abridges the fundamental rights to equality, freedom, or property set out in Articles 14, 19, or 31 respectively. It was argued that this amendment destroys the harmony between Parts III and IV of the Constitution by making the fundamental rights conferred by Part III

---

[49] Compare Chapter IV, '"Integral Part" but not Basic Features', pp. 142–7.

subservient to the directive principles of State Policy set out in Part IV of the Constitution. It was suggested that the basic structure doctrine protected the interrelation of the different parts of the Constitution and the 'harmony' between the socio-economic principles in Part IV and the civil and political rights in Part III of the Constituion was a basic feature of the constitution. Chandrachud speaking for the majority agreed and observed that the 'basic structure of the Constitution rests on the foundation that while the directive principles are the mandatory ends of government, those ends can be achieved only through permissible means which are set out in Part III of the Constitution.'[50]

The respondents argued that identifying the principle of harmony between fundamental rights and directive principles as a basic feature of the Constitution resulted in the question of constitutional validity of amendment in 'too wide and academic'[51] a fashion. To assess this claim it is important for us to analyse how Chandrachud identified basic features in this case. He draws heavily from Granville Austin's political history of the freedom movement and drafting history of the Constituent Assembly[52] to identify fundamental rights and directive principles of state policy as the 'conscience of the Constitution'.[53] As the 'Indian Constitution is founded on the bedrock of the balance between Parts III and IV'[54] any amendment which gives absolute primacy to one over the other disturbs this harmony and balance and hence is a violation of the basic structure of the constitution. He emphatically states that anything 'that destroys the balance between the two parts will ipso facto destroy an essential element of the basic structure of our constitution'.[55]

While constitutional history sourced from the Constituent Assembly Debates or from a respected treatise of political history by Granville Austin does provide useful perspectives for the inter- pretation of the constitution. Rules of statutory and constitutional

[50] *Minerva Mills*, supra n. 10, p. 1800.

[51] Ibid., p. 1802.

[52] G. Austin, *Working a Democratic Constitution: A History of the Indian Experience*, New Delhi: Oxford University Press, 2002.

[53] *Minerva Mills*, supra n. 10, pp. 1804–6.

[54] Ibid., p. 1806.

[55] Ibid., p. 1807.

interpretation generally guide and control the extent to which such materials are used to interpret words and phrases in the constitution. In *Minerva Mills* Chandrachud's reliance on such materials to identify basic features such as the harmony between Parts III and IV of the Constitution disregards the text of the Constitution.

Granville Austin suggests that the Indian Constitution is tensely strung between three objectives: preserving national unity, achieving a social revolution, and sustaining democracy. He understands the legal disputes relating to land reform policy as an instance of conflict between the latter two objectives: namely, social revolution and democracy. Whether this is a useful way to understand our early constitutional history is open to considerable doubt![56] In any event Austin's conclusion that conflicting constitutional objectives are reconciled by making directive principles in Part IV of the Constitution subject to fundamental rights in Part III of the Constitution is unsupported by the constitutional text. Chief Justice Chandrachud's reliance on this conclusion results in faulty identification of the 'harmony' between these two parts as a basic feature of the Constitution.

Bhagwati's dissent in *Minerva Mills* is a fitting rebuke to such an approach to identifying basic features. He recognizes the varied approaches to the identification of basic features of the constitution in *Indira Gandhi*, but finds himself in agreement with Mathew 'on one position of a basic and fundamental nature: that whether a particular feature forms part of the basic structure has necessarily to be determined on the basis of the specific provisions of the Constitution.'[57] He examines the key provisions in Part IV, particularly Article 37, to find that the 'socio-economic rights embodied in the Directive Principles are as much a part of human rights as the Fundamental Rights'[58] in Part III. He categorically rejects the idea that these parts of the Constitution conflict with each other, but reasons that in the contingent event that a conflict arose between fundamental rights

---

[56] See U. Baxi '"The Little Done, The Vast Undone"—Some Reflections on Reading Granville Austin's *The Indian Constitution*' in (1967) *Journal of the Indian Law Institute*, 9, p. 323 and R. Dhavan, *Supreme Court of India: A Socio-Legal Critique of its Juristic Techniques*, Bombay: N.M. Tripathi P. Ltd, 1977.

[57] *Minerva Mills*, supra n. 10, p. 1821.

[58] *Minerva Mills*, supra n. 10, p. 1845 (Bhagwati J).

and directive principles, Parliament may respond as it deems fit as the constitution is silent on this question.[59] Bhagwati engaged with the constitutional history behind the provisions being interpreted and analysed the differential legal force of fundamental rights of citizens and directive principles which imposed obligations directly on the state[60] but reiterated that a basic feature may be identified primarily by an interpretation of the constitutional text.

Bhagwati identified two basic features of the Constitution which were applicable in *Minerva Mills*: judicial review and the limited amending power of Parliament. Both these features rest on an interpretation of the provisions of the Constitution: Articles 32 and 226 which provide for judicial review and unamended Article 368 which regulates amending power respectively. These provisions read together led Bhagwati to the conclusion that the judiciary was the institution with a constitutional mandate, and especially equipped to interpret the Constitution as a legal document, to maintain the constitutional distribution of powers and functions and the supremacy of the constitution.

So far in this section I have considered the process of identifying basic features of the constitution with a particular focus on the use of the preamble and constitutional history as an aid to this task. The analysis of *Minerva Mills* suggests that both these aids are unsuitable as they give inadequate attention to the core task of constitutional interpretation, where the court pays attention to the constitutional text and identifies only such principles which may be understood to be a part of the normative core of constitution. The preamble and constitutional history are relevant only in so far as they provide additional justifying reasons in support of a conclusion adequately supported by the constitutional text.

Before I conclude this section, I briefly consider two other modes of identifying basic features where the court may disregard the textual provisions to varied extents. First, the court may consider basic features to be those common law principles which are pre-constitutional in origin and second, basic features may be viewed as natural law or higher law principles. The Indian court has not considered either

---

[59] Ibid., p. 1851 (Bhagwati J).
[60] Ibid., pp. 1842–53 (Bhagwati J).

of these options at length and hence the analysis of these issues will be brief.

The Canadian court's use of unwritten constitutional principles, including the rule of law, democracy, federalism, in addition to the written constitutional rules, has led some commentators to suggest that these unwritten principles are best understood as pre-existing common law principles or natural law values or some combination of the two. Where such underlying constitutional principles are traced back to Coke in *Dr Bonham's Case*[61] the argument is legal and historical in character. However, these fundamental principles may be understood to 'articulate basic legal assumptions that inhere in the human social condition itself and that therefore possess normative force independent of legislative enactment'.[62] In this case the argument is moral and political in character. Sometimes, as T.R.S. Allan proposes,[63] these two types of arguments are combined together and offered as a comprehensive theory of constitutional justice. Even this sketchy account of these plausible sources of basic features of the constitution alerts us to considerable difficulties that 'fit' with the historical, doctrinal, and philosophical understandings manifest in the Indian cases. Keeping aside the merits of such approaches[64] for the moment I proceed by noting that the Indian court has not seriously attempted to ground basic features in either of these approaches and for the purposes of this work our enquiry need not proceed any further.

I conclude this section by reiterating that the Indian courts have, in Bhagwati's words, denied that basic features

consist of any abstract ideals to be found outside the provisions of the Constitution. The Preamble no doubt enumerates the great concepts embodying the ideological aspirations of the people but these concepts are particularized and their essential features delineated in the various provisions of the Constitution. It is these specific provisions in the body of the Constitution which determine the type of democracy which the founders

[61] (1610) 8 Co Rep 114.

[62] Mark D. Walters, 'The Common Law Constitution in Canada: Return of Lex Non Scripta as Fundamental Law', in 51 *U Toronto LJ* 91 (2001) 93.

[63] Trevor Allan, *Constitutional Justice*, Oxford: Oxford University Press, 2003.

[64] See John Leclair, 'Canada's Unfathomable Unwritten Constitutional Principles', in 27 *Queen's LJ* 389 (2002) for criticism of such theories.

of that instrument established; the quality and nature of justice, political, social, and economic which they aimed to realize, the content of liberty of thought and expression which they entrenched in that document and the scope of equality of status and of opportunity which they enshrined in it. These specific provisions enacted in the Constitution alone can determine the basic structure of the Constitution. These specific provisions, either separately or in combination, determine the content of the great concepts set out in the Preamble. It is impossible to spin out any concrete concept of basic structure out of the gossamer concepts set out in the Preamble. The specific provisions of the Constitution are the stuff from which the basic structure has to be woven.[65]

The paragraph above is worth quoting in full only to take note of the emphasis on the central role that the text of the Constitution plays in identifying basic features and the unwillingness to deploy the preamble or other extra-constitutional materials to this task. This marked distinction between text and extra-textual resources may be taken in the extreme to reflect a formalist conception of constitutional interpretation where the words of the Constitution yield meaning in a stable and determinate fashion unaided by other linguistic resources. More nominally it clarifies that any interpretation of the constitution should *begin* with the constitutional provisions and that modes of interpretation which find no support in the constitutional text are inappropriate to the task of identifying basic features of the Constitution. No part of this work argues for a formalist or literalist model of constitutional adjudication and all that the preceding section seeks to do is to discard modes of identifying basic features of the constitution which fail to meet the threshold requirements of the task of 'interpreting' the 'text' of the constitution.

THE BASIC FEATURES OF THE CONSTITUTION: IN LIEU OF A CONCLUSION

I think there is near unanimity that there are at least five features that can be regarded as essential and basic. The first is secularism; second, democracy; third, rule of law; fourth, federalism; and the fifth is an independent judiciary with the power of judicial review.[66]

[65] *Minerva Mills*, supra n. 10, pp. 1821–2.
[66] Soli Sorabjee, 'The Ideal Remedy: A Valediction', in Pran Chopra (ed.) *The Supreme Court versus the Constitution* , New Delhi: Sage Publications, 2006, p. 204.

So far in this chapter I have analysed the nature and character of basic features of the Constitution as general constitutional rules which are identifiable by an interpretation of constitutional provisions on a case-by-case basis. These clarifications, though crucial to the enterprise of identifying basic features, do not help us isolate among the many features of the constitution which enjoy textual support those which may be said to be 'basic'. In other words, of all the features of the Constitution what marks features which are basic to the Constitution. In this concluding section I critically examine the extent to which the courts have provided us with an answer to this question. Further, I explore whether any particular theoretical approach to constitutional adjudication helps us cast an explanatory and justificatory framework around the courts' effort. I conclude by noting that the task of identifying basic features is inherently prone to disagreement, and the best that I can do is to prune the range of justifying reasons which may properly be offered in support of the claim that a particular feature of the Constitution is basic in character.

I began this section with a bold and forthright assertion by the ex-Attorney General of India, Soli Sorabjee, speaking at a seminar examining whether the basic structure doctrine was inimical to the development of Indian constitutional law. He proposes that at the least five features of the Constitution—secularism,[67] democracy,[68] rule of law,[69] federalism,[70] and independence of the judiciary[71]—are 'unanimously' thought to comprise the basic features of the Constitution. While reiterating the possibility that the court may add to these features of the constitution, his statement would draw

[67] *S.R. Bommai* v. *Union of India*, AIR 1994 SC 1918; *R.C. Poudyal* v. *Union of India*, AIR 1993 SC 1804: *Pravin Bhai Toghadia* v. *State of Karnataka*, AIR 2004 SC 2081.

[68] *Indira Gandhi* v. *Raj Narain*, AIR 1975 SC 2299; *Kihoto Hollohan* v. *Zachilhu*, 1992 (Supp) 2 SCC 651; *Union of India* v. *Association of Democratic Reforms*, AIR 2002 SC 2113.

[69] *Indira Gandhi* v. *Raj Narain*, supra n. 68; *Rameshwar Prasad* v. *Union of India*, (2006) 2 SCC 1.

[70] *S.R. Bommai*, supra n. 67 and *Rameshwar Prasad*, supra n. 69.

[71] *Sambamurthy* v. *State of AP, Minerva Mills*, AIR 1987 SC 663, *Kihoto Hollohan*, supra n. 68; *Chandra Kumar* v. *Union of India*, AIR 1997 SC 1125; *Sampath Kumar* v. *Union of India*, AIR 1987 SC 386.

adequate support from the court's precedents across the last three decades. Arguably socialism[72] and equality[73] merit a mention as two other features which have played a significant, though not consistent, role in basic structure review cases. Sorabjee's confidence in naming these basic features rests assuredly on a reading of the court's precedents, but this masks the several disagreements over how the court has, and should go about identifying these basic features.

In the previous section I noted that the courts were keen to establish that the basic features were not to be identified using resources extrinsic to the constitution. The basic features identified are particular to the Indian constitution and need not be generally applicable to all constitutions in all places. This point may be illustrated by two useful examples. First, in *R.C. Poudyal v. Union of India*[74] the reservation of a seat in the legislative assembly of Sikkim for the elected representative of the Buddhist clergy and the reservation of seats for a tribe far in excess of its proportion in the population were challenged as damaging or destroying the basic features, democracy, and secularism. The court upheld the legislative reservations in this case but for our purposes I must turn to the argument in court that a prohibition against discrimination on the ground of religion is not a basic feature of a democratic state. He contended that the constitution of Cyprus had no provision on prohibiting discrimination on the basis of religion and was nevertheless a democratic state; this was evidence that religious non-discrimination was not a necessary feature of a democratic constitution. Chief Justice L.M. Sharma, speaking for the majority ruled that the 'example is fallacious as it assumes that fundamental features of all constitutions are same or similar. The basic philosophy of a constitution is related to various elements including culture and tradition, social and political conditions, and the historical background.'[75] The court clearly establishes in this case that the basic feature enquiry is one rooted in the Indian Constitution as it is, and such features are not to be identified by evaluating

[72] *Minerva Mills*, supra n. 10; *Samatha v. State of AP*, AIR 1997 SC 3297; *Sanjeev Coke v. Bharathi Coking Coal*, AIR 1983 SC 239.

[73] *Indira Gandhi*, supra n. 69; *Indra Sawhney v. Union of India (I)*, 1992 Supp (3) SCC 217.

[74] AIR 1993 SC 1804.

[75] *Poudyal* 1823 (Sharma, CJ).

constitutional practice in other countries or the correlation between theoretical conceptions of democracy and secularism. In this case, the court's particularist approach to interpreting the constitution highlights the embedded character of basic features in the text and constitutional practice in India.

The rooted character of basic features may be illustrated in a different fashion. The principle of subsidiarity has come to occupy a very important role in organizing the distribution of powers and functions among multi-tier institutions of government. It is argued that subsidiarity is a preferred principle for the distribution of power as it promotes the twin objectives of deepening democracy and promoting efficiency.[76] After the Constitution (73rd Amendment) Act, 1993 and the Constitution (74th Amendment) Act, 1993 the Indian constitution has institutionalized a multi-tier state structure but does not articulate a principled basis for the distribution of powers and functions across these layers of government. The principle of subsidiarity may offer the best constitutional principle to systematize what presently appears to be a haphazard distribution, but the court cannot confer on it the status of a 'basic feature' of the constitution on this basis. The constitutional provisions certainly support the claim that 'federalism' is a basic feature as the principle which governs the centre-state relationship. The constitution is silent on principles which will govern a multi-tier governance structure and in these circumstances it is not open to the court to infer into the constitution the best available theoretical principle to organize these relations.

In this section, I have identified two senses in which basic features of the constitution are intrinsic to the Indian constitution: first, basic features are not general constitutional rules which must be 'basic' or central to the integrity of every constitutional document but only those which are central to the Indian Constitution. Second, identifying basic features is not about finding the best general constitutional rules by which Indian Constitutional law may be organized but identifying the general constitutional rules which provide the foundations for our constitutional provisions, however

[76] Nick Barber, 'The Limited Modesty of Subsidiarity', 11 *European LJ* 308–25 (2003).

imperfect such principles may be. Hence, by protecting basic features of the constitution the court is safeguarding the moral and political precommitments in the constitutional text.

While there is unanimity that the basic feature enquiry must begin by interpreting the constitutional text, controversy breaks out on how general constitutional rules are to be derived from the detailed constitutional provisions and which of these rules is basic to the Constitution. Though Sorabjee is right in asserting that there is a rather stable set of basic features of the constitution, I have in this section set out the manner in which basic features are grounded in the constitutional text of the Indian Constitution.

I began this Chapter with the criticism that the Supreme Court identifies basic features in a whimsical adhoc fashion. I set out to show that this criticism is misplaced as the court has developed an interpretive technique to identify basic features appropriate for a common law court interpreting a constitutional text. I have identified, analysed, and subsequently discarded several methods proposed by the court and academic commentators and carefully set out the most viable method by which basic features may be identified. In order to provide a fuller account of the sense in which a basic feature may be said to be interpretation of the constitution I must articulate the model of constitutional adjudication which I adopt in this work. I may begin to address these controversies about the nature of constitutional interpretation by developing a typology of the methods by which principles may be said to arise from the constitutional provisions.

Basic features of the constitution are those constitutional principles which arise by implication from the constitutional provisions. It is suggested that as they are not directly expressed in the constitution, there is a greater degree of ambiguity attached to the identification of these principles. As I discuss in the next chapter, where we consider the question of constitutional adjudication in greater detail, this is not necessarily the case. There is no doubt that identifying basic features of the Constitution raises difficult problems of ambiguity and uncertainty in constitutional adjudication, but these difficulties are neither unique nor devastating to basic structure review or the task of identifying basic features of the constitution.

5
Legitimacy of the
Basic Structure Doctrine

This essay proceeds from the standpoint that the 'basic structure' doctrine is anti-democratic and counter-majoritarian in character, and that unelected judges have assumed vast political power not given to them by the constitution.[1]

The basic structure doctrine has, since its inception in *Kesavananda* in 1973, often been criticized as being illegitimate. In this work I have anticipated and countered many dominant strands of these criticisms. By breaking basic structure review into its component parts—constitutional justification; nature, scope and standards of review, and the grounds of review—and then identifying and analysing the relevant case law on each element of the doctrine. This elaboration and analysis of the scope and content of the doctrine and its precise contours in practice allows for a nuanced and accurate assessment of its legitimacy.

In this chapter I will respond to the key challenges to the legitimacy of the basic structure doctrine by engaging directly with the normative arguments about legitimacy of the doctrine while building on arguments of legal doctrine carried out so far. While there is no doubt that the range of appropriate criticisms of the basic structure doctrine is limited by its actual content and practice, I will begin by classifying and consolidating all the significant arguments against the

[1] Raju Ramachandran, 'The Supreme Court and the Basic Structure Doctrine' in B.N. Kirpal et al. (eds) *Supreme But Not Infallible*, New Delhi: Oxford University Press, 2000, p. 108.

doctrine into types of legitimacy arguments and then respond to each type of argument in turn.

In the quotation excerpted above, Raju Ramachandran questions the anti-democratic character, and more generally the political legitimacy, of the basic structure doctrine. In this chapter I am concerned with the overall legitimacy of the doctrine which includes its political, moral, and sociological legitimacy. Any assessment of the legitimacy of the basic structure doctrine will draw on a general theoretical understanding of constitutional adjudication and legitimacy. I begin the chapter by sketching out how I understand the legitimacy question.

Legitimacy may be generally understood to be an assessment of whether an authority or a particular action is justifiable by reference to a set of criteria. The criteria by which legitimacy is assessed will vary greatly depending on the type of authority—a state regime or a parent—as well as the relevant circumstances kind of action taken. Legitimacy acquires a positive or normative character depending on the kinds of criteria that one employs in your assessment. Even where normative legitimacy is assessed, often this enquiry is fact-sensitive and temporal in character. The kind of criteria by which legitimacy is assessed allows us to categorize legitimacy to be legal, political, moral, or sociological. Often, claims of illegitimacy, particularly with reference to judicial decisions, combine these varied criteria to make a cumulative assessment. I now briefly examine how the constitutional legitimacy of a judicial decision may be assessed.

Richard Fallon advances a sophisticated account of the concept of legitimacy[2] in constitutional theory which aids the enquiry in this chapter immensely. He follows Joseph Raz in suggesting that '[c]onstitutional theory comprises two major parts, an account of the authority of constitutions and an account of the way constitutions should be interpreted'.[3] These two aspects of constitutional theory are partially interdependent but may also be explored independently.

[2] Richard Fallon, 'Legitimacy and the Constitution', 118 *Harvard L Rev* 1789 (2005).

[3] Joseph Raz, 'On the Authority and Interpretation of Constitutions: Some Preliminaries' in L. Alexander (ed.) *Constitutionalism*, Cambridge: Cambridge University Press, 1998, p. 157.

An enquiry into constitutional legitimacy of the basic structure doctrine rests on the authority of the Indian Constitution and a model of constitutional interpretation consistent with this account of constitutional authority.

In this chapter I focus on the mode of constitutional interpretation and do not fully explore the extent to which this is an adequate account of constitutional authority. As I am concerned with the legitimacy of the basic structure doctrine—and not the legitimacy of the constitution in its entirety, I confine the discussion to an evaluation of the judicial role in creating and sustaining the use of the doctrine.

Fallon's three-part division of legitimacy into legal, sociological, and moral concepts depending on the criteria by which legitimacy is assessed allows us to organize the varied criticisms of the basic structure doctrine. The concluding part of this chapter will bring together these strands of analysis to present an integrated account of how the basic structure doctrine is constitutionally legitimate.

LEGAL LEGITIMACY

To assess the legal legitimacy of a judicial decision one evaluates whether it complies with the legal norms applicable to the case. The legal norms which guide judicial decision making include those written into the constitution as well as those norms developed by the court interpreting the constitutional text. Both these types of norms do not determine the judicial outcome in all cases: they may be indeterminate or under-determinate in their guidance in particular cases. In these circumstances the decision maker enjoys some discretion in the interpretation of particular norms. Even where constitutional norms are determinate courts may consider other moral reasons to develop the law with an innovative decision. But such moral reasons for change must be weighed against the moral duties on judges to maintain continuity in a legal system. This is a matter I consider more fully in the section on moral legitimacy below.

Before I examine the legal legitimacy of basic structure doctrine we must take note of the objection that the classification of legitimacy into moral and legal assumes a positivist view of law. More specifically it seems to assume that criteria for legal legitimacy do not include moral values, and that these two types of legitimacy may be evaluated separately. The separation of law and morals in positivist legal theory is an axiom related to the identity and validity of laws and not to the evaluation of the legitimacy of a legal rule.[4] There is significant theoretical disagreement about whether moral criteria should play any role in answering the question as to whether a law exists. Once it is agreed that a law does exist, as the basic structure doctrine undoubtedly does, an enquiry into whether the law is justifiable or legitimate requires a wider and more multi-dimensional enquiry using various normative criteria including moral criteria. Even a positivist scholar would insist that an account of legitimacy should rely on moral reasoning and would simultaneously hold the view that the separation of law and morals is critical to debates about the identity and validity of law. A non-positivist scholar may argue that moral legitimacy lies at the core of the enquiry into what the law is, and not merely an assessment of its legitimacy. It is not necessary for the purposes of this chapter for me to deny the truth of the non-positivist claim about the relationship between law and morals. In this chapter, I do not fully engage with the philosophical debates on the nature of law as a view on this important question does not settle the legitimacy of the basic structure doctrine. To the extent that I respond to the moral legitimacy of basic structure review, I certainly am not avoiding the key issues raised by a non-positivist account of law.

So while the enquiry into legitimacy in this chapter will evaluate the basic structure doctrine using moral criteria, the separation of legitimacy into legal, moral, and sociological categories allows us to approach these discrete criteria in independent sections. The analytical benefits of such an exercise are manifold: the clarity of exposition is supplemented by our ability to respond to the varied strands of the existing Indian debates on the basic structure doctrine appropriately. The unequivocal admission that these are intricately connected and interdependent enquiries accommodates the non-positivist view that legal legitimacy should include moral criteria. Now I proceed to critically analyse the debates on legal legitimacy.

---

[4] Contrast W.J. Waluchow, *Inclusive Legal Positivism*, Oxford: Clarendon Press, 1994.

The *Kesavananda* opinion sparked an efflorescence of constitutional criticism and commentary through the 1970s and 1980s,
the intensity of which has never been repeated again in Indian
constitutional history. Almost every constitutional lawyer of the
period, and several political commentators, strenuously denounced
or commended the court's decision, and many of them subsequently
revised and modified their stand.[5] Many of these earlier criticisms,
together with more recent ones, dispute whether the basic structure
doctrine can be understood as an interpretation of the constitution.
Three arguments regarding the legal illegitimacy of the basic structure
doctrine are often raised. Firstly, that the *Kesavananda* court had no
textual basis for its conclusion; secondly it is argued that the doctrine
is not supported by the constitutional text and establishes implied
limitations divined by the judges unaided by the constitution. This
second objection is supplemented by the claim that the court has no
authority to read implied limitations into the constitution. Thirdly, it
is argued that if the objections above are valid then it follows that the
court effectively amended the constitution in the guise of interpreting
it, an action it has no legal authority to do. These three arguments
rest on particular understandings of the nature of constitutional
interpretation and are dealt with in turn.

Express Constitutional Meaning

A significant strand of the criticism of the basic structure doctrine
is rooted in the claim that the doctrine is not warranted by the
constitutional text. More specifically it is suggested that no article of
the constitution contains the phrase 'basic structure' or any equivalent
phrase. Further, it is argued that the constitutional text does not even
indirectly support the impact and consequences of the doctrine.
These are arguments about the express and implied meanings of the
constitution and I will deal with express meanings in this section and
implied meanings in the next. They draw support in part from the
lack of clarity in the justifications offered by the plurality opinions

[5] S.P. Sathe, *Judicial Activism in India*, New Delhi: Oxford University Press,
2002, pp. 77–8 on H.M. Seervai's volte face on the question of judicial review of
constitutional amendments. See 'Introduction' Chapter for a fuller account of the
constitutional debates of the time.

of the court in the early basic structure cases but ultimately rest on a misunderstanding of the nature of interpretive activity engaged in by courts.

These arguments assume that the words in the constitution present neatly carved out textual formulae which resolve complex interpretive problems which come before the court, thereby rendering unnecessary any further interpretation of the text or enquiry into constitutional design or function. This literalist approach to constitutional interpretation ostensibly requires limited resources: the text of the constitution, lexicographical aids to interpretation, and the rules of interpretation developed in the common law.[6] By adopting such a view of constitutional interpretation commentators seldom find it necessary to articulate substantive reasons to support one interpretation of the constitution as superior to the other, and by denying the possibility of real interpretive choice the conclusions of the court are presented as indisputably right or wrong.

In Chapters 2 and 3 I have carefully analysed several cases to ascertain the constitutional basis for the basic structure doctrine. There is no argument in this work that the basic structure doctrine is expressly set out in any particular article or set of articles read together. This is not an altogether surprising feature of any constitutional doctrine: the doctrine of separation of powers which maintains the distribution of powers between the branches of government and the doctrine of pith and substance which assists the court to determine the zones of legislative and executive competence between state and union governments are similarly not spelt out in any constitutional provision. There is no doubt that both these doctrines are valid and legitimate constitutional law despite the lack of express constitutional sanction.

The expectation that every proposition or doctrine of constitutional law will have an express constitutional basis relies on an incorrect literalist understanding of constitutional law and adjudication. It gives no account of the extensive role played by constitutional

---

[6] A survey of constitutional commentaries in India will confirm that the literalist mode of constitutional interpretation still reigns supreme. For example see H.M. Seervai, *Constitutional Law of India*, Bombay: N.M. Tripathi P. Ltd., 1994 (4th edn Vol. 1), pp. 172–200.

interpretation of the court in fleshing out the inert provisions of any constitution. Decided cases become binding legal propositions through their application and refinement in subsequent cases where courts control the scope and application of these decisions through relevant rules of precedent. These legal propositions in various areas of constitutional law, taken together, constitute a body of constitutional common law which has developed enormously over the last fifty-seven years. There may be significant differences in weight and malleability of legal rules which rest on the constitutional text and those that are identified as constitutional common law. This is not a topic which I will explore further in this work.[7] For the limited purposes of the argument in this chapter, it is sufficient for us to show that constitutional doctrine not expressly warranted by the constitutional text may still be a legitimate interpretation of the constitution.

If I am correct about the nature of constitutional doctrine spelt out above, then the illegitimacy of the basic structure doctrine cannot be because it is not expressly supported by the constitutional text. Then such a doctrine may be illegitimate as it goes beyond the proper limits of using implied meanings in constitutional interpretation. In Chapters 1 and 2 I argued that the court developed a novel approach to the interpretation of the constitution in *Kesavananda*, where the court no longer interpreted words or phrases set out in specific articles in isolation and instead sought to make sense of the relevant articles in the context of the wider constitutional mandate gleaned from the constitution as a whole. For example, Sikri in *Kesavananda* interpreted the word 'amendment' in Article 368 by first conducting a conspectus or survey of a wide range of constitutional provisions paying special attention to the fundamental rights and directive principles chapters to gather insights into the appropriate scope of the amending power under Article 368. Sawant adopts a similar approach in *Bommai* to conclude that the constitutional value of secularism constrains and guides the executive power to issue proclamation of President's Rule

---

[7] For varied accounts of the nature and significance of constitutional doctrine see D. Strauss, 'Common Law Constitutional Interpretation', 63 *Univ Chicago L Rev*, pp. 877–935 (1996) and C. Fried, 'Constitutional Doctrine', 107 *Harvard L Rev*, pp. 1140–57 (1994).

under Article 356. This approach to constitutional interpretation, which may be described as a 'structural approach', has not been consistently adopted by all judges in these cases or by other courts deciding basic structure review cases. Despite this lack of unanimity in judicial opinion, arguably a structural approach to constitutional interpretation offers a potential explanation for the legal legitimacy of the basic structure doctrine.

Implied Meaning

Implied constitutional meanings have played a significant role in the court's constitutional interpretation in basic structure review cases. Implied meaning plays a significant role in arguments about the constitutional basis of basic structure review and the identification of basic features of the constitution. The process of implication in constitutional interpretation has been differently expressed in three types of arguments in basic structure cases: first, the doctrine of implied limitations; second, the doctrine of necessary implication and third, the claim that the basic structure doctrine involves a 'structural' interpretation of the constitution. Before I explore each of these in turn I will critically examine the nature of implications in constitutional interpretation and more specifically, ascertain the extent to which it needs special justification over and above what is usually provided for express meanings.

The distinction between implied and express meanings rests on the directness with which meaning is conveyed.[8] As meaning in constitutional interpretation is conveyed through written text, the text may communicate with varied degrees of directness. For example, one of the enduring debates in Indian constitutional law is the interpretation of Article 21 of the constitution which provides that 'No person shall be deprived of his life or personal liberty except according to procedure established by law.'[9] The provision directly imposes restraints on the executive branch of government to act within the boundaries of the enacted law. Whether this provision imposes any restraints on the legislative branch of government has been the

---

[8] Jeremy Kirk, 'Constitutional Implications (I): Nature, Legitimacy, Classification and Examples', *Melbourne Univ L Rev*, pp. 645–76 (2000).

[9] Constitution of India, 1950, Article 21.

subject of intense debate.[10] As the fundamental rights entrenched in Part III of the constitution generally bind all three branches of government, the proposition that Article 21 binds the legislature is a reasonable one. Moreover, restraints on legislative power to protect the life and liberty of citizens arguably have as much significance as the restraints on executive power. In this instance, as in many others, the important questions in constitutional interpretation cannot be resolved by resorting to the direct meaning ascertained from the constitutional provision. Further, the relatively indirect meaning of the provision is more significant in its impact on the protection of life and liberty and allows for the fundamental rights in Part III of the constitution to be read consistently.

This example illustrates a few crucial insights into the distinction between express and implied meaning: first, I do not examine the implied meanings of a provision because it is necessarily ambiguous or uncertain. Implications need to be taken into account even where the provision is phrased clearly and plainly in order to respond to situations to which the provision clearly applies but is under-determinate as to outcomes. Second, it is not always the case that express meanings are more important or significant than implied ones. The relative importance of express and implied meanings is contingent on the context in which they are applied. Finally, the directness with which a constitutional provision conveys meaning is a matter of degree which rests on the language conventions of the community of speakers and interpreters. So where a batsman in a cricket match being sledged by the bowling side is asked to 'occasionally try to use his bat to hit the ball', the implied suggestion that he should stop leaving the ball or using his pads is the more immediate purpose of the sledge than the direct request for him to use the bat.

In constitutional interpretation the 'important question is always what the constitution means; whether the ideas are communicated directly or indirectly is incidental'.[11] Hence, for many of the reasons explored above the justifying reasons which make one interpretation

---

[10] S.P. Sathe, *Judicial Activism in India*, New Delhi: Oxford University Press, 2002, pp. 107–12.

[11] J. Kirk, supra n. 8, p. 629.

of a constitution better or more legitimate in any case need not be weighted differently whether I am applying express or implied meanings. Nevertheless, the courts have historically been suspicious of the role of implications in interpretations and have attempted to develop doctrines to fence in the range of implications which may be legitimately considered. The Indian courts have been no exception to this general trend. In basic structure review cases implied meanings have been restrained through three distinct doctrinal formulations. I will examine each of these critically to ascertain the character and scope of these limits and whether they are successful in bestowing basic structure review with more legitimacy.

Doctrine of Implied Limitations

The doctrine of implied limitations was put forth with great conviction by lead counsel in *Kesavananda*, Nani Palkhivala. The doctrine draws on the administrative law rule relating to jurisdiction which posits that every grant of power is limited both explicitly and implicitly by the nature of the grant. In other words, a statute must be construed in a manner that maintains the balance between its parts by applying those explicit and inherent limitations necessary to promote the scheme and design of the instrument. [12] Palkhivala argued that this principle should apply to Parliament's power to amend the constitution which was, like its ordinary legislative power, conferred by the constitution and relied on varied precedents of the Privy Council, Canadian, Irish, Australian, and US courts to support this claim. Six majority judges in *Kesavananda* led by Sikri accepted this claim, but seven judges including Khanna explicitly rejected the doctrine of implied limitations as having no foundation in the constitution. Since its rejection in *Kesavananda* the doctrine of implied limitations has played no part in the future judicial discourse on basic structure review.

The attempt to import the doctrine of implied limitations from its common law milieu to aid constitutional interpretation has several limitations. First, the constitutional version of the administrative law doctrine drew little support from the constitutional text. As the Indian

[12] Nani Palkhivala, *Our Constitution Defaced and Defiled*, Delhi: Macmillan Co. of India, pp. 32–7.

courts have relied on text based implications in basic structure review cases, the doctrine found little support. Moreover, as Rajeev Dhavan carefully points out, the doctrine could draw little or no support from other jurisdictions where it was considered by the courts.[13] Any effort to articulate a sound doctrine of implied limitations will need to be grounded in a wider theoretical understanding of the nature of sovereignty and the distinction between amending and constituent power.[14] These operate as broader justifying reasons and are particularly critical to the success of the doctrine of implied limitations as the version argued before the Indian courts and accepted by six of the *Kesavananda* judges paid scant attention to the constitutional text.

Dhavan, in an early review of the basic structure doctrine concludes that the *Kesavananda* court 'managed to invent a whole new theory of implied limitations'.[15] Coming as it does, at the end of his effective criticism of the doctrine of implied limitations, this conclusion is ambiguous about whether he understands the basic structure doctrine to rest on the common law doctrine of implied limitations or simply that it is sustained by constitutional implications of a different sort. In this section I have suggested that the doctrine of implied limitations plays no role in the judicial discourse on the basic structure doctrine since *Kesavananda* and this is a good outcome. In the sections below I will explore the role that implied meaning does play in basic structure cases and demonstrate why these implications offer a legitimate and persuasive interpretation of the constitution.

Doctrine of Necessary Implication

The most well-developed common law test for identifying those implications which may be legitimately drawn is the 'doctrine of necessary implication'. This test is often portrayed as investing the

[13] Rajeev Dhavan, 'The Basic Structure Doctrine-A Footnote Comment', in R. Dhavan and A. Jacobs (eds), *Indian Constitution: Trends and Developments*, Bombay: N.M. Tripathi P. Ltd, 1978, pp. 160–78, 164–5.

[14] D. Conrad, 'Limitation of Amendment Procedures and Constituent Power', in D. Conrad (ed.) *Zwischen Den Traditionen: Probleme Des Verfassungsrechts Und Der Rechtskultur in Indien and Pakistant*, Stuttgart: Franz Steiner Verlag, 1999, pp. 48–9.

[15] R. Dhavan, supra n. 13, p. 164.

task of judicial interpretation drawing on implications with objectivity and neutrality thereby restricting judicial choice and enhancing the legitimacy of legal decisions. However, on closer examination the doctrine does not deliver on this promise.

The 'necessity' invoked by the doctrine clearly requires a greater degree of persuasiveness of acceptable implications and rules out frivolous and stray implications. However familiar problems which plague the interpretive task return to haunt this canon of interpretation. First, it is unclear whether the necessity required is logical or practical. Logical necessity exists where the implications sought to be drawn follow from the propositions of law as a matter of logical deduction. I may illustrate logical necessity by an example from the game of tennis that a player, who fails to keep the ball within the boundaries of the playing area, and a second rule provides that the boundaries of the playing area are measured from the inside edge of the marker line, then it logically follows that if a ball hits the boundary markers and no part of the ball touches the insides of the line, the point is lost. Though the two rules read together do not expressly set out the consequences of a ball hitting the boundary marker lines, it may be logically implied that in this instance the ball should be ruled out of the playing area. In this case, the rules fully determine the outcome but there may be cases where logical necessity may under-determine outcomes or may be indeterminate. It is clear from the above example that the outcome of the rules is not a practical necessity. The game of tennis would sustain the same level of skill and achievement even if a ball hitting the boundary markers was taken to be in rather than out. The doctrine of necessary implication may, in a particular case, sustain various implications that are logically or practically necessary and this ambiguity may result in different outcomes with the same set of rules.

The doctrine of necessary implication has not engaged the attention of the Indian courts in basic structure review cases. However, Seervai, in his *Commentaries on the Constitution*, seeks to justify the doctrine using this canon of construction and this explanation has gained significant currency. A critical examination of these efforts is both insightful and essential for an understanding of the basic structure doctrine. Seervai begins his explanation of the basic structure doctrine by citing a passage from the Privy Council's ruling in *R* v. *Burah*[16] on the principles of interpretation of a constitution. The court held:

If what has been done is legislation within the general words which give the power, and if it violates no express condition or restriction by which that power is limited... it is not for a Court of Justice to inquire further or to enlarge constructively these conditions and limitations.[17]

There is some disagreement whether this opinion on the scope of legislative power in a legal system where the doctrine of Parliamentary sovereignty is the norm applies without modification to a different constitutional tradition such as India. Seervai suggests that this interpretive principle does apply with two important caveats. First, the word 'express' 'does not exclude what is necessarily implied.'[18] Second, he proposes that 'the nature of a constitution may be important on a question of construction'.[19] For the purposes of this section, I will focus on the first caveat on necessary implications.

Seervai proceeds to show how the ambiguities resident in Article 368 necessarily imply that amending power in the Indian Constitution is limited in character. Let us examine one such ambiguity to ascertain the type of necessity that Seervai employs in this discussion. The central issue in Article 368 is whether the 'constituent power' to amend 'any' article allows Parliament to repeal all of the provisions of the constitution. Seervai answers the question in the negative as Article 368(2) provides that when an amending bill receives the assent of the President 'the constitution shall stand amended'. Thus he concludes that:

[A] constitution which is repealed does not stand at all, much less does it stand amended. It is a necessary implication of the constitution standing amended, that all its provisions cannot be repealed, and the word 'any' does not mean 'all'.[20]

The necessity invoked by Seervai is logical and rests on the premise that every word in a constitutional or statutory document should be

---

[16] *R* v. *Burah* (1878) 3 AC 889 (PC) (India).

[17] Ibid., 193–4.

[18] H.M. *Seervai, Constitutitonal Law of India*, Bombay: N.M. Tripathi P. Ltd, 1994 (4th edn, 1994) p. 3140.

[19] Ibid.

[20] H.M. Seervai, supra n. 18, p. 3141.

invested with significant meaning. This style of argument seems to be circular, as it assumes its conclusion: and moreover, fails to provide a strong justification. The logical necessity only makes sense if one assumes, with Seervai, that the phrase 'the constitution shall stand amended' carries with it both a formal consequence of the amending procedure as well as the substantive requirement that a full-fledged constitutional text must subsist at the end of the amendment carried out under Article 368. Even where the constitution is repealed in its entirety, there is no doubt that a constitutional arrangement continues to exist. This arrangement will consist of an amalgam of political conventions, statutory laws, and the common law rules much like the British Constitution. No doubt these constitutional norms are not contained in a single document but they are sufficient to satisfy the nominal and formal requirements of the phrase 'the constitution shall stand amended'. To sustain the logical necessity that Seervai tries to show, he will need to find another mode of reasoning which does not assume that some part of the Constitution of India, 1950 must continue to exist.

The use of canons of constitutional interpretation like the doctrine of necessary implication, irrespective of the type and the strength of implication they seek to draw from textual resources, may at times operate satisfactorily unaided by more substantive arguments about constitutional values and principles. Such arguments are considered a satisfactory basis on which to justify a legal conclusion in court rooms and among the legal profession. Notwithstanding the merit of these professional uses of the doctrine, I find that Seervai's use of the doctrine fails to decisively settle a rigorous academic debate over the interpretation of Article 368 amending power as I have shown that logical necessity invoked admits conclusions that he seeks to avoid. There is no way to sustain his argument unless one assumes that some conclusions, like total repeal of the constitution, are so absurd a result that it is not envisaged by the constitution. However, to assume this proposition as a premise would be to assume the conclusion sought to be justified. The doctrine of necessary implication unsupported by any of the substantive moral or political reasons which justify one interpretation over another is unlikely to provide decisive or convincing reasons on which the basic structure doctrine may legitimately rest. Structural interpretation offers us a superior approach to understand the nature of constitutional implications and I will turn to this in the next section.

Structural Interpretation

In ... structuralism, the Constitution is interpreted liberally, as a totality, in the light of the spirit pervading it and the philosophy underlying it ... Structuralist interpretation can also be teleological, meaning that it understands the Constitution to be intended to achieve certain purposes. It is, in that sense, result-oriented. [21]

Sathe suggests that the Indian court's movement from a positivist to a structuralist mode of interpretation explains the emergence and development of the basic structure doctrine. This is a descriptive claim about the practice of constitutional adjudication in the Indian Supreme Court on which further analysis has the potential to provide a better legal justification for the basic structure doctrine. In the sections above I argued that the doctrine of implied limitations and the doctrine of necessary implications have not been endorsed, and do not help us understand the interpretive techniques deployed by the Supreme Court in basic structure cases. In this section I critically examine the character of structural interpretation and examine whether it helps us understand basic structure adjudication better and if it enhances the legal legitimacy of the basic structure doctrine.

It is not enough to affix the label 'structural interpretation' as a justification for the basic structure doctrine unless I can address several related questions. First, is structural interpretation a discrete method of interpretation? If so, what are the ingredients of such an approach? Second, is structural interpretation an appropriate or justified method of interpretation? A response to these questions will require a deeper and more sustained investigation into the character of 'structural interpretation' than that offered by Sathe. This investigation can draw usefully from the careful analysis that structural interpretation has received in other constitutional jurisdictions.

Sathe tells us that a structural interpretation views the constitution in totality, accounting for its philosophy and spirit. This description

---

[21] S.P. Sathe, 'India: From Positivism to Structuralism', in J. Goldsworthy (ed.), *Interpreting Constitutions: A Comparative Study*, Oxford: Oxford University Press, 2006, p. 226.

portrays structural interpretation to be a cipher through which metaphysical meaning is extracted from the constitution. In Chapters 2 and 3 I observed that the courts drew on various provisions of the constitution to clarify the scope of the amending power in Article 368 and the emergency power in Article 356. In these cases it is the words of the constitutional text which are the main resource in constitutional interpretation. There is little or no weight attached to the philosophy or spirit of the constitution. Any useful understanding of basic structure review as structural interpretation will need to account for text-dependent character of such judicial interpretation. While drawing justifiable implications lies at the core of a structural interpretation of the constitution, by understanding the character and strength of the implications drawn by the court I will analyse the legal legitimacy of the conclusions arrived at in basic structure cases. I begin by assessing the extent to which such implications rest on the constitutional text.

The implications in basic structure cases are multi-provisional in character.[22] For example, limited amending power under Article 368 is implied not merely from the phrasing of the provision itself,[23] but from other provisions: the preamble and directive principles which set out the objectives of government; fundamental rights, the division of power between levels of government and the separation of power between institutions of government which limit governmental power. I must be clear that multi-provisional implications are not necessarily superior or stronger than mono-provisional implications. In either case the strength of particular implications is grounded in the soundness of the reasons offered in support of the implications. However, multi-provisional implications allow the court to interpret the constitutional document in 'totality' so that integrity of the document is maintained. Further, such implications allow the court to reconcile various provisions which apparently conflict with each other in a principled fashion.

[22] J. Kirk, supra n. 8, pp. 658–60.

[23] Khanna in *Kesavananda* rests his conclusion on the limited amending power under Article 368 almost exclusively on the interpretation of the term 'amendment'. The other majority opinions in *Kesavananda* and the opinions in subsequent cases where basic structure review has been extended to other forms of state action and basic features are identified draw implications from multiple provisions in the constitution.

Interpretations are frequently referred to as being structural in a different sense. Robin Elliot, analysing the interpretive approach of the Canadian Supreme Court, defines structural argumentation as a form of 'argumentation that proceeds by way of drawing of implications from the structures of government created by' the constitution and the 'application of the principles generated by those implications—which can be termed the foundational or organizing principles of the Constitution—to the particular constitutional issue at hand'.[24] The principles so generated are 'not simply aids to the interpretation of provisions in the text of our Constitution, or otherwise to provide assistance in the resolution of difficult constitutional issues, but to be taking on a legal status equivalent to that enjoyed by provisions found in the text of our Constitution'.[25]

Eliot critically identifies the key interpretive technique in a structural interpretation to be implications drawn from the constitutional text but calls such implications 'structural' as they draw on the 'structures of government' set out under the constitution. It may well be that the Canadian Supreme Court implies constitutional principles from the provisions setting out the structures of government, but the Indian Supreme Court draws multi-provisional implications from a wider range of constitutional provisions which are not confined to structures of government but extends to substantive values. Further, the Canadian court may accord these constitutional principles with a different legal status than that occupied by basic features in basic structure review. For the purposes of the argument in this chapter it is sufficient to note that while both the courts draw implied meanings from multiple provisions of the constitutional text the phrase 'structural interpretation' points towards different interpretive methods in each court.

The second axis along which I analyse structural interpretation in basic structure cases is the extent to which such implications reflect the intentions of the framers. In Chapters 1 and 2 I had noticed that a significant part of the arguments raised in support of, and against, the basic structure doctrine drew support from the speeches of the

---

[24] Robin Elliot, 'References, Structural Argumentation and the Organizing Principles', 80 *Canadian Bar Review* 67 (2001), p. 68.

[25] Elliot, supra n. 24, p. 69.

framers in the Constituent Assembly as well as the history of the freedom movement. After carefully assessing the evidence I had reached the conclusion that the weight of historical evidence did not clearly settle the question of the scope of amending power under the constitution. In these circumstances it is impossible to assert that the framers had a deliberate and clear intention which they had communicated using deficient means of expression. So far as it is possible to assert that basic structure review reflects the framers' intentions, I may only suggest that these intentions were in the nature of 'implicit assumptions'[26] about matters not expressly considered by them but taken for granted as integral to the exercise of designing the constitution.

Implicit assumptions are implications drawn from the intellectual and social context in which the constitution was drafted. This is not merely an exercise of identifying the expectations of the framers of the constitution, but of uncovering the theoretical and practical convictions on which the particular constitutional rules were adopted. The constant refrain of the courts in basic structure cases that the constitution was not designed to be the playthings of the majority reflects an assumption about the limitations inherent in the constitutional project where the political life of the collective is sought to be governed by a framework of rules. Though communication of ideas in everyday life, as well as through constitutions, cannot take place without implicit assumptions about the nature of the communicative act, there is no doubt that varied assumptions are consistent with the constitutional text and choosing between these assumptions is not a cut-and-dried process. Despite the significant role played by such assumptions about constitutional design in basic structure cases, using implicit assumptions allows the court to avoid the difficult task of articulating substantive and coherent justifications for the interpretations they choose. By adopting a moderate originalist stance the court hitchhikes on the legal legitimacy of the founders' assumed intentions and thereby fails to confront the essential ingredient of judicial choice.

[26] J. Goldsworthy, 'Implications in Language, Law and the Constitution', in G. Lindell (ed.), *Future Directions in Australian Constitutional Law*, Annadale: Federation Press 1994, pp. 150, 154–61.

The third axis along which I will analyse Sathe's proposal for structural interpretation as an explanation for the basic structure doctrine is the extent to which such interpretation is purposive or 'teleological' in character. I must be clear at the outset that a purposive interpretation is not intrinsically a 'structural' interpretation. Simply put, a purposive interpretation identifies the objectives sought to be achieved by the provision of the constitution and then secures that objective even if this requires a strained construction of words in the case at hand. To the extent that the objectives to be achieved are identified through multi-provisional implications, such an interpretation may be structural in nature. So in this sense, a structural interpretation may also be purposive in character.

Dhavan argues that in *Kesavananda* the court has abandoned a common law inspired 'literal approach'[27] to constitutional interpretation and adopted a 'teleological theory of interpretation which saw statutes and constitutions in their teleological context and purpose'.[28] He approves of this shift as long as the courts clearly outline institutional safeguards by specifying the limits to which this 'context-purpose'[29] approach may be used thereby limiting the discretion of the judges. Structural interpretation through multi-provisional implications offers us one possible institutional safeguard to the use of this context-purpose mode of constitutional interpretation. By requiring all claims about the objectives of the constitution to satisfy a rigorous multi-provisional test there is a reasonable safeguard against the callous recognition of constitutional objectives.

Structural interpretation offers us useful insights into the approach to constitutional interpretation I have come across in basic structure review cases discussed in this work. Structural interpretation allows us to satisfactorily explain the nature of implications employed by the Indian courts in establishing the constitutional basis of basic structure review and identification of basic features. By eliminating metaphysical arguments about the spirit of the constitution as the kind of structural interpretation on which the basic structure doctrine is founded and substituting it with an understanding of

[27] R. Dhavan, *Supreme Court of India: A Socio-Legal Critique of its Juristic Techniques*, Bombay, N.M. Tripathi P. Ltd, 1977, p. 68.
[28] Ibid.
[29] Ibid., supra n. 27, p. 69.

multi-provisional implications as structural interpretation I am better able to explain judicial performance by specifying the different ingredients in constitutional interpretation involved in such cases. In this sense, structural interpretation offers us the best explanation of Indian courts' approach to constitutional interpretation in basic structure cases.

In order to assess whether structural interpretation enhances the legitimacy of the basic structure doctrine I will need to develop a richer account of constitutional interpretation more generally. I had observed at the beginning of this part of the chapter on implied meaning that conventionally the common law and rules of statutory interpretation attempted to eliminate judicial choice in interpretation. In this conveyor belt model of legitimacy, judicial decisions are legitimate when they translate authoritative constitutional or statutory pronouncements without exercising any judicial creativity. Irrespective of the general viability of this model of constitutional interpretation, it provides us no guidance when the constitutional provisions under-determine the specific solution to which the basic structure doctrine responds. In such a context, interpretive techniques which are based on sound reasoning and are principled judicially manageable formulae offer us the only means by which to regulate otherwise open-ended judicial choice. To the extent that structural interpretation circumscribes the range of choices that judges may resort to in such cases, it offers a partial restriction on judicial choice. Structural interpretation, or any other model of interpretation, does not eliminate judicial choice but that model of interpretation or legal legitimacy is unavailable in the conditions of under-determination in which the basic structure doctrine is grounded.

Amending or Interpreting the Constitution

The third key argument made against the legal legitimacy of the basic structure doctrine is whether the Supreme Court, by creating this doctrine, is amending and not interpreting the constitution. This argument is put forth with varied convictions and motivations.[30] At the core of the argument lies a distinction between judges declaring

---

[30] For a recent collection of such criticisms see Pran Chopra (ed.) *The Supreme Court versus the Constitution*, New Delhi: Sage Publications, 2006.

the law and making the law and a particular understanding of the judicial role. Before I engage with the theoretical debates around judicial creativity it is essential for us to recapitulate on the extent of creativity involved in basic structure review cases. It is to this that I now turn.

In the early basic structure cases, the Supreme Court was confronted with a question about the scope of Parliament's amending power to which the constitutional text did not provide an unambiguous answer. The court had grappled with the question in previous cases and had come up with divergent responses: first, by allowing Parliament unlimited power to amend the constitution and then second, by holding that the power did not extend to the fundamental rights enshrined in Part III of the constitution.[31] In *Kesavananda* the court overruled these precedents and held that Parliament's amending power was plenary but did not extend to the basic features of the constitution. Hence, the *Kesavananda* court was creative or innovative in two senses: firstly, it answered the question regarding the scope of Parliament's amending power in a novel fashion and second, by overruling the existing precedent on the point of contention. Since the *Kesavananda* opinion, the creativity of the court in basic structure cases has found expression in the extension of basic structure review to forms of state action beyond constitutional amendment and in the identification of basic features of the constitution.

The preliminary objection to any form of judicial creativity emerges from the formalist claim that it is the duty of judges merely to declare the law as it is. Hart's critique of the formalist's failure to understand the open-texture of language and the epistemic incapacities of the author, of a generally phrased rule, to anticipate the several factual circumstances to which it may potentially apply has made the case for legal indeterminacy in an emphatic and yet unchallenged manner.[32] Raz extended this argument by showing the existence of, and the need for, judicial creativity in regulated disputes, covered by the existing law, as well as unregulated disputes or gaps in the law.[33] For the purposes of the argument in this chapter, it is

---

[31] Compare Chapter 1.

[32] H.L.A. Hart, *Concept of Law*, New Delhi: Oxford India Paperbacks, 2002, pp. 124–54.

[33] J. Raz, *Authority of Law*, Oxford: Clarendon Press, 1983, pp. 53–78.

the distinction between interpretation and amendment that is critical and it is beyond the scope of this work to fully engage with the arguments about the existence and extent of judicial creativity. I will assume that judicial creativity exists and argue that a meaningful distinction may be drawn between constitutional interpretation and constitutional amendment.

In basic structure cases the court has been confronted by legally regulated and unregulated disputes where the law is indeterminate. If I accept that the judicial role is to interpret the law to resolve the disputes before it, then the court has to deploy a range of techniques which do not amount to amending the constitution. The distinction between interpretation and amendment in the context of constitutional adjudication is analogous to the distinction between interpretation and legislation in the context of statutory adjudication. As I noted earlier in this section, interpretation as I understand it here includes both declaring and making the law. The distinction I seek to draw is between judicial law making and legislative law making[34] and extending that distinction to constitutional interpretation and constitutional amendment.

I may begin with an uncontroversial distinction between these two types of constitutional change: constitutional amendment always entails constitutional change by changing constitutional provisions through the appropriate legal process prescribed by the Constituion. Judicial interpretation, even where it makes new law or changes existing law, it does not alter the constitutional provisions themselves but only chooses from a range of possible meanings attached to the constitutional text and thereby alters constitutional meaning through a change in constitutional doctrine. Though it is often asserted that the constitutional text enjoys overall supremacy over constitutional doctrine, the relative weight of text and doctrine in deciding particular cases is not fixed and unchanging. Moreover, while constitutional text is invested with the authority of its makers, constitutional doctrine acquires authority by the strength of its reasoning and its acceptance by legal and political elites as well as the people at large.

---

[34] This section of the chapter develops on the distinctions drawn in A. Kavanagh, 'The Elusive Divide between Interpretation and Legislation under the Human Rights Act 1998' 24 *OJLS*, pp. 259–85 (2004).

The distinction between interpretation and amendment is established by several institutional safeguards which continuously operate to regulate the scope and extent, as well as the types of constitutional change possible under each category of constitutional change. First, constitutional interpretation can take place only when parties bring a case before the court. The constitutional jurisdiction of the Indian Supreme Court is rather wide and allows a range of cases to come before it including cases which are not strictly bivalent disputes brought to the court at the instance of affected parties. These include presidential references of important constitutional matters[35] and the expanding sphere of public interest litigation jurisdiction including some cases where the court has recognized some rights violations acting of its own accord.[36] Even if I account for this expanded jurisdiction I may safely claim that the court does not effectively choose when, or on what subject, it may initiate constitutional change. Unlike Parliament which may amend any portion of the constitution at the time of its choosing, the court's ability to interpret the constitution is necessarily structured around the interests of the parties who choose to engage it.

When a court is engaged by parties to resolve a dispute between them, the court must engage in 'interpretive reasoning'[37] to arrive at a justifiable conclusion. In order to 'interpret' the constitutional text the judge must isolate the meaning of the constitutional provision and provide justifying reasons for the conclusions that they reach in the particular case. As I have pointed out earlier in this work, this is not always a mechanical task as interpretation often requires a careful weighing of conflicting interests and values. The reasons which judges articulate must pay due regard to the reasons and purposes embedded in the constitutional text to be an interpretation of the text. Further, judges must engage with relevant precedent and integrate the reasoning in the present case with the reasons offered in previous cases. Even where judges choose to distinguish past precedents and develop the law in new directions they must articulate sound reasons

---

[35] Constitution of India, 1950, Article 143.

[36] S. Ahuja, *People, Law and Justice: Casebook on Public Interest Litigation*, Hyderabad: Orient Longman, 1997.

[37] A. Kavanagh, supra n. 34, p. 271.

for this choice. The discussion so far on the constraints on the type of reasoning that judges may employ is at great variance with the reasoning adopted by legislators amending the constitution. Though legislators do take into account the legal history and practice of the constitution they are free to develop an entirely novel approach to designing constitutional rules. They may rearrange the weights attached to different constitutional principles and introduce new constitutional arrangements motivated entirely by forward-looking reasons. This distinction between the types of reasoning in constitutional interpretation and constitution amendment hints at the varied extent to which these modes of reasoning may alter the constitutional law of the land. I will now examine if the distinction between constitutional interpretation and constitutional amendment defines the extent of constitutional change that can be brought about by each mode.

The restrictions on the judiciary related to the matters it takes up and the constraints on types of reasoning it employs in resolving them suggests that constitutional interpretation is amenable only to piecemeal constitutional change. Even where the court goes beyond the legal dispute before it and makes observations on larger constitutional issues, these observations are considered to be obiter dicta and do not operate as binding law in future cases. As amendments to the constitution may 'reform a whole area of the law in a root-and-branch fashion'[38] there is some truth to the suggestion that interpretation is suited to making small-scale constitutional changes. However, this observation should not be misunderstood to lead to the conclusion that the scale of constitutional change bears a linear relationship to the significance and impact of such change.

So far in this section I have tried to draw a general distinction between two types of constitutional change: through constitutional amendment and constitutional interpretation. I argue that these types of constitutional change may be distinguished using several criteria including the scope of permissible changes, the types of reasoning the respective institutions apply, and the type of constitutional changes possible under each category. Applying these criteria to the judicial performance in basic structure cases I

[38] A. Kavanagh, supra n. 36, p. 271.

argue that the courts have adhered to the key elements of this distinction satisfactorily.

The *Kesavananda* case was brought to the court by interested parties who argued that the court should overrule its precedent in *Golaknath*. The court agreed with the petitioners and developed the basic structure doctrine while interpreting the scope of the amending power in Article 368 while relying on the multi-provisional implications drawn from salient provisions of the constitution. Since *Kesavananda* the court has scrupulously avoided 'amending' the constitution by listing out a catalogue of basic features and has developed them on a case by case basis. Moreover, it has expanded the scope of the doctrine incrementally to bring other forms of state action under its ambit.

At this stage I may safely conclude that the constitutional changes through which the basic structure doctrine originated and developed satisfy the criteria of constitutional interpretation. The judiciary has developed the doctrine while adhering to the institutional constraints, styles of reasoning, and other interpretive obligations which are central to the distinction between constitutional amendment and constitutional interpretation. The argument that the judiciary has amended the constitution to introduce the basic structure doctrine rests on a fundamental misunderstanding about the nature of constitutional interpretation and may safely be disregarded.

I began the enquiry into legal legitimacy by identifying three key challenges to the legitimacy of the basic structure doctrine. First I examined whether the basic structure doctrine was expressly set out in the constitutional text and clarified that no part of this work advances this unsustainable proposition. Then I investigated whether implied meanings may be drawn from the constitutional text and whether there are limits to such an exercise. I noticed that various doctrines have been developed to circumscribe the range of implications which may be legitimately considered in constitutional interpretation. The phrase 'structural interpretation', when taken to indicate the use of multi-provisional implications which are sensitive to the context and purpose of the provisions, provide the best explanation for the type of interpretation adopted in basic structure cases. These structural implications are extensively used in arguments about the constitutional basis of the basic structure doctrine and the identification of basic features of the constitution.

Insofar as drawing structural implications is a well understood mode of constitutional interpretation it contributes to the legal legitimacy of the basic structure doctrine. As legal legitimacy is a scalar category which admits of measurement by degrees, structural interpretation makes a significant contribution to enhancing the legal legitimacy of the basic structure doctrine. I conclude the first part of this chapter by outlining the key distinctions between constitutional interpretation and constitutional amendment and show that the argument that the Supreme Court amended the constitution to introduce the basic structure doctrine rests on a fundamental mistake about the nature of constitutional interpretation and an inadequate understanding of the distinction between interpretation and amendment as modes of constitutional change. Next I turn to the arguments regarding the moral legitimacy of basic structure review.

Moral Legitimacy

In this part of the chapter I assess whether the basic structure doctrine is morally legitimate. When I say that a constitutional law doctrine is morally legitimate we mean that it is respect-worthy and capable of moral justification.[39] Clearly not all the evaluative aspects of a constitutional doctrine bear on the question of its moral legitimacy.[40] Some doctrines may be virtuous as they are elegantly crafted and applied with clarity while others may be practically useful in a particular historical setting. An enquiry into legitimacy is concerned with those evaluative aspects which help us decide whether the doctrine is, all things considered, morally worthy, and therefore at least deserving of our respect, if not our obedience.

I will show that the basic structure doctrine is morally legitimate in the context of its evolution and practice in Indian constitutional adjudication. While it is not part of the argument here that such

[39] R. Fallon, 'Legitimacy and the Constitution', 118 *Harvard L Rev* p. 1789, p. 1796.

[40] A. Marmor, 'Are Constitutions Legitimate?', USC Legal Studies Research Paper No 6–9 (http://ssrn.com/abstract=89952) 4 (27 April 2006).

a doctrine is ideal or necessary for all constitutions, or for all times, neither am I focused on the specific legitimacy of the basic structure doctrine in a particular historical context. In this chapter I am interested in a partly general and partly particular account of the moral legitimacy of the basic structure doctrine where I take the Indian Constitution and the Supreme Court decisions as the background conditions for our assessment but take no other specific historical or factual factors into account.

The moral legitimacy of judicial doctrine in constitutional law rests primarily on considerations of political morality of the institutions it creates and sustains, though in some fundamental rights cases we may be concerned with the personal morality of citizen action or the consequences of state action on the moral choices of citizens. The moral legitimacy of the basic structure doctrine, which is our concern in this part of the chapter, rests entirely on the political morality of the institutional arrangements and relationships between the three branches of government and the people at large.

I may assess the moral legitimacy of the basic structure doctrine in one of two ways: first, by sketching out a general account of criterion by which legitimacy is ideally measured and then demonstrate that these criteria are satisfied by the basic structure doctrine. In the alternative I may identify the main arguments that have been, or may be, raised against the moral legitimacy of the basic structure doctrine and then show that these arguments fail to identify, misunderstand, or misapply, the criteria by which moral legitimacy is assessed. Here I adopt the latter negative strategy to show that the doctrine is legitimate in a minimal, even if not in an ideal, sense.

The question of the moral legitimacy of judicial doctrine, when posed as starkly as I have at the start of this part of the chapter, suggests that a simple yes or no answer is available. In order to respond to the question in this binary fashion I must assume that the evaluation of legitimacy that I seek to make is guided by clearly identified, discrete criteria, shared by all participants in the legitimacy discourse who agree about the precise scales by which each of these criteria are to be satisfied. None of these assumptions are valid as the discourse around ideal type theories of legitimacy is mired in deep disagreement about the criteria and measures of moral legitimacy. Moreover, even if there was unanimity and certainty about the moral criteria by which legitimacy may be appraised since 'moral justification can come in degrees',[41] I can only assert that the basic structure doctrine is more or less justified. Our effort in this part, and in the chapter as a whole, is to show that the basic structure doctrine enjoys a substantial degree of legitimacy.

The basic structure doctrine is a doctrine of judicial review which allows the High Courts and the Supreme Court to invalidate state actions which damage or destroy the basic features of the constitution. The power of judicial review in itself, is not controversial[42] in the Indian context as the constitution clearly vests the courts with a wide range of judicial review powers to ensure that state action is jurisdictionally competent, compliant with fundamental rights, and follows proper administrative process. Hence, those parts of the basic structure review which complement or supplement existing models of constitutional judicial review have not provoked a great deal of controversy and do not require extensive moral justification. The controversial aspect of basic structure review is the court's regulation of the scope of Parliament's constitution amending power. Hereafter, I will identify and respond to the criticisms of this part of basic structure review. If the justification of the basic structure doctrine as it applies to the judicial review of constitutional amendments are valid then they contribute significantly to support the application of basic structure review to other less popular forms of state action.

Basic structure review allows the court to review constitutional amendments for compliance with the basic features of the constitution. The key concerns about the moral legitimacy of such a doctrine include the following. Firstly, by proposing limits to the scope of amending power, the court entrenches certain constitutional principles permanently beyond the reach of the people and this is undemocratic. Secondly, even if limitations on amending power are defensible, there is no reason why a court exercising judicial review power should police those limits. Both these related concerns are addressed in the section below. Next, I consider the argument

[41] A. Marmor, supra n. 40, p. 5.

[42] This was pointed out with clarity by Patanjali Sastri in *V.G. Row* v. *State of Madras*, (1952) Supreme Court Reporter 597.

that the possibility of the court declaring a constitutional amendment to be unconstitutional fundamentally misunderstands the nature of sovereignty and the related concepts of constituent power and revolution. I will explore these arguments in the second section below.

Democracy, Limited Amending Power, and Judicial Review

The principle of democratic decision-making requires a method of group decision where every member of the group is treated equally. There are no *a priori* reasons to assume that it is desirable that all decisions in all types of groups should be submitted to a democratic process. Since many complex political societies adopt the democratic principle as a legitimate model of decision making and institutional design in the political sphere, democracy has emerged as a pre-eminent normative standard for decision-making more generally. Most constitutions modify the democratic principle of group decision making insofar as they insulate important moral and political decisions against change by ordinary lawmaking by the government. This entrenchment of moral and political values may be overcome only by the process of constitutional amendment which usually requires some form of super-majoritarian political process of decision making. Once amendments secure this super-majoritarian political authority they are understood to be capable of undoing entrenched provisions of the constitution.

Insofar as constitutionalism is taken to be a legitimate political principle, it follows that the entrenchment against ordinary legislation and the role of constitutional amendment is legitimate too. Irrespective of whether constitutionalism and democracy are reconcilable as a matter of abstract principle,[43] the Indian Constitution unambiguously reconciles between the two principles as a matter of constitutional design. The constitution subjects all ordinary law making power to the provisions of the constitution while other articles specifically provide for the special conditions under which various parts of the constitutional text may be amended.

[43] For a recent argument against the legitimacy of robust constitutionalism see A. Marmor, 'Are Constitutions Legitimate?', University of Southern California Legal Studies Research Paper No 6–9 (2006).

This conventional understanding of the relationship between constitutionalism and democracy embraced by the Indian Constitution is modified by the basic structure doctrine which imposes substantive limits on the scope of the amending power. The key question addressed in this section is whether limited amending power entailed by the basic structure doctrine is merely an extension of the conventional reconciliation of the constitutional and democratic principles, and if it develops rather than abandons this principle of constitutional design. In other words, does the basic structure doctrine adopt and extend the distinction between the ordinary law-making process and the constitutional law-making process or does the doctrine decisively reject the majoritarian premise of law making: that the only legitimate outcome to a decision-making process is a decision that a majority or plurality of citizens favours?[44]

In this section I will explore this question in two parts: firstly, I examine whether the basic structure doctrine rejects the majoritarian premise or merely denies the exclusivity of amending power in changing the constitution. I will show that while the basic structure doctrine deepens the entrenchment of some constitutional values against conventional constitutional amendments it retains the option for radical constitutional change by the people. In other words the doctrine envisages a dualist model of democracy which distinguishes between a decision by Parliament and a decision by the people.[45]

Secondly, I examine whether basic structure judicial review is illegitimate as it is anti-democratic. I respond to this argument in two ways: firstly, I argue that in a constitutional democracy the court may insist that certain background moral conditions be met before majoritarian decision making may be considered democratic and secondly, I show that basic structure review is essential to sustain a dualist democratic model which distinguishes between the decisions of a government and decisions by the people.

Exclusivity of Amending Power

The Indian Constitution envisages two levels of law making: ordinary law making where the legislature enacts laws subject to the

[44] R. Dworkin, *Freedom's Law*, Harvard: Harvard University Press, 1997, pp 15–16.
[45] B. Ackerman, *We the People*, Boston: Balknap Press, 1993 (Vol. 1) p. 6.

provisions of the constitution and constitutional law making where the provisions of the constitution may be amended following a special procedure. The distinction between these two types of law making is maintained by the device of entrenching constitutional rules by insulating them from the ordinary law making process and requiring a special majority to alter or remove them. Hence, the constitution prescribes different levels of majoritarian support as threshold requirements for valid constitutional change. These thresholds typically distinguish between how specific majorities are constituted and the deliberative quality of their decision making. Most existing accounts of Indian constitutional law embrace this reconciliation of democracy with constitutionalism as providing a complete picture of constitutional change. Embedded in this account is the assumption that amending power set out in the constitution is the exclusive instrument of constitutional change.

In our preliminary survey of the modes of amendment authorized by the constitution in Chapter 1 of this work, I had suggested that besides the general amending power in Article 368, there are several other provisions which provide for the amendment of specific provisions of the constitution.[46] So in this sense, clearly Article 368 is not the exclusive source of the power of constitutional amendment in the Indian constitution as other provisions of the constitution provide for its amendment. In this chapter I am concerned with exclusivity of amending power in a different sense. I enquire into whether Article 368, together with all other provisions of the constitution which authorize amendment, exhausts the legal and political avenues for legitimate constitutional change. This may also be understood as an enquiry into whether amendment under Article 368 is boundlessly inclusive[47] as it encompasses all modes of constitutional change. The exclusivity of the amending clauses in this latter sense has a critical bearing on our understanding of the legitimacy of the basic structure doctrine.

[46] Constitution of India 1950, Article 4 on the admission of new States and Article 169 which provides for the creation of Legislative Councils in States are examples of constitution amending power outside Article 368.

[47] F.I. Michelman, 'Thirteen Easy Pieces', *Michigan L Rev* (1995) 1297, 1306–08.

In *Kesavananda* the court held that amending power in Article 368 was not exclusive by holding that the amendment provisions in the constitution taken together did not exhaust the formal modes of constitutional change. As the court held that amending power was incapable of changing the basic features of the constitution, it had to develop the concept of the constituent power of the people. I have examined how the court interpreted the constitution to arrive at this conclusion in Chapter 1 and in the section on 'Sociological Legitimacy' below. I will now assess whether the non-exclusivity of amending power in Article 368 is morally defensible.

There has been no critical enquiry into this question in the Indian academic and legal debates on the basic structure doctrine. As there has been rigorous engagement with this issue in American constitutional scholarship I will begin by examining the central arguments on this issue in the debate on the exclusivity of Article V of the United States constitution. A useful starting point is Walter Dellinger's argument for limited judicial review of constitutional amendments under Article V to ensure compliance with the amendment process.[48] While Dellinger does anticipate several informal mechanisms for constitutional change, he concludes on the basis of limited historical evidence that the 'formal amendment process... in Article V represents a domestication of the right to revolution.'[49] Akhil Amar Reed challenges this view after conducting an extensive review of the historical evidence to conclude that the people of the United States 'retain an unenumerated, constitutional right to alter our Government and revise our Constitution in a way not explicitly set out in Article V'.[50]

The exclusivist versus non-exclusivist interpretation of the amending process in a constitution does not have to rest on a historical argument particular to the founding history of the constitution of the United States. One may make a distinction between different modes

---

[48] Walter Dellinger, 'The Legitimacy of Constitutional Change: Rethinking the Amendment Process', 97 *Harvard L Rev* 386 (1983–4).

[49] Ibid., p. 431.

[50] A.A. Reed, 'The Consent of the Governed: Constitutional Amendment Outside Article V', 94 *Columbia L Rev* 457 (1994) 458–9. See also A.A. Reed, 'Philadelphia Revisited: Amending the Constitution Outside Article V', 55 *U Chicago L Rev* 1043.

of constitutional change by assessing the quality and scope of deliberation which precedes it. Ackerman developes a 'dualist democracy' model which understands the United States Constitution as putting in place a two-tiered practice of democratic law making: ordinary law making through the legislative process and higher law making through constitutional amendment and other heightened deliberative modes of constitutional change—constitutional moments.[51]

In this model, higher law making goes beyond amendments to the constitution to include a process of: 'signalling' a shift from ordinary law making and amendment to a mode of fundamental revision of the constitution going beyond interest group positions; the making of proposals 'in language the majority of the population can support';[52] a period of mobilized deliberation where the proposals secure 'deeper and broader support from the general citizenry'[53] and finally a process by which these new constitutional proposals are legally codified. Ackerman claims that this four-part process of higher law making results in a constitutional politics of a deliberative quality superior to that achieved through the formal amendment process.

The dualist democracy model is neither a necessary nor complete account of how majoritarian democracy and constitutionalism may be reconciled in constitutional design. Wherever constitutional politics resembles ordinary politics and is driven by interest group proposals which are not subject to extensive deliberation then the concerns arising out of popular majoritarianism in ordinary lawmaking with constitutional amendment and higher law making.[54] However, as several courts including the Canadian Supreme Court[55] and the Indian Supreme Court through the basic structure doctrine insert themselves as guardians of the deliberative quality of constitutional politics they may well be able to ensure the integrity of this process.

---

[51] B. Ackerman, supra n. 45, pp. 267–8. M. Vargova 'Democratic Deficits of a Dualist Deliberative Constitutionalism: Bruce Ackerman and Jürgen Habermas', 18 *Ratio Juris*, pp. 365–85 (2005).

[52] Ibid., p. 290.

[53] Ibid., p. 287.

[54] R. Bellamy, *Constitutionalism and Democracy*, Dartmouth: Ashgate Publishing, 2006, p. xxxviii.

[55] Reference re *Secession of Quebec* (1998) 2 SCR 217.

A second criticism of the dualist democracy argument is that it is built on, and therefore limited to, the American constitutional experience. Hence, it is suggested that it does not help us explain or justify the non-exclusivity of amendments under Article 368 as a process of constitutional change in India. This objection may be overcome in two ways: firstly by recognizing that Bruce Ackerman's efforts in the first volume of *We The People* has both descriptive and normative elements. The descriptive elements of the book are focused on the reconstruction of American constitutional history 'without the assistance of guides imported from another time and place'.[56] The normative argument in the book is that the dualist democratic ideal offers a better explanation of the process of radical constitutional change than monist or foundationalist democratic models. This is a general argument about the best reconciliation of democracy and constitutionalism as political concepts which may have application beyond the American constitutional context.[57] Secondly, recent comparative constitutional law scholarship has successfully applied a modified version of Ackerman's argument to the debates on constitutional amendment in Canada.[58] Sen in a recent work argues that 'the Indian constitutional tradition may be best understood through the Ackermanian distinction between democratic discourses occurring during normal political periods of self-interested political bargaining and those that involve leader–citizen engagement in debating issues of higher law principles'.[59] These sophisticated applications of the dualist democracy model to understand non-American constitutions suggest that this path is worth exploring.

In Chapter 1 a critical examination of the constitutional basis of the basic structure doctrine with respect to constitutional amendments led me to conclude that the Supreme Court distinguished between two modes of changing the constitutional text: amending power

[56] B. Ackerman, supra n. 45, p. 3.

[57] S. Levinson, 'Transitions', 108 *Yale LJ* 2215 (1999).

[58] Sujit Choudhry and Bernadette Mount, 'Ackerman's Higher Lawmaking in Comparative Constitutional Perspective: Constitutional Moments as Constitutional Failures?' (15 August 2006) ExpressO Preprint Series, Working Paper 1544, available at: http://law.bepress.com/expresso/eps/1544 (20 April 2007).

[59] S. Sen, *Popular Sovereignty and Democratic Constitutions*, New Delhi: Oxford University Press, 2007, p. 25.

and constituent power. Both these modes of constitutional change mobilized popular support albeit through different mechanisms. While the first was exercised indirectly through representative institutions like Parliament and State legislatures, the latter is exercised directly by the people. By holding that the amending power in Article 368 was circumscribed by the substantive limitation of basic features the court is not denying the democratic principle or the power of the people to change the constitution, but merely denying the exclusivity of amendment under Article 368 as a mode of formal constitutional change.Seen in this light, the basic structure doctrine is best understood as a rejection of a monist and foundationalist democratic model and an endorsement of the dualist democratic model whereby courts scrutinize proposals for radical constitutional change to ensure that they comply with the deep deliberative requirements necessary for radical constitutional change.

Judicial Review

The argument that judicial review is undemocratic is on the ascendant in constitutional theory.[60] Critics argue that judicial review is politically illegitimate as it allows non–representative judges to override legislative or executive choices thereby defeating cherished political principles like political equality and representation. This is a criticism that rests on the principles of composition and institutional character of governmental institutions in liberal democratic states and the process by which they arrive at their conclusions. A second type of criticism would be that judicial review has indeed resulted in worse decisions than legislative or executive action. This outcomes-based criticism would be contingent on adequate data on the decisions made by these institutions in a particular jurisdiction and a critical analysis of the decisions made.

Most criticism of the legitimacy of the basic structure doctrine has been of the former variety that rests on the institutional character of governmental institutions in India and their processes of decision-making. This is not surprising as an outcomes–based assessment of institutional performance to secure basic constitutional values

---

[60] Compare J. Waldron, 'The Core of the Case Against Judicial Review', 115 *Yale LJ* 1346 (2006).

would unanimously lead to the conclusion that basic structure review is justified. As discussed earlier in Chapter 3, and in more detail below, the court has struck down only the most flagrant abuses of parliamentary power under basic structure review. There is no reason to assume that the legitimacy of political institutions should be assessed only by non–instrumentalist reasons. An instrumentalist concern with the ends of political authority—good government—may allow us to choose between political decision-making processes and institutions.[61]

However, in this section I will focus on the non–instrumentalist argument against basic structure review and review the institutional and process based arguments raised in the literature. The general argument against judicial review is most frequently concerned with a court overturning the decision of a legislature or executive for failure to comply with fundamental rights. This argument has two salient features that must be emphasized: first, it is concerned with strong judicial review where the court is allowed to effectively override another institution's decision.[62] In Chapter 3, I had argued that basic structure review as an independent model of judicial review empowered courts to strike down state action and in cases where basic features are applied in conjunction with other models of judicial review they serve as interpretive aids. Despite the courts' reluctance to strike down state action under basic structure review it must be acknowledged that basic structure review resembles a strong form of judicial review. To this I must add a crucial caveat: the Supreme Court has time and again recognized that the basic structure of the constitution may be undone by the 'people' and thereby preserves an override by popular sovereign action.

Secondly, the general argument against judicial review is focused on review to ensure compliance with fundamental rights. The prevalence of widespread disagreement about the content and application of fundamental rights in popular and academic circles is thought to be a key ingredient in the argument against judicial review. I have argued

---

[61] Compare A. Kavanagh, 'Participation and Judicial Review: A Reply to Waldron', 22 *Law and Philosophy* 451–86 (2003).

[62] J. Waldron clearly identifies his target as strong judicial review of legislative action. J. Waldron, supra n. 60, p. 1353.

that basic features of the constitution are not fundamental rights, and are general constitutional rules of a substantive character, the meaning of which may be subject to, as much, if not more moral disagreement. The substantive character of basic structure review and the capacity of the court to order strong remedies would mean that the general argument against judicial review would apply substantially to basic structure review.

A third important distinction between the general argument against judicial review and basic structure review is that the general argument is conducted in a legal context where the constitution does not expressly authorize strong judicial review such as in the United States. In newer constitutions, like those in India or South Africa, the court is expressly conferred with the power to overturn the decisions of other governmental institutions on predetermined grounds. The impact of these pre-commitments on institutional design and the relationship between the legislature and the courts on the general argument against judicial review is a matter of controversy. In any event, it is not the argument in this work that the Indian constitution expressly provides for basic structure review and hence this argument may not carry any special weight.

Having cleared a few preliminary concerns about the applicability of the general argument against judicial review to basic structure review in the discussion above, I will now respond to this argument in two ways: firstly, I will argue that the general argument assumes that democracy is equivalent to the right to participate in the process of decision-making. Secondly, I argue that by privileging the right to participation such a conception of democracy adopts majoritarian voting arrangements as the sole source of all political legitimacy.

There are profound philosophical disagreements about the meaning and objectives of a democracy as a political principle by which decision-making in our societies is organized. Even if I begin with the assumptions about equal political participation as being an important value in our democracy there are significant disagreements about the decision-making processes and institutions that such a value requires. Most general arguments against judicial review emphasize the representative character of legislatures and executives and contrast this with the unrepresentative character of judiciaries. Such an argument makes mistakes at two levels: firstly, it proposes that voting systems respect the principle of equal political participation without further scrutiny and secondly, it suggests that majoritarian decision-making is equivalent to democracy. I will examine each in turn.

Most liberal democracies constitute their legislatures and executives through some system of aggregating voting preferences of its adult citizens. While Waldron recognizes that voting systems are not perfect he argues that a reasonably functioning democracy will confer more political legitimacy on their elected organs. Most careful analyses of voting systems in mature democracies like the UK or India point out that the first-past-the-post system invariably creates legislatures and executives which do not enjoy a mandate from a majority of voters. Further, when I speak about a democratic judiciary, I imagine an institution which draws on 'legal professionals of all ranks of society, and where access to legal education, information, legal advise and expertise, and a legal career are all widely dispersed, rather than being the prerogative of a small or relatively small group of people.'[63] While it is not the argument here that the Indian judiciary, or for that matter the judiciary in any other country, is composed in this fashion I only need to show that such a principle of composition can be understood to be democratic in character. Moreover, it is often possible that judicial review itself becomes a viable channel of political participation which overcomes the institutional barriers inherent in the majoritarian voting process. When I consider that there is considerable scepticism about the precise institutional mechanisms through which the democratic principle should be realized the elevation of the voting mechanism as the sole vehicle to ensure equal participation is unjustifiable.

The Indian constitution confers fundamental rights on citizens and ordains the court with the authority to enforce these rights and override state action which violates these rights. Thereby the constitution recognizes that there may be circumstances in which the representative institutions of the state do not have the power to decide on certain issues. Hence it may be asserted that, as Dworkin argues in another context, the Indian constitution embraces a constitutional conception of democracy where collective decisions are 'made by political institutions whose structure, composition, and practices

[63] Annabelle Lever 'Is Judicial Review Undemocratic?' (2007) PL 280, 286.

treat all members of the community, as individuals, with equal concern and respect.'[64] The constitutional conception of democracy requires that the state institutions respect democratic conditions such as equal status for all citizens in order to be politically legitimate. Further such a conception of democracy would elevate the conditions under which a decision-making process can be said to be collective to be more than a 'statistical function of individual action.'[65] In other words government by the people would require 'that in a democracy political decisions are taken by a distinct entity—the people as such—rather than by any set of individuals one by one.'[66]

Constitutions which embrace strong judicial review commit themselves to an understanding of democracy which requires that decisions taken by representative governmental institutions respect democratic conditions and hence restrict these institutions through the mechanism of judicial review. Further, in order to claim that a decision is supported by a majority of persons in a political community I must be able to show that such a decision-making process is a communal collective action by the 'people'. Basic structure review embraces both these facets of the Dworkin's conception of constitutional democracy. Though some basic features of the constitution protected by the court go further than the 'democratic conditions' of equal status and respect for all citizens, the version of basic structure review defended in this work envisages that this doctrine will not stand in the way of radical constitutional change carried out by the 'people' directly exercising their sovereign power.

I will now turn to the background assumption that Waldron makes to sustain the general argument against judicial review. Waldron suggests that his general criticism is not unconditional 'but depends on certain institutional and political features of modern liberal democracies'.[67] In this section, I will critically examine these background conditions on which the criticism of judicial review rests and argue that relatively young complex democracies such as India often fail to meet these conditions and that basic structure review is

[64] R. Dworkin, *Freedom's Law*, Oxford: Oxford University Press, 1996, p. 17.
[65] Ibid., p. 20.
[66] Ibid.
[67] J. Waldron, supra n. 60, p. 1353.

carefully crafted to deal with such exceptions to the general argument against judicial review.

Waldron identifies four fundamental assumptions on which he builds his argument about the political illegitimacy of judicial review. In this part I will focus our attention on the first assumption about the character of democratic institutions. Waldron assumes that: 'This society has a broadly democratic political system with universal adult suffrage, and it has a representative legislature, to which elections are held on a fair and regular basis'.[68] He then goes on to elaborate that such a society must practise a democratic culture of 'responsible deliberation and political equality'[69] and clarifies that the core of this assumption is 'process values and not outcome values'.[70] In other words, Waldron argues that the political legitimacy of an institutional framework should be assessed by examining whether it follows a democratic deliberative process of a quality which authorizes the outcomes of the process. Waldron's concerns are with the judicial review of legislation and the legislative deliberative process which produces legislation—in other words, normal politics.

In the previous section, I elaborated on the dualist democratic model as a sound justification for basic structure review. This dualist model distinguishes between normal politics, which Waldron is concerned with, and the constitutional politics of higher law-making. If I accept this distinction between two modes of democratic decision-making as a normative claim, I would need to modify Waldron's argument to require the 'process values' of higher law-making to be background assumptions against which I assess the legitimacy of basic structure review. If the argument in the previous section, where I claimed that basic structure review ensures that the deliberative quality for higher law-making is achieved before radical constitutional change is possible is correct, then basic structure review falls within the exceptions of the case against judicial review.

While Waldron does concede that the case against judicial review fails if one of the background conditions is not satisfied, he clarifies that this does not amount to a positive justification for judicial

---

[68] Waldron, supra n. 60, p. 1361.
[69] Ibid.
[70] Ibid., p. 1362.

review.[71] In order to make a positive argument for basic structure review as a politically legitimate form of judicial review, I must be able to show that this form of judicial review responds to some identifiable deliberative dysfunction. Basic structure review allows the court to mark the distinction between ordinary and higher law-making by declaring that certain forms of state action affect core constitutional principles which requires a heightened deliberative scrutiny. As the court does not decide the substantive constitutional principles to which all higher deliberative action must comply it does not impose any normative values on the people. It merely signals to the political institutions of the state that they have overlooked or ignored the level of deliberative scrutiny necessary for this type of constitutional change to be legitimate.

So far I have argued that basic structure review defeats the central argument against judicial review as it responds to the failure of democratic institutions to recognize and protect a dualist democratic model whereby the constitutional validity of constitutional change is assessed by requiring the appropriate deliberative democratic process to be followed. In other words, it responds to a deliberative dysfunction in higher law-making under the Indian constitution. I conclude by making a brief positive argument for the legitimacy of basic structure review by showing that it is primarily concerned with the process values of democratic deliberation that must attach to each proposal for constitutional change and does not allow the court to posit its normative choices on the political institutions or the people at large. Irrespective of the general viability of this argument, it does not provide adequate support for the substantive character of basic structure review that protects core constitutional principles.

In this section, I have responded to the general argument against judicial review. I began by conceding that the general argument would apply to basic structure review even though it reviews constitutional amendments for damage to basic features or general constitutional rules. Two types of responses against the general argument have been proposed: firstly, arguments that challenge the equivalence of representative institutions composed by voting procedures to democracy and secondly, arguments that advance a constitutional

---

[71] Ibid., p. 1404.

conception of democracy as the appropriate model for the Indian constitution. The second type of argument proposed assumes the validity of the general argument against judicial review but argues that basic structure review distinguishes between the two levels of democratic deliberation required for ordinary law-making and higher law-making, and therefore reiterates the deliberative process to be followed for higher law-making to be successful.

An evaluation of the arguments marshalled above leads me to conclude that while a reasonable justification for basic structure review can be made using non-instrumentalist reasons, an overwhelming argument remains to be made using an instrumentalist justification for basic structure review. As Raz observes, in a political society where there is disagreement about principles 'the institutional question should be decided in a way sensitive to the traditions and the conditions of different countries at different times, and that the institutions which are most likely to best implement the correct considerations be entrusted with the task'.[72]

Rethinking Sovereignty

No Supreme Court and no judiciary will sit in judgment over the sovereign will of Parliament ... Ultimately, the whole Constitution is a creature of Parliament.[73]

The concept of sovereignty and its relationship with the constitution is central to any understanding of the legitimacy of the basic structure doctrine. Jawaharlal Nehru, the first Prime Minister of India, in the quotation above embraces the view that Parliament is sovereign and the constitution and the institutions created by it are subordinate to it. The concept of sovereignty plays a critical role in both political and legal discourse—this dual character is critical to the argument in the rest of this section. The version of parliamentary sovereignty put forth by Nehru is difficult to reconcile with the constitutional text or with the basic structure doctrine. In this section I show that this strong version of parliamentary sovereignty rests on a misinterpretation of the Constitution of India, 1950 and an inadequate understanding of the concept of sovereignty in constitutional democracies. These

[72] J. Raz, 'Disagreement in Politics', 1998 *American Journal of Politics*, 25–52.
[73] Constituent Assembly Debates (10 September 1949) <http://164.100.24.208/ls/condeb/vol9p31a.htm > (2 October 2007).

errors arise, among other reasons, from the peculiar circumstances in which the Constituent Assembly continued to exist as the first Parliament in independent India.

If the doctrine of parliamentary sovereignty is indeed mistaken and plays no role in Indian constitutional law then I go on to explore what notion of sovereignty should replace it. Critics of the basic structure doctrine suggest that the Supreme Court has 'usurped' the sovereignty of Parliament.[74] This criticism caricatures the basic structure doctrine and its impact on the concept of sovereignty. I conclude this section by advancing a concept of sovereignty which can explain the reality of a legal system where there are 'multiple unranked sources of legal power'.[75] Such a concept of sovereignty best explains the place of sovereignty in Indian constitutional law and the role played by the basic structure doctrine. Let us begin by first setting out the understanding of sovereignty and how I develop on it in this section.

Sovereignty is a central concept in our understanding of the nature of political authority. The term is used to describe the phenomenon of 'supreme authority in a territory'.[76] The nature of supremacy of a political authority necessary for sovereignty to exist, the precise institutional forms or legal rules through which the sovereign may be identified, and the territorial basis by which members of a distinct political society are to be identified has been the subject of significant theoretical debates. This is not the place for this wider enquiry into the historical character of these debates.[77] In this section I am primarily concerned with the role that debates on sovereignty plays in constitutional law and constitutional theory.[78]

[74] P. Chopra, *The Supreme Court versus the Constitution: A Challenge to Federalism*, New Delhi: Sage Publications, 2006, pp. 13–17.

[75] N. Barber, 'Sovereignty Re-examined: The Courts, Parliament and Statutes' in 20 *Oxford J Legal Studies* 131–54 (2000) 134.

[76] D. Philpot 'Sovereignty', in *Stanford Encyclopedia of Philosophy*, alailable at: http://plato.stanford.edu/entries/sovereignty 2003, (accessed 20 September 2006).

[77] P.C. Oliver, 'Sovereignty in the 21st Century', 14 *Kings College LJ* 137–78 (2006).

[78] For a history of parliamentary sovereignty in England see J. Goldsworthy, *The Sovereignty of Parliament, History and Philosophy*, Oxford: Oxford University Press, 1999.

Parliamentary Sovereignty

I began this section with Nehru's views on the nature of parliamentary sovereignty and its relationship with the constitution. Nehru was not alone in proposing parliamentary sovereignty to be the model of sovereignty embraced by the Indian Constitution. Distinguished academic commentators[79] and several other prominent political leaders[80] laboured under the same premise. The persistence of the doctrine of parliamentary sovereignty in Indian constitutional law even after the inauguration of the Republic of India under the 1950 Constitution has much to do with the hold of the Diceyan formulation of English constitutional doctrine of parliamentary sovereignty[81] on the Indian constitutional imagination.

The doctrine of parliamentary sovereignty occupies a central place in English constitutional law and history.[82] The history of the doctrine reveals the changing relationship between parliament and the courts over time. The evolution of the doctrine in English constitutional law is best understood as a 'blend of the normative and the empirical'.[83] Dicey's formulation of the doctrine of parliamentary sovereignty has come to occupy an iconic status and bears repetition. He proposed that Parliament 'has under the British Constitution, the right to make or unmake any law whatever; and further, that no person or body is recognised by the law of England as having a right to override or set aside the legislation of Parliament'.[84] Dicey asserted that it was empirically true that Parliament enjoyed these positive and negative aspects of sovereignty and that the ascription of sovereignty could be justified as Parliament 'represented the most authoritative expression

---

[79] R. Dhavan, *The Supreme Court and Parliamentary Sovereignty*, New Delhi: Sterling Publishers 1976 undertakes a detailed and exhaustive analysis of *Kesavananda* and Parliamentary Sovereignty.

[80] G. Austin, *Working a Democratic Constitution*, New Delhi: Oxford University Press, 2003.

[81] A.V. Dicey, *An Introduction to the Study of the Law of the Constitution* (10th edn), London: Macmillan, 1958, p. ??.

[82] P. Craig, 'Public Law, Political Theory and Legal Theory', (2000) *Public Law* 211–39.

[83] P. Craig, supra n. 82, p. 212.

[84] A.V. Dicey, supra n. 81, pp. 39–40.

of the will of the nation'.[85] Though these arguments were taken to reflect the constitutional position of Parliament in the late nineteenth and first half of the twentieth century, this is the subject of a wider debate in contemporary political and legal debates.

The Diceyan doctrine of parliamentary sovereignty posits that the foundation of the legal authority of Parliament's omnipotent law-making power rests on the legal fact that the courts enforce all Acts of Parliament. Since Dicey, the English constitutional debates have gone on to consider whether parliamentary sovereignty is of a continuing or self-embracing character[86] and how these distinctions may explain the legal impact of the European Communities Act, 1972 and more recently the Human Rights Act, 1998. Moreover, there has been considerable theoretical debate on the contours of the doctrine of parliamentary sovereignty examining whether it is necessarily illimitable or indivisible or for that matter whether a Diceyan model of sovereignty provides an adequate account of the practice of English constitutional law today.[87] This is not the place for an extensive account of the debate on the sovereignty and its place in English constitutional law as I am concerned with whether the doctrine of parliamentary sovereignty provides the best understanding of parliamentary amending power in the Indian Constitution.

The word 'sovereignty' appears once in the Constitution of India, 1950 in the preamble which proclaims India to be a 'Sovereign Democratic Republic'.[88] The court has not interpreted the word 'sovereign' in the preamble to provide substantive reasons for its judgments. Further, some judges have expressed the view that it is not 'necessary to enter the academic question as to where sovereignty resides ...'.[89] Though it may well be prudent for judges to avoid an extensive journey into political theory to base their opinions in

---

[85] P. Craig, supra n. 82, p. 221.

[86] P. Mirfield, 'Can the House of Lords Lawfully be Abolished?' 95 *LQR* 36 (1995), and G. Winterton, 'Is the House of Lords Immortal?', 95 *LQR* 386 (1979).

[87] N. MacCormick, *Questioning Sovereignty*, Oxford: Oxford University Press, 1999.

[88] Constitution of India, 1950.

[89] *Golaknath* v. *State of Punjab*, AIR 1967 SC 1643 (Wanchoo, J), 1679.

constitutional law cases, this is an enquiry someone investigating the legitimacy of the basic structure doctrine cannot avoid.

There is no doubt that some understanding of sovereignty underlies the reasons offered by the court in support of its decisions in a range of constitutional cases where the court is required to specify where ultimate political power rests. In order to justify the basic structure doctrine which circumscribes Parliament's amending power, I must necessarily develop a view on the nature of sovereignty in the Indian Constitution. It has been argued that the doctrine substitutes parliamentary sovereignty with judicial supremacy. In the rest of this section, I will examine this claim critically and show that it rests on a misunderstanding of the doctrine and the concept of sovereignty in the Indian Constitution.

The doctrine of Parliamentary sovereignty has never been seriously advanced as a doctrine in Indian constitutional law. The unsuitability of its application was noted in one of the earliest cases before the Supreme Court. Fazl Ali in *re Delhi Laws Act 1912*[90] discussing the doctrine of parliamentary sovereignty pointed out that the 'sovereignty of Parliament is an idea fundamentally inconsistent with the notions which govern inflexible and rigid constitutions existing in countries which have adopted any scheme of representative government'.[91] This was emphatically restated by Gajendragadkar in *Re Special Reference 1964*[92] who noted:

In a democratic country governed by a written Constitution, it is the Constitution which is supreme and sovereign…. Therefore, there can be no doubt that the sovereignty which can be claimed by the Parliament in England cannot be claimed by any Legislature in India in the literal absolute sense.[93]

This observation has been reaffirmed subsequently in several cases[94] and most recently in *Kuldip Nayar* v. *Union of India*.[95] Surprisingly, the discussions on the nature of sovereignty in the amendment

[90] AIR 1951 SC 332.
[91] Ibid.
[92] AIR 1965 SC 745.
[93] Ibid. (Gajendragadkar, CJ).
[94] *Sub Committee on Judicial Accountability* v. *Union of India*, AIR 1992 SC 320 (Ray, J) 332.
[95] *Kuldip Nayar* v. *Union of India*, (2006) SCC 1 (Sabharwal, CJ).

cases did not refer extensively to these important precedents on the inapplicability of the doctrine of parliamentary sovereignty in Indian constitutional law.[96] Perhaps most judges, including those dissenting judges who expressed an opinion, took the inapplicability of the doctrine of parliamentary sovereignty to be a settled legal proposition which required no restatement.[97]

If the doctrine of Parliamentary sovereignty finds no judicial support from the earliest cases to more recent ones as I have shown above, the stubborn persistence of this doctrine in political and academic discourse on the basic structure is remarkable. This may, in part, be due to the tendency to conflate the concept of sovereignty with Parliament's constituent or amending power. It is assumed that the amending power in Article 368 is the same as the sovereign power and constituent power of the Constituent Assembly. In the previous section I have adequately dealt with the distinction between amending and constituent power. The relationship between constituent power and the nature of sovereignty is one that requires careful theoretical elaboration, which is beyond the scope of this work.[98] By responding to these two distinct, though related, categories separately I avoid several confusions which plague the present debate and present a clearer and better understanding of the doctrine.

Judicial Supremacy, Popular Sovereignty, or Shared Sovereignty

The basic structure doctrine, in the mind of many observers, appears to have replaced parliamentary sovereignty and the separation of powers with judicial supremacy.[99]

[96] *Indira Gandhi v. Raj Narain*, AIR 1975 SC 2299 (Beg, J) p. 2441 affirms the holding in *Re Special Reference* 1964.

[97] *Keshavananda Bharati v. State of Kerala*, AIR 1973 4 SCC 225 (Shelat and Grover, JJ) 640. 'But the doctrine of parliamentary sovereignty as it obtains in England does not prevail here except to the extent provided by the Constitution. The entire scheme of the Constitution is such that it ensures the sovereignty and integrity of the country as a Republic and the democratic way of life by parliamentary institutions based on free and fair elections.'

[98] P.C. Oliver, *The Constitution of Independence*, Oxford: Oxford University Press, 2005, for a discussion on sovereignty and constituent power in Commonwealth jurisdictions.

[99] P.B. Mehta, 'The Inner Conflict of Constitutionalism', in Z. Hasan (ed.) *India's Living Constitution*, New Delhi: Permanent Black, 2004, p. 180.

In the previous section I argued that the courts have correctly taken the view that the doctrine of parliamentary sovereignty plays no role in the interpretation of the constitution. In this section I will examine whether the basic structure doctrine developed by the court accommodates an adequate understanding of the concept of sovereignty. I will now examine whether the courts advance an alternative to parliamentary sovereignty which is an adequate political conception of the relationship between the institutions of state and the people. If I can show that this is indeed the case, then the argument that the doctrine misunderstands the concept of sovereignty is mistaken and may be set aside.

I explore alternative accounts of the concept of sovereignty advanced by the court and academic commentators as underlying the basic structure doctrine: namely judicial supremacy, popular sovereignty, and shared sovereignty. I conclude that the only satisfactory account of sovereignty in the Indian Constitution must embrace an institutionally dispersed concept of sovereignty which is both legal and political in character and is composed of multiple and unranked sources of sovereign power. Let us begin this section by examining the argument relating to judicial supremacy in greater detail.

Judicial Supremacy

There is no doubt that the effect of the basic structure doctrine is to dislodge Parliament's pre-eminent role in the constitution amending process and circumscribe its powers. When viewed against background assumptions of the doctrine of parliamentary sovereignty the doctrine was perceived to be a naked usurpation of sovereign power by the Supreme Court. The *Kesavananda* opinion which set out the basic structure doctrine prompted a shrill denunciation by the political class, which claimed that the court had usurped Parliament's sovereign powers. This charge did not find significant academic or professional legal support though some scholars suggested that the court had now declared itself to be supreme as 'it has an undefined ... and therefore inexhaustible power to annul any amendment to the constitution'.[100]

---

[100] P. Chopra, *The Supreme Court versus the Constitution*, New Delhi: Sage Publications, 2006, p. 27.

The argument that the basic structure doctrine is a cloak for the proclamation of judicial supremacy misunderstands the nature and practice of the basic structure doctrine. First, this argument wrongly assumes that the basic structure doctrine allows the judiciary to exercise power whimsically and without limits, and fails to pay adequate attention to the form and substance of the doctrine elaborated in Chapters 3 and 4 of this work. In these chapters I elaborated on the nature and standard of basic structure review and the identity of basic features of the constitution to demonstrate that judicial interventions in the amending process are only likely in the most extreme cases of constitutional amendment. Further, where the basic structure doctrine is applied to other forms of state action it allows for judicial intervention only for the most egregious violations of basic features and is supplementary to other forms of constitutional judicial review available to test these forms of state action.

This low level of judicial intervention under the basic structure doctrine is best understood to be a result of the 'damage or destroy' standard of review as well as the general level at which basic features are identified, both of which are essential parts of the doctrine. This low standard of review as well as the other ingredients of the doctrine have been delineated, like many other constitutional doctrines used by the Supreme Court, at a level of clarity to be expected of the constitutional common law. As this standard of review is an integral part of the basic structure doctrine, it can hardly be argued that the doctrine offers a basis for asserting judicial supremacy.

Secondly, the argument of judicial supremacy pays inadequate attention to the practice of basic structure review in the past thirty-three years. Though the thrust of the arguments in this work is not quantitative, a cursory survey of reported Supreme Court cases which refer to the basic structure doctrine would indicate a steady increase in the invocation of the doctrine from its inception in 1973 to the present day. However, on closer scrutiny if the cases in which the Supreme Court strikes down state action using basic structure review are tabulated then this is a very small number. Sathe in a recently concluded survey of basic structure review cases in the Supreme Court found that the Court struck down state action very rarely....[101]

[101] S.P. Sathe, *Judicial Activism*, New Delhi: Oxford University Press, 2004.

Moreover, a cursory analysis of the ratio of the number of cases in which basic structure review is invoked to the number of cases where state action is struck down on the basis of the basic structure doctrine remains extremely low. The claims made here refer only reported Supreme Court cases in the *Supreme Court Cases Reporter* series for the period under consideration and does not allow us to generalize beyond that limited data set. However, even this limited survey confirms Sathe's observation that the Supreme Court has used the doctrine sparingly and it suggests that any claim that basic structure review is a doctrine that establishes judicial supremacy runs counter to the evidence available.

Before I conclude this part, I must consider one other sense in which basic structure review may provide for judicial supremacy. It may be argued that basic structure review allows the court to be supreme as it has the last word. That is to say that the court is supreme as it cannot be overruled by the legislature or the executive. Judicial supremacy in this sense is relatively uncontroversial in India, as it is embedded in our constitutional system which explicitly recognizes judicial review and allows the court to strike down state action on the grounds of jurisdictional competency, compliance with fundamental rights, and principles of administrative law. Basic structure review may only extend this type of judicial supremacy in two ways: first, in its application to constitutional amendments to which other forms of judicial review are inapplicable and second, by providing for another basis for judicial review of state action in addition to existing models of review.

While at first glance there seems to be some basis for the claim that basic structure review enhances judicial supremacy, a closer examination of some recent constitutional practice suggests other-wise. For the purposes of this section I will look to a recent example of the modes of interaction possible between Parliament and the courts. In *Indra Sawhney* v. *Union of India*[102] the Supreme Court held that equality was a basic feature of the constitution and that the 50 per cent limit on reservation quotas, the ban on quota based promotions in public employment, and the exclusion of the creamy layer in the identification of 'Other Backward Caste' beneficiaries

---

[102] *Indra Sawhney* v. *Union of India*, AIR 1993 SC 477.

are binding legal propositions which emerge from this basic feature. Parliament has subsequently amended the constitution to expressly overcome these restrictions and when these amendments were challenged under the basic structure doctrine, the court upheld the constitutional amendment.[103]

The court did not articulate clear reasons for upholding these amendments. The court could have articulated justifications related to the nature and standard of basic structure review or gone further to refashion basic structure review as a dialogue between the courts and the other branches of government. First, the court could have clarified that its holding that equality is a basic feature of the constitution in *Indra Sawhney* does not entail the further legal propositions regarding the 50 per cent limit, the exclusion of the creamy layer, and the bar on reservations in promotions in public employment, as these propositions are derived from the court's doctrine on the fundamental right to equality. This clarification would allow the court to distinguish the abstract nature of basic structure review, where the court assesses if the state action challenged before it 'damages or destroys' the basic feature of equality, from the fundamental rights compliance review where the court examines whether the state action complies with the court's doctrine on the right to equality. The recognition that the concrete legal propositions advanced in *Indra Sawhney* are rooted in the court's interpretation of the constitutional right to equality, it becomes apparent that these legal propositions may be overcome by a constitutional amendment. This equality doctrine articulated by the court is not an integral part of basic feature of equality with which basic structure review is concerned. Even if this equality doctrine is remoulded by constitutional amendment, the basic feature of equality can survive in the constitution. Basic structure review would strike down only such state actions which go so far as to efface any meaningful guarantee of equality from the constitution and the constitutional amendments in this case do not have such an effect.

A second type of justification which the court may have explored in support of its conclusions in *Indra Sawhney* would be to characterize basic structure review as a softer model of judicial review

[103] *M. Nagaraj* v. *Union of India*, AIR 2007 SC 71.

which promotes a 'democratic dialogue' between the branches of government. Where a judicial decision in a basic structure case is open to reversal, modification, or avoidance[104] then the remedy in basic structure review cases must be accurately characterized to be more like a declaration of incompatibility. Unlike fundamental rights compliance review, competence review, and administrative law review, where the relationship between the court and the legislature and executive is static; under basic structure review the court has the opportunity to advance a dynamic model of review where the court's finding triggers a public debate about the basic features of the constitution and the ensuing dialogue between the institutions of government deepens our constitutional culture.[105] Such a dialogue promotes democracy in two senses: first, the court allows the democratically elected arms of government to participate in the process of identification and elaboration of basic features of the constitution and secondly, it secures pan-institutional commitment to features of a constitutional democracy apart from majority rule.

So far in this part I have considered whether the basic structure doctrine makes the judiciary sovereign or the supreme institution of government. I argue that such a claim pays inadequate attention to the nature and standard of basic structure review and the low level of judicial intervention under the doctrine. Moreover, the court has tentatively used remedies in basic structure review cases to foster a democratic dialogue around key constitutional principles between the institutions of government thereby deepening our constitutional culture without reserving to itself the 'last word' on these matters. Further, in the next part of this section I will show that the doctrine does not establish the judiciary as the ultimate arbiter of basic constitutional values and expressly recognizes that this power rests with the people at large. If this is indeed the case, then the charge that basic structure doctrine elevates the judiciary to the supreme branch of government completely mischaracterizes the basic structure doctrine.

[104] R. Clayton, 'Judicial Deference and "Democratic Dialogue": The Legitimacy of Judicial Intervention under the Human Rights Act 1998', 2004 PL 33–47, 41.

[105] P. Hogg and A. Bushell, 'The Charter dialogue between courts and legislatures (or perhaps the Charter of Rights isn't such a bad thing after all) 35 *Osgoode Hall LJ* 75 (1997).

Popular or Shared Sovereignty

The claim that the Indian Constitution embraces a principle of popular sovereignty rests partly on a historical and normative argument and partly on legal arguments in the courts. The Constituent Assembly invested with the responsibility of drafting the Indian Constitution by the Indian Independence Act, 1947 proclaimed that it was acting in the sovereign interests of the people of India and not under the British legal authority which formally constituted it. This claim was reinforced by the Assembly adopting rules which gave it the power to dissolve itself.[106] It would be incorrect to claim that the Constituent Assembly was composed democratically and represented all sections of society. Though Austin is sympathetic to the view that the Constituent Assembly was meticulously composed to be a microcosm of the country it was ultimately 'a one–party assembly in a one–party country.'[107] The preamble of the Constitution of India, 1950 reiterates the vesting of sovereign power by expressly proclaiming that 'We, the People of India,'[108] give unto ourselves this constitution. If I take these assertions of popular authorship of the constitution seriously, as normative claims about where sovereignty is located there is no doubt that framers of the constitution embraced some version of popular sovereignty. Dietrich Conrad's careful analysis of the drafting of the Indian Constitution and the preamble led him to conclude that:

the legal authority of the Indian Constitution is to be assumed to derive from the authorship of the Indian people and that the Constitution is based upon the notions of popular, and *not* parliamentary, sovereignty.[109]

Despite the strength of the historical and normative argument for recognizing popular sovereignty in the Indian Constitution, the courts have not advanced a robust legal doctrine in support of such

[106] Constituent Assembly Rules of Procedure and Standing Orders Ch III Rule 7 cited in G. Austin, *The Indian Constitution: The Cornerstone of a Nation*, New Delhi: Oxford University Press, (Pbk edn) 2005, p. 7.

[107] G. Austin, *The Indian Constitution: The Cornerstone of a Nation*, New Delhi: Oxford University Press (Pbk edn) 2005, p. 8. For a fuller description of the composition of the Constituent Assembly see pp. 8–25.

[108] Constitution of India, 1950, Preamble.

[109] D. Conrad, *Zwischen Den Traditionen*, Stuttgart: Fran Steiner Verlag, 1999, p. 92.

a claim. In *Golaknath* v. *State of Punjab*[110] where the Supreme Court first introduced constitutional limits on the power of amendment, Subba Rao, confronting the argument on the nature of limits imposed by his ruling observed: 'the residuary power of Parliament may be relied upon to call for a Constituent Assembly for making a new Constitution or radically changing it'.[111] In *Kesavananda*, petitioner's counsel advanced an argument of popular sovereignty which Hegde[112] seemed to embrace, but most of the judges either rejected[113] such a proposition or found that it was unnecessary to decide the question.[114]

It was in *Indira Gandhi* v. *Raj Narain*[115] that the court moved towards a concept of shared sovereignty as an explanation of the basic structure doctrine. Chandrachud suggests that the distinction between legal and political sovereignty is useful to understand the basic structure doctrine. He proposes that the dicta speaking of 'sovereignty is of the people'[116] is best understood to be about political sovereignty. Legal sovereignty, on the other hand, is entrusted by the people to 'the three organs of the Sovereign Democratic Republic'[117] to exercise power on their behalf. He is alive to the possibility that 'political theory, faced with the complexities of modern life, finds location of sovereignty as a power concept too elusive and difficult a task to be satisfactorily carried out.'[118]

Beg developed an extensive analysis of the concept of sovereignty in his concurring opinion in *Indira Gandhi*. He suggests that the only concept of sovereignty which is compatible with Indian constitutional law is one that is denuded of 'all its customary connotations'.[119] He endorses a view of sovereignty which is 'divisible

---

[110] AIR 1967 SC 1643.

[111] *Golaknath* supra n. 110, p. 1670 (Subba Rao, CJ). Hidayatullah concurs p. 1705.

[112] AIR 1973 SC 1861 (Hegde, J), 1623–4.

[113] Ibid., 1603 (Matthew, J).

[114] Ibid., (Chandrachud, J).

[115] AIR 1975 SC 2299.

[116] Ibid., p. 2443 (Chandrachud, J).

[117] *Indira Gandhi*, supra note 115.

[118] Ibid., p. 2444 (Chandrachud, J).

[119] Ibid., p. 2436 (Beg, J).

and not... absolute and unlimited'.[120] He anticipates that a proposal for radical constitutional change 'must be shown to have the
sanction of all the three organs of the Republic, each applying its own
methods and principles and procedure for testing the correctness or
validity of the measure'.[121] Baxi endorses Beg's view that the 'constitution... could... be regarded as the true or "ultimate" sovereign'.[122]
Such a view of the supremacy of the constitution entails that 'the
Court is a co-ordinate branch of government with a constitutional
mandate to ensure that purported amendment has become "in fact
and in law"[123] a part of the constitution'.[124]

Conclusion

As the *Indira Gandhi* case was the last case in which there was a
rigorous judicial enquiry into the nature of sovereignty in the Indian
constitutional and political framework and its impact on the basic
structure doctrine, there is no benefit of a further enquiry into the
reasoning of the Supreme Court on this issue. In the first part of this
section I argued that the doctrine of parliamentary sovereignty has
little or no basis in Indian constitutional law. A cursory glance at
the provisions of the constitution which distributes legislative power
between central and state legislatures, separates powers and functions
of the legislative, executive, and judicial branches of government, and
imposes limits on the capacity of parliament to act in contravention
of citizens' fundamental rights confirms that the Diceyan model of
parliamentary sovereignty finds no place in the Indian constitutional
scheme. The Indian Constitution clearly adopted the American
model of constitutionalism with limited government and strong
judicial review. Though some elements of the English Parliamentary
system were adapted to Indian conditions—the composition of the
higher executive and collective cabinet responsibility—it is difficult to

---

[120] Ibid.

[121] *Indira Gandhi*, supra n. 115, 2436 (Beg J).

[122] Ibid., p. 2436.

[123] *Sajjan Singh* v. *Union of India*, AIR 1965 SC 845 (Mudholkar, J).

[124] U. Baxi, 'Some Reflections on the Nature of Constituent Power', in
R. Dhavan and A. Jacob (eds), *The Indian Constitution: Some Trends and Issues*,
Bombay: N.M. Tripathi P. Ltd, 1978, p. 123.

support the conclusion that this entails the doctrine of Parliamentary sovereignty.

I may surmise that the persistence of the doctrine of parliamentary sovereignty in Indian constitutional law is largely due to the historical legacy of Indian public law tradition being rooted in the English public law and the particular historical circumstances under which the Constituent Assembly which drafted the constitution continued to exist as the first provisional Parliament of independent India. This institutional continuity prompted the claim that this provisional Parliament had a special role in interpreting the constitution as it drafted the constitution and this enhanced interpretive role was sanctified through the 'doctrine of contemporaneous exposition'.[125] This method of interpretation cannot justify the accompanying assertions of parliamentary sovereignty which otherwise have no historical, political, or legal basis.

I then considered the claim that the judiciary was supreme and sovereign and found that this claim did not appreciate the nature of the basic structure doctrine and its practice over the last three decades. I noted that the court's dicta has recognized that the people acting directly could give themselves a new constitution using a process which is yet to be determined. Moreover, the court has in recent cases developed remedies in basic structure cases which allow for an institutional dialogue between the institutions of government and this blunts the argument that the judiciary is having the last word on all these issues.

In the last part of this section I considered two alternative views of the nature of sovereignty which have found some support from the Supreme Court and academic commentators: first, popular sovereignty where sovereign power rests with the people at large and second, shared sovereignty or constitutional sovereignty[126] where the constitution is supreme and all constitutional amendment has to be approved by the three branches of government. These two versions of sovereignty are sought to be reconciled by the court

[125] *Minerva Mills* v. *Union of India*, AIR 1980 SC 1789 (Chandrachud) 1791.

[126] For recent confirmations of constitutional sovereignty see *I.R. Coelho* v. *State of Tamil Nadu* (2007) SC Almanac 197 (Sabharwal CJI) 212–14 and *M. Nagaraj* v. *Union of India* (2006) 8 SCC 212 (Kapadia, J) 244.

which takes shared sovereignty to be about political sovereignty and constitutional sovereignty to be about legal sovereignty. This reconciliation suggests that this is a 'working theory' which 'should be acceptable to lawyers'.[127]

This uneasy reconciliation between popular and shared constitutional sovereignty proposed by the courts is convoluted and unnecessary. At the root of these arguments is an outmoded and static conception of sovereignty which assumes that it is 'logical or empirical necessity for a legal force to one institution, or to have a legal rule that will, or can, decisively resolve conflict between different legal sources'.[128] To provide an adequate account of sovereignty which can explain and allow for better understanding of the basic structure doctrine one needs an institutionally dispersed version of sovereignty which accommodates a 'continuing legal system' whose identity is determined by the continuity of its political institutions rather than a static rule of recognition. Such a theory of sovereignty would require a different account of judicial legitimacy which acknowledges that judges have a dual authority—legal and political[129]—and hence require a revised account of the appropriate boundaries for the judicial exercise of power with multiple unranked sources of legal power.

At this point I have gone beyond what I set out to do at the start of this Chapter: to provide a minimalist account of the legitimacy of the basic structure doctrine that counters the primary criticisms of the doctrine. In this section, I have argued that the doctrine of parliamentary sovereignty cannot be the basis of a serious challenge to the constitutionality of basic structure review. I have proposed that the best understanding of the basic structure doctrine and sovereignty in a political and legal sense will require the development of a new account of sovereignty itself and this is a task that I will take up on another occasion.

The moral legitimacy of the basic structure doctrine has been the primary focus of the political and academic criticism of the doctrine. In this part of the Chapter I have responded to the three

---

[127] Indira Gandhi, supra n. 115, p. 2436 (Beg, J).
[128] N. Barber, Sovereignty Re-examined, *OJLS*, 131–54 (2000) 139.
[129] Ibid., pp. 150–2.

primary criticisms of the doctrine: firstly, that it is an undemocratic limit on the amending power; secondly, that judicial review of constitutional amendment is illegitimate and thirdly, that the doctrine misunderstands the nature of sovereignty. I have argued that the basic structure doctrine imposes limits on Parliaments amending power but acknowledges that the constitution can be radically changed by the people themselves. The general argument for the illegitimacy of judicial review overemphasizes the representative character of elected political institutions and underplays the democratic pedigree earned by non–representative institutions. Further, such an argument does concede that judicial review may be legitimate in some circumstances where representative institutions fail to maintain democratic essentials and basic structure responds to these situations. Finally, I show that the argument for parliamentary sovereignty has very little support in the Indian constitution or in the decisions of the court. An adequate understanding of basic structure review would require a revised account of sovereignty which is institutionally dispersed and envisages a legal system with multiple unranked sources of power.

SOCIOLOGICAL LEGITIMACY

Kesavananda did not enjoy legitimacy in 1973 … It was the Election case that earned legitimacy for Kesavananda.[130]

Sociological legitimacy exists when the people at large, or a narrow segment of legal and political elites, regard the institutional arrangements of the state or some particular decisions made by it as 'justified, appropriate, or otherwise deserving of support for reasons beyond fear of sanctions or mere hope for personal reward'.[131] Legitimacy in this sense is an empirical category which requires the measurement of the extent to which the people, or a particular section of them, obey the legal system and the reasons for this obedience. A quantitative or qualitative social survey or a more focused ethnography may be

---

[130] S.P. Sathe, 'Limitation on Constitutional Amendment', in R. Dhavan and A. Jacobs (eds), *Indian Constitution: Trends and Issues*, Bombay: N.M. Tripathi P. Ltd, 1977, p. 183.

[131] R. Fallon, 'Legitimacy and the Constitution', 118 *Harvard L Rev* 1989 (2005) 1795.

possible ways of gathering this empirical evidence. More often, the very fact that a majority of the people do not rise up in revolt or active disobedience of the political system is taken to be adequate evidence of the tacit legitimacy of the legal system or some ingredient of it. Thus, active agreement or mere acquiescence may be taken as ideal or minimal benchmarks against which sociological legitimacy may be measured.

Sathe's invocation of legitimacy in the quotation above is best understood as evaluating the sociological legitimacy of the basic structure doctrine among legal and political elites in the 1970s. He suggests that popular legitimacy among the people at large is conditioned by the legitimacy of the basic structure doctrine among legal and political elites as 'the ordinary people do not understand the intricacies of the law'.[132] He does not support his conclusions with any quantitative empirical evidence on how wide-spread the acceptance of the basic structure doctrine is and he rests his conclusions on his, and Seervai's, reasons for changing their view on the legitimacy of the doctrine.

Evaluations of the sociological legitimacy of the basic structure doctrine have been one of the central concerns in Indian constitutional law scholarship. The practice of conducting large surveys to ascertain the legitimacy of a judicial doctrine, though popular and widely used in other countries,[133] is not common in India. Thus debates about the legitimacy of the basic structure doctrine are primarily concerned with the views of scholars of constitutional law and politics. In this section I will first critically respond to the two phases of intense argument about the legitimacy of the basic structure doctrine; namely early years of the doctrine beginning with the 1970s and then a second phase which begins after the *Indira Gandhi* up to the present times. I conclude this section by assessing the extent to which the sociological legitimacy of a judicial doctrine is contingent on its legal and moral legitimacy and what the insights into this complex relationship between the three strands hold for the future debates on the legitimacy of the basic structure doctrine.

---

[132] S.P. Sathe, supra n. 130, p. 185.

[133] J.L. Gibson, 'Measuring Attitudes Toward the United States Supreme Court', 47 *American J Political Science* (2003) 354.

The 1970s: Basic Structure Doctrine in its Early Years

In *Golaknath*,[134] the Supreme Court for the first time imposed substantive limits on the amending power of Parliament to the extent that it abridged fundamental rights in Part III of the constitution. Seervai[135] and Tripathi[136] took the lead in demonstrating that this judgment was wrong and that the court was guilty of overstepping constitutional boundaries. They were joined in this chorus by almost every prominent legal academic and political commentator of the period. While some of them are categorical in their rejection[137] of the *Golaknath* formula, others equivocate on the key issues.[138] The one discordant note in this chorus of denunciation was that of Dietrich Conrad, a constitutional law scholar from the University of Heidelberg, who presented papers and then subsequently published an article[139] for limitations on amending and constituent power. This careful analysis of the theoretical basis of the constitutional principles underlying the *Golaknath* decision had a decisive influence in *Kesavananda*.[140] When the *Kesavananda* opinion was announced, Tripathi was emphatic that as 'academic research had completely undermined the foundations of the arguments supporting the majority opinions in *Golak Nath*'[141] this view was abandoned by the court without argument.

The hostile reception to *Golaknath* was more muted when the court delivered the *Kesavananda* judgment. However, Tripathi attacked the judgment with a strongly worded and carefully argued

---

[134] AIR 1967 SC 1643.

[135] H.M. Seervai, *Constitutional Law of India*, Bombay: N.M. Tripathi P. Ltd, 1968 (1st edn Vol. I) 1088–1119.

[136] P.K. Tripathi, *Some Insights into Fundamental Rights*, Bombay: University of Bombay, 1972, pp. 1–45.

[137] S.P. Sathe, 'Supreme Court, Parliament and the Constitution', 6 *Economic and Political Weekly* 1821–8, 1972–9 (1971).

[138] R. Dhavan, *The Supreme Court of India: A Socio-Legal Critique of its Juristic Techniques*, Bombay: N.M. Tripathi P. Ltd, 1977, p. 410.

[139] D. Conrad (ed.), 'Limitation of Amendment Procedures and the Constituent Power' in D. Conrad (ed) *Zwischen Den Traditionen*, Stuttgart: Franz Steiner Verlag, 1999, pp. 47–86.

[140] *Kesavananda Bharati* v. *State of Kerala*, AIR 1973 SC 1861, 2020.

[141] P.K. Tripathi, '*Keshavananda Bharati* v. *State of Kerala*: Who Wins?' 1974 SCC Journal 1–6.

article which was extremely influential at the time.[142] Other writers like Dhavan,[143] Baxi,[144] and Sathe[145] published guarded appraisals of the *Kesavananda* judgment. Political elites of the Congress party were particularly disenchanted with the judgment and published extensive journalistic criticisms and organized seminars to denounce the doctrine for being anti-revolutionary and other related ills.[146]

An overall assessment of the sociological legitimacy of the basic structure doctrine in this period among legal and political elites leads us to the conclusion that the doctrine was perceived to be illegitimate. A richer analysis of the sources of this perception will require a careful understanding of the intellectual and political setting in which this early assessment took place. The assumption that the concept of parliamentary sovereignty as a political principle was foundational to the constitution and the political discourse of socialist revolution which polarized political judgment of the period are particularly important factors which framed the reception of the basic structure doctrine among legal and political elites. A careful analysis of the social and intellectual history of the doctrine will allow for a nuanced and heightened appreciation of the remarkable performance of the court in generating the doctrine in rather adverse historical circumstances. But this analysis is beyond the scope of the work and best left to another author and another book. At this point it is sufficient to note that the basic structure doctrine at its inception found no willing and articulate support and it is fair to conclude that it was perceived to be illegitimate among legal and political elites of the time.

[142] Ibid.

[143] R. Dhavan, *Supreme Court of India and Parliamentary Sovereignty*, New Delhi: Sterling Publishers, 1976.

[144] U. Baxi, 'The Constitutional Quicksands of *Kesavananda Bharati* and the Twenty-fifth Amendment' in (1974) 1 SCC Journal 45 and U. Baxi, 'Some Reflections on the Nature of Constituent Power', in R. Dhavan and A. Jacobs (eds), *Indian Constitution: Trends and Issues*, Bombay: N.M. Tripathi P. Ltd, 1978, pp. 122–43.

[145] S.P. Sathe, 'Limitations on Constitutional Amendment: "Basic Structure" Principle Re-examined', in R. Dhavan and A. Jacob (eds), *Indian Constitution: Trends and Issues*, Bombay: N.M. Tripathi P. Ltd, 1978, pp. 179–91.

[146] For a rich overview of the views of the political elites and a survey of newspaper editorials of the time see G. Austin, *Working a Democratic Constitution: The Indian Experience*, Delhi: Oxford University Press, 1999.

Indira Gandhi and Beyond: The Basic Structure Doctrine Today

The *Indira Gandhi* case marks a significant inflection point in the sociological legitimacy of the basic structure doctrine. The willingness of the Congress government to amend the constitution and enact laws to overcome the electoral disputes of Indira Gandhi was challenged in *Indira Gandhi*.[147] The proclamation of the national emergency soon after and the passing of the radical (Constitution 42nd Amendment) Act, (1976), dramatically altered the perception of legal and political elites regarding the constitution and its relationship with the political process. In this context, the basic structure doctrine emerged as the bulwark against the excesses of political majoritarianism.

The political upheavals of the time were complemented in equal measure by the legal gymnastics of leading counsels and constitutional commentators of the time. H.M. Seervai's volte face on the correctness and legitimacy of the basic structure doctrine was both, legally the most significant, and academically the most poorly articulated justification.[148] Seervai proposed that the *Indira Gandhi* case had modified the basic structure doctrine to such an extent that 'a critical discussion of *Kesavananda's* case, taken by itself would be inaccurate and misleading without a discussion of the deeper analysis of the amending power in the *Election* case'.[149] This is an outrageous claim when one considers that the constitutional basis of the basic structure doctrine was taken to be binding precedent by the court in *Indira Gandhi* and the court confined itself to applying the doctrine to a new set of legal and factual circumstances.[150]

Sathe's reassessment of the legitimacy of the basic structure is more forthright and reflective. He points out that 'the *Kesavananda* decision acquired legitimacy because of the subsequent developments'[151] and reflecting on Seervai's change of opinion observes that

---

[147] AIR 1975 SC 2299.

[148] H.M. Seervai, *Constitutional Law of India*, Bombay: N.M. Tripathi P. Ltd, 1994 (4th edn Vol. II), pp. 3109–71.

[149] Ibid., supra n. 150, pp. 3109–10.

[150] Ibid., pp. 3135–6. Seervai acknowledges this in passing while discussing the impact of the basic structure doctrine.

[151] S.P. Sathe, 'Limitations on Constitutional Amendment', supra n. 148, 181.

'he and many of us came to favour that doctrine mainly because of the experience, during the Emergency'.[152] Writers who appraised the basic structure doctrine in *Kesavananda* cautiously now endorsed the doctrine more emphatically.[153] But this substantial turnaround in the appreciation of the basic structure doctrine did not lead to an elite consensus.

The dissenting voices gained prominence with the formation of the first Bharatiya Janata Party-led coalition government at the Centre. Their decision to constitute the National Commission to Review the Working of the Constitution[154] at the turn of the century gave sceptics of the doctrine a new forum.[155] Though not all criticisms of the doctrine were motivated by the political agenda of the government,[156] they are indicators that the sociological legitimacy among Indian legal and political elites is far from unanimous. Much of the recent criticism concedes that the basic structure doctrine did play an important role at a particular juncture in India's constitutional history but then goes on to argue that in our present political and

[152] Ibid.

[153] Contrast U. Baxi's caution in U. Baxi, 'The Constitutional Quicksands of *Keshavananda Bharati* and the Twenty-fifth Amendment', (1974) 1 SCC Journal 45 with the exuberant criticism of Chandrachud's basic structure opinions in U. Baxi, *Courage, Craft and Contention: The Indian Supreme Court in the Eighties*, Bombay: N.M. Tripathi P. Ltd, 1985, pp. 64–110. A similar contrast can be made between R. Dhavan's critical assessment of the doctrine in R. Dhavan, *Supreme Court and Parliamentary Sovereignty*, New Delhi: Sterling Publishers, 1976 and its full endorsement in R. Dhavan, 'Judges and Indian Democracy: the lesser evil?', in F. Frankel (ed.), *Transforming India: Social and Political Dynamics of Democracy*, New Delhi: Oxford University Press, 2005, p. 315.

[154] For a fuller discussion of the political context against which the National Commission was set up. See 'Introduction'.

[155] S. Kashyap, *The Need to Review the Working of the Constitution*, New Delhi: Shipra Publishers, 2000 and S.N. Mishra, S.C. Hazary, and A. Mishra, *Constitution and Constitutionalism in India*, New Delhi: ABH Publishing Corporation, 1999.

[156] R. Ramachandran, 'The Supreme Court and the Basic Structure Doctrine', in B.N. Kirpal, A.H. Desai, G. Subramanium, R. Dhavan, and R. Ramachandran (eds), *Supreme but not Infallible: Essays in Honour of the Supreme Court of India*, New Delhi: Oxford University Press, 2000, and P. Chopra, *The Supreme Court versus the Constitution: A Challenge to Federalism*, New Delhi: Sage Publications, 2006.

economic context the doctrine hinders rather than advances our development.

The brief historical survey of the sociological legitimacy of the basic structure spanning the three decades of its existence makes it clear that the doctrine continues to face significant challenges. 'As is generally true with sociological legitimacy, the acceptance was probably never unanimous'[157] at any point in time. Like moral and legal legitimacy I may usefully speak only in terms of the extent and degree of sociological legitimacy at any point in time. By those standards it would be a fair assessment to say that the doctrine was widely perceived to be illegitimate among legal and political elites at its inception in the 1970s but secured a great deal of legitimacy in the Emergency period and soon after. At the turn of the century the doctrine is buffeted by new political and legal challenges which threaten to unseat it from the lofty perch it enjoys in Indian constitutionalism.

By paying attention to complex inter-relationships between moral, legal, and sociological legitimacy, I would emphasize the relative independence of legal and moral legitimacy of the basic structure doctrine from its sociological legitimacy at different points in time. Even if the doctrine was morally and legally legitimate when it was announced in *Kesavananda* it did not enjoy the same degree of sociological legitimacy. As the doctrine came to be accepted as legitimate by the legal and political elites in dramatically different political circumstances, this had little to do with the arguments for the legal or moral legitimacy of the doctrine which remained constant across this period even if they were articulated in a more nuanced fashion. We will explore the overall legitimacy of the basic structure doctrine in a composite fashion in the concluding section of this chapter.

OVERALL LEGITIMACY OF THE DOCTRINE

The sociological legitimacy of the basic structure doctrine in significant measure rests on elite and popular understanding of the workings of the doctrine and the legal and moral legitimacy that it enjoys. In Chapter 1 of this work I identified key contemporary issues in

---

[157] R. Fallon, supra n. 131, p. 1803.

Indian constitutional law and argued that the basic structure doctrine was one issue that needed better explanation and justification. In Chapters 2 and 3, I re-examined the constitutional basis for the application of the basic structure doctrine to constitutional amendment and other forms of state action respectively. I rejected the argument that the basic structure doctrine is a fanciful invention of the Supreme Court without constitutional foundation and proposed that it is a justifiable interpretation of the constitutional text. In Chapter 4, I showed that basic structure review operates as an independent type of judicial review through which the court ensures that state action does not 'damage or destroy' basic features of the Constitution. I argued in Chapter 5 that the court has committed itself to identify basic features as key constitutional principles at the core of the normative identity of the constitution through a common law adjudication technique. The careful reconstruction of the constitutional basis and working of the doctrine of basic structure in Chapters 2 to 5 allowed me to isolate and respond to the core legitimacy challenges to basic structure review in Chapter 6.

In this final chapter, I have responded to the key arguments against the legal, moral, and sociological legitimacy of basic structure review. I have argued that the utilization of multi-provisional implications to ascertain constitutional meaning is a justified model of constitutional interpretation. The constitutional basis of basic structure review and the identification of basic features of the constitution employ this mode of constitutional interpretation. Secondly, I have argued that while basic structure review does not allow Parliament to have the final word on constitutional amendments which damage the basic features of the constitution; this is not usurped by the courts but left to the people to exercise their constituent power. I have suggested that arguments against the illegitimacy of basic structure review takes too limited a view of the democratic qualities of institutions and the requirements of political participation and equal representation. Basic structure review enhances the degree of political participation in radical expansive constitutional change by requiring a higher level of deliberative decision-making to support such constitutional amendment. I conclude this chapter with a brief survey of the ebbs and flows of the sociological legitimacy of the basic structure doctrine. Clearly the basic structure doctrine does not enjoy unanimous endorsement among Indian political and legal elites. This is not surprising in a vast complex democracy.

Insofar as this work is successful in better portraying the constitutional basis and workings of the basic structure doctrine and refuting arguments against its illegitimacy it will contribute to enhancing the sociological legitimacy of the doctrine. It would be naive to imagine that the sociological legitimacy or popular approval of the basic structure doctrine would be contingent on an academically oriented work like this. It is certainly my hope and ambition to take this work forward by developing the arguments brought out here and contributing to this goal.

Bibliography

BOOKS

Ackerman, B. *We the People* (The Belknap Press of Harvard University Press, Cambridge Massachusetts, 1991, Vols 1-2).

Ahuja, S. *People Power and Justice: A Casebook of Public Interest Litigation* (Orient Longman, New Delhi, 1997).

Allan, T.R.S. *Constitutional Justice* (Cambridge University Press, Cambridge, 2000)

Alexander, L. (ed.). *Constitutionalism* (Cambridge University Press, Cambridge, 1998).

Austin, G. *The Indian Constitution: Cornerstone of the Nation* (Clarendon Press, Oxford, 1966).

————. *Working a Democratic Constitution: A History of the Indian Experience* (Oxford University Press, Oxford, 2003).

Baxi, U. *The Indian Supreme Court and Politics* (Eastern Book Company, Lucknow, 1980).

————. *Courage, Craft and Contention: The Indian Supreme Court in the Eighties* (N.M. Tripathi Pvt Ltd, Bombay, 1985).

Bellamy, R. *Constitutionalism and Democracy* (Dartmouth Ashgate Publishing, Aldershot, 2006).

Bhandari, M.K. *Basic Structure of the Indian Constitution: A Critical Reconsideration* (Deep & Deep Publications, New Delhi, 1993).

Cane, P. and M. Tushnet (eds). *The Oxford Handbook of Legal Studies* (Oxford University Press, Oxford, 2003)

Chopra, P. *The Supreme Court versus the Constitution: A Challenge to Federalism* (Sage Publications, New Delhi, 2006).

Conrad, D. (ed.). *Zwischen Den Traditionen: Probleme Des Verfassungsrechts in Indien and Pakistant* (Franz Steiner, Verlag, Stuttgart, 1999)

Dhavan, R. and A. Jacobs (eds). *Indian Constitution: Trends and Developments* (N.M. Tripathi Pvt Ltd, Bombay, 1978).

Dhavan, R. *The Supreme Court of India and Parliamentary Sovereignty* (Sterling Publishers Private Ltd, New Delhi, 1976).

Dhavan, R. *The Supreme Court of India: A Socio-Legal Critique of its Juristic Techniques* (N.M. Tripathi Pvt Ltd, Bombay, 1977).

Dworkin, R.M. *Freedom's Law: The Moral Reading of the American Constitution* (Oxford University Press, Oxford, 1999).

————. *Taking Rights Seriously* (Gerald Duckworth & Co., London, 1977).

Dyzenhaus, D. *The Unity of Public Law* (Hart Publishing, Oxford, 2004).

Ely, J.H. *Democracy and Distrust: A Theory of Judicial Review* (Harvard University Press, Cambridge, Massachusetts, 1980).

Epp, C. *The Rights Revolution* (The University of Chicago Press, Chicago, 1998).

Fish, S. *The Trouble with Principle* (Harvard University Press, Cambridge, Massachusetts, 1999).

Frankel, F., Z. Hasan, R. Bhargava, and B. Arora (eds). *Transforming India: Social and Political Dynamics of Democracy* (Oxford University Press, New Delhi, 2000).

Goldsworthy, J. (ed.). *Interpreting Constitutions: A Comparative Study* (Oxford University Press, Oxford, 2006)

————. *The Sovereignty of Parliament, History and Philosophy* (Oxford University Press, Oxford, 1999).

Hart, H.L.A. *Concept of Law* (Oxford India Paperbacks, New Delhi, 2002).

Hasan, Z., E. Sridharan, and R. Sudarshan (eds). *India's Living Constitution: Ideas, Practices, Controversies* (Permanent Black, New Delhi, 2002).

Hobsbawm, E. *On History* (Weidenfeld and Nicolson, London, 1997).

Iyer, V. (ed.). *Democracy, Human Rights and the Rule of Law* (Butterworths India, New Delhi, 2000).

Jacobsohn, G.J., *The Wheel of Law: India's Secularism in Comparative Constitutional Context* (Oxford University Press, New Delhi, 2003).

Kashyap, S. *Reforming the Constitution* (UBS Publishers' Distributors Pvt Ltd, New Delhi, 1992).

————. *Basic Constitutional Values* (Ajanta Publications, New Delhi, 1994).

————. (ed.). *The Framing of India's Constitution* (Universal Law Publishing Co. Ltd, New Delhi, 2004).

————. *Constitution Making Since 1950* (Universal Law Publishing Co. Ltd, New Delhi, 2004).

Kashyap, S., D.D. Khanna, and G.W. Kueck (eds). *Need to Review the Working of the Constitution* (Shipra Publishers, New Delhi, 2004).

Kirpal, B.N., A.H. Desai, G. Subramanium, R. Dhavan, and R. Ramachandran (eds). *Supreme but not Infallible: Essays in Honour of the Supreme Court of India* (Oxford University Press, New Delhi, 2000).

Kramer, L.D. *The People Themselves: Popular Constitutionalism and Judicial Review* (Oxford University Press, Oxford, 2004).

Lakshminath, A.R. *Basic Structure and Constitutional Amendments: Limitations and Justiciability* (Deep and Deep Publication Pvt Ltd, New Delhi, 2002).

Larry, A. (ed.). *Constitutionalism: Philosophical Foundations* (Cambridge University Press, Cambridge, 1998).

Lindell, G. (ed.). *Future Directions in Australian Constitutional Law* (Federation Press, Annandale, 1994)

Loughlin, M., *The Idea of Public Law* (Oxford University Press, Oxford, 2004).

Lutt, J. and M.P. Singh. *Dieter Conrad: Zwischen den Traditionen* (Franz Steiner, Verlag, Stuttgart, 1999).

MacCormick, N. *Questioning Sovereignty* (Oxford University Press, Oxford, 1999).

Marmor, A. (ed.). *Law and Interpretation* (Clarendon Press, Oxford, 1998).

Marshall, G. *Constitutional Conventions* (Clarendon Press, Oxford, 1984).

Palkhivala, N. *Our Constitution Defaced and Defiled* (Macmillan Co. of India, Delhi, 1974).

Mishra, S.N., S.C. Hazary, and A. Mishra (eds). *Constitution and Constitutionalism in India* (APH Publishing Corporation, New Delhi, 1999).

Patapan, H. *Judging Democracy: The New Politics of the High Court of Australia* (Cambridge University Press, Cambridge, 2000).

Raman, S. *Amending Power under the Constitution of India: A Politico–Legal Study* (Eastern Law House, Calcutta, 1990).

Rao, S. *The Framing of India's Constitution* (The Indian Institute of Public Administration and N.M. Tripathi Pvt Ltd, Bombay, 1968, Vols 1–5).

Raz, J. *Authority of Law: Essays on Law and Morality* (Oxford University Press, Oxford, 1979).

—————. *Ethics in the Public Domain: Essays in the Morality of Law and Politics* (Clarendon Press, Oxford, 1994).

Sathe, S.P. *Judicial Activism in India: Transgressing Borders and Enforcing Limits* (Oxford University Press, New Delhi, 2002).

Seervai, H.M. *Constitutional Law of India* (4th edn, N.M. Tripathi Pvt Ltd, Bombay, 1993).

Sen, S. *Popular Sovereignty and Democratic Transformations: The Constitution of India* (Oxford University Press, New Delhi, 2007).

Sharma, J. *Terrifying Vision: Golwalkar, the RSS and India* (Penguin Books, New Delhi, 2007).

Shourie, A. *Courts and their Judgments: Promises, Prerequisites, Consequences* (Rupa & Co., New Delhi, 2001)

Singh, M.P. (ed.). *V.N. Shukla's Constitution of India* (10th edn, Eastern Book Co., Lucknow, 2003).

Subramanium, G., R. Dhavan, and R. Ramachandran (eds), *Supreme but not Infallible: Essays in Honour of the Supreme Court of India* (Oxford University Press, New Delhi, 2000).

Trevor, A. *Constitutional Justice: A Liberal Theory of the Rule of Law* (Oxford University Press, Oxford, 2001).

Tripathi, P.K. *Some Insights into Fundamental Rights* (University of Bombay, Bombay, 1972).

Tribe, L.H. *Constitutional Choices* (First Indian Reprint, Universal Law Publishers, New Delhi, 2000).

Verma, K. and S.K. Verma (eds). *Fifty Years of the Supreme Court of India— Its Grasp and Reach* (Oxford University Press, New Delhi, 2000).

Wade, H.W.R. *Constitutional Fundamentals* (Stevens & Sons, London, 1980).

Waldron, J. (ed.). *Theories of Rights* (Oxford University Press, Oxford, 1984).

Waluchow, W.J. *Inclusive Legal Positivism* (Clarendon Press, Oxford, 1994).

Wheare, K.C. *Modern Constitutions* (Oxford University Press, Bombay, 1966).

Zavos, J. A Wyatt, and V. Hewitt (eds), *The Politics of Cultural Mobilization in India* (Oxford University Press, New Delhi, 2004).

ARTICLES

Ackerman, B. 'The Common Law Constitution of John Marshall Harlan' 36 *New York Law School L Rev*, pp. 5–32 (1991).

Garg, R.D. 'Phantom of Basic Structure of the Constitution: A critical appraisal of the *Kesavananda* Case', 16 *Journal of the Indian Law Institute*, pp. 243–69 (1974).

Adler, M. 'Popular Constitutionalism and the Rule of Recognition: Whose Practices Ground US Law?' University of Pennsylvania Law School Public Law and Legal Theory Research Paper Series Research Paper No. 54 http://papers.ssrn.com/abstract=603442

Allan, T.R.S. 'Doctrine and Theory in Administrative Law: An Elusive Quest for the Limits of Jurisdiction', *Public Law*, pp. 429–54 (2003).

Barber, N.W. 'Professor Loughlin's Idea of Public', 25 *Oxford J of Legal Studies*, pp. 157–67 (2005).

————. 'Sovereignty Re-examined: The Courts, Parliament, and Statutes', 20 *Oxford J of Legal Studies*, pp. 131–54 (2000).

ü, U. '"The Little Done, The Vast Undone"—Some Reflections on Reading Granville Austin's The Indian Constitution', 9 *Journal of the Indian Law Institute*, pp. 322–430 (1967).

————. 'The Constitutional Quicksands of *Kesavananda Bharati* and the Twenty Fifty Amendment' (1974), 1 Supreme Court Cases Journal 45.

————. 'On How Not To Judge the Judges: Notes Towards Evaluation of the Judicial Role', 25 *Journal of the Indian Law Institute*, pp. 211–37 (1985).

————. 'Saint Granville's Gospel: Reflections', 36 *Economic and Political Weekly*, pp. 921–30 (2001).

————. 'Constitutional Changes: An Analysis of the Swaran Singh Committee Report' (1976) 2 Supreme Court Cases (Journal), 17.

————. 'Kar Seva of the Indian Constitution? Reflection on Proposals for Review of the Constitution', 35 *Economic and Political Weekly*, p. 891 (2000).

————. 'A known but an indifferent judge: Situating Ronald Dworkin in Contemporary Indian Jurisprudence', 1 *International Journal of Constitutional Law*, pp. 557–89 (2003).

Bhargava, R. 'Words save lives: India, the BJP and the Constitution' <http://www.opendemocracy.net/themes/article-3-504.jsp> (10 April 2007).

Black, C. 'Amending the Constitution: A Letter to a Congressman', 82 *Yale L J*, p. 189 (1972).

Choudhry, S. and B. Mount. 'Ackerman's Higher Lawmaking in Comparative Constitutional Perspective: Constitutional Moments as Constitutional Failures?' (15 August 2006). ExpressO Preprint Series. Working Paper 1544 <http://law.bepress.com/expresso/eps/1544>

Claus, L. 'Implication and the Concept of a Constitution', 69 *Australian L J*, p. 887 (1995).

Clayton, R. 'Judicial Deference and "Democratic Dialogue": The Legitimacy of Judicial Intervention under the Human Rights Act 1998', *Public Law*, pp. 33–47 (2004).

Cohn, M. 'Judicial Activism in the House of Lords: A Composite Constitutionalist Approach', *Public Law*, pp. 95–115 (2007).

Corwin, E. 'The Higher Law Background to the American Constitutional Law', 42 *Harv L Rev*, 149 (1928).

Craig, P. 'Public Law, Political Theory and Legal Theory', *Public Law*, pp. 211–39 (2000).

Dellinger, Walter. 'The Legitimacy of Constitutional Change: Rethinking the Amendment Process', 97 *Harvard L Rev*, p. 386 (1983–4).

Dicey, A.V., 'An Introduction to the Study of the Law of the Constitution' (10th edn Macmillan, London, 1958).

Dworkin, Ronald. 'Rawls And The Law' 72 *Fordham L. Rev.*, p. 1387 (2003–4).

Elliot, R. 'References, Structural Argumentation and the Organizing Principles of Canada's Constitution', 80 *The Canadian Bar Review*, p. 67 (2001).

Ely, J.H. 'On Discovering Fundamental Principles', 92 *Harvard L Rev*, pp. 5–92 (1978–9).

Endicott, T. 'Putting Interpretation in its Place', 13 *Law and Philosophy*, pp. 451–79 (1994).

———. 'Linguistic Indeterminacy', 16 *Oxford Journal of Legal Studies*, pp. 667–97 (1996).

Fallon, R.H. 'How to Choose a Constitutional Theory', 87 *California L Rev*, p. 535 (1999).

———. 'Legitimacy and the Constitution', 118 *Harvard L Rev*, p. 1789 (2005).

Freeman, S. 'Constitutional Democracy and the Legitimacy of Judicial Review', 9 *Law and Philosophy*, pp. 227–70 (1990).

Fried, C. 'Constitutional Doctrine' 107 *Harvard L Rev*, pp. 1140–157 (1994).

Garg, R.D. 'Phantom of Basic Structure of the Constitution: A critical appraisal of *Kesavananda* case' 16 *Journal of the Indian Law Institute*, p. 243 (1974).

Gibson, D. 'Constitutional Amendment and the Implied Bill of Rights', 12 *McGill L J.*, p. 497 (1967).

———. 'Constitutional Vibes: Reflections on the Secession Reference and the Unwritten Constitution', 11 *National J Constitutional L*, p. 49 (1999).

Gibson, J.L. Measuring Attitudes Toward the United States Supreme Court 47 *American J Political Science*, p. 354 (2003).

Goldsworthy, J. 'Homogenizing Constitutions', 23 *Oxford J of Legal Studies*, 483–505 (2003).

———. 'Raz on Constitutional Interpretation', 22 *Law and Philosophy*, pp. 167–93 (2003).

Hogg, P. and A. Bushell. 'The Charter dialogue between courts and legislatures (or perhaps the Charter of Rights isn't such a bad thing after all), 35 *Osgoode Hall L.J.* p. 75 (1997).

Jacobsohn, G.J. 'An unconstitutional constitution? A comparative perspective', 4 *International J Constitutional L*, pp. 460–87 (2006) at p. 462.

Kavanagh, A. 'Original Intention, Enacted Text and Constitutional Interpretation', 47 *American J of Jurisprudence*, p. 255 (2002).

———. 'The Idea of a Living Constitution', 16 *Canadian J of Law and Jurisprudence*, p. 55 (2003).

——. 'The Elusive Divide between Interpretation and Legislation under e Human Rights Act 1998', 24 *Oxford J Legal Studies*, pp. 259–85 2004).

——. 'Participation and Judicial Review: A Reply to Waldron', 22 *Law and Philosophy*, pp. 451–86 (2003).

.elbley, C.A. 'Are There Limits To Constitutional Change? Rawls On Conprehensive Doctrines, Unconstitutional Amendments, and The Basis of Equality', 72 *Fordham L. Rev.*, p. 1487 (2003–04).

Kirk, J. 'Constitutional Implications: Nature, Legitimacy, Classification, Examples' (Pt 1), 25 *Melbourne Univ L Review*, p. 26 (2000).

——. 'Constitutional Implications: Doctrines of Equality and Democracy' (Pt 2), 25 *Melbourne Univ L Review* (2001).

Leclair J. 'Canada's Unfathomable Unwritten Constitutional Principles', 27 *Queen's LJ*, p. 389 (2002).

Levinson, S. 'Transitions' 108 *Yale L.J.*, p. 2215 (1999).

Loughlin, M. 'Theory and Values in Public Law: An Interpretation' *Public Law*, pp. 48–66 (2005).

Loveland, I. 'Public Law, Political Theory and Legal Theory—A Response to Professor Craig's Paper', *Public Law*, pp. 205–10 (2000).

MacCormick, N. 'Argumentation and Interpretation in Law', 5 *Ratio Juris*, pp. 12–29 (1993).

Marmor, A. 'Are Constitutions Legitimate?' USC Legal Studies Research Paper Nos 06–9 (27 April 2006) Constituent Assembly Debates (Lok Sabha Secretariat New Delhi Rep 1999 Vol. 7). <http://ssrn.com/abstract=89952>.

De Marneffe, P. 'Popular Sovereignty, Original Meaning, and Common Law Constitutionalism', 23 *Law and Philosophy*, pp. 22–260 (2004).

Michelman, F.I. 'Justice As Fairness, Legitimacy, and The Question of Judicial Review: A Comment', 72 *Fordham L Rev*, p. 1487 (2003–4).

Minnatur J. 'The Ratio in the Kesavananda Bharati Case', 1 *Supreme Court Cases* (Journal), p. 74 (1974).

Mirfield, P. 'Can the House of Lords Lawfully be Abolished?', 95 *LQR*, p. 36 (1995).

Morgan, D.G. 'The Indian "Essential Features" Case' 30 *International and Comparative Law Quarterly*, p. 307 (1981).

Nayak, Venkatesh. 'The Basic Structure of the Indian Constitution' (Commonwealth Human Rights Initiative <http://www.humanrightsinitiative.org/publications/const/the_basic_structure_of_the_indian_constitution.pdf>)

Neuborne, B. 'The Supreme Court of India', 1 *International J of Constitutional Law*, pp. 476–510 (2003).

Palkhivala, N.A. 'Fundamental Rights Case: Comment', 4 *Supreme Court Cases* (Journal), 57 (1973).

Poole, T. 'Dogmatic Liberalism? TRS Allan and the Common Law Constitution', 65 *Modern L Review*, pp. 463–75 (2002).

Rao, P.P. 'Basic Features of the Constitution', 2 *Supreme Court Cases Journal*, p. 1 (2000).

Raz, J. 'Rights and Politics', 71 *Indiana Law Journal*, pp. 27–44 (1995).

————. 'Why Interpret?', 9 *Ratio Juris*, pp. 349–63 (1996).

————. 'Disagreement in Politics', 43 *American J of Jurisprudence*, pp. 25–52 (1998).

Reed, A.A. 'Philadelphia Revisited: Amending the Constitution Outside Article V', 55 *U Chicago L Rev*, p. 1043.

————. The Consent of the Governed: Constitutional Amendment Outside Article V, 94 *Columbia L Rev*, p. 457 (1994) at pp. 458–459.

Steinman, Adam. 'A Constitution for Judicial Law Making', 65 *U of Pittsburg Law Review*, p. 545 (2004).

Sathe, S.P. 'Amendability of Fundamental Rights: Golaknath and the Proposed Constitutional Amendment', *Supreme Court Journal* 33 (1969).

————. 'Supreme Court, Parliament and the Constitution', 6 *Economic and Political Weekly*, pp. 1821–8, 1972–9 (1971).

Schauer, F. 'Giving Reasons', 47 *Stanford L Rev*, p. 633 (1995).

Shourie, A. 'Protector of the Democratic Citizen', *Indian Express*, 20 January 2005.

Strauss, D. 'Common Law Constitutional Interpretation', 83 *U Chi L Rev*, p. 880 (1996).

————. 'Reply: Legitimacy and Obedience', 118 *Harvard L Rev*, p. 1854 (2005).

Tripathi, D. 'Foreign Precedents and Constitutional Law', 57 *Col L Rev*, p. 319 (1957).

Tripathi, P.K. '*Kesavananda Bharati* v. *State of Kerala*: Who Wins?', 1 *Supreme Court Cases* (Journal) p. 3 (1974).

de Vos, Pierre. 'A Bridge too Far? History as Context in the Interpretation of the South African Constitution', 17 *South African J of Human Rights*, p. 1 (2001).

Waldron, J. 'The Core of the Case Against Judicial Review, 115 *Yale L J*, p. 1346 (2006).

Walters, M. 'The Common Law Constitution in Canada: Return of the Lex Non Scripta as Fundamental Law', 51 *U Toronto L J*, p. 91 (2001).

Winterton, G. 'Is the House of Lords Immortal?', 95 LQR, p. 386 (1979).

ography

S

, R. *Unwritten Norms and Principles as a Basis for Constitutional view in Canada* (MPhil Thesis, Faculty of Law, University of xford, 2002).

an, A. *Constitutional Adjudication in South Africa* (DPhil Thesis, Faculty of Law, University of Oxford, 1997).

avanagh, A. *Fidelity and Change in Constitutional Adjudication* (DPhil Thesis, University of Oxford, 2000).

Kirk, J. *'Implied Rights' in Constitutional Adjudication by the High Court of Australia since 1983* (DPhil Thesis, Faculty of Law, University of Oxford, 1998).

Tortell, L.A. *The Monetary Remedy for Breach of Constitutional Rights in the USA, India, New Zealand, and the United Kingdom* (DPhil Thesis, Faculty of Law, University of Oxford, 2002).

Thiruvengadam, A. *Comparative Law in India and South Africa* (SJD Thesis, University of New York, unpublished).

Statute Index

Case Index

Subject Index